D0122269

OUR COUNTRY,
RIGHT OR WRONG

OUR COUNTRY, RIGHT OR WRONG

The Life of
Stephen Decatur,
the U.S. Navy's
Most Illustrious
Commander

LEONARD F. GUTTRIDGE

A TOM DOHERTY ASSOCIATES BOOK
New York

OUR COUNTRY, RIGHT OR WRONG: THE LIFE OF STEPHEN DECATUR,
THE U.S. NAVY'S MOST ILLUSTRIOUS COMMANDER

This book is printed on acid-free paper.

A Forge Book
Published by Tom Doherty Associates, LLC
175 Fifth Avenue
New York, NY 10010

www.tor.com

Forge® is a registered trademark of Tom Doherty Associates, LLC.

Library of Congress Cataloging-in-Publication Data

Guttridge, Leonard F.
 Our country, right or wrong : the life of Stephen Decatur, the U.S. Navy's most illustri-
ous commander / Leonard F. Guttridge.–1st ed.
 p. cm.
"A Tom Doherty Associates book."

ISBN-13: 978-0-765-30701-9
ISBN-10: 0-765-30701-4
 1. Decatur, Stephen, 1779–1820. 2. United States. Navy–Biography. 3. Admirals–
United States–Biography. 4. United States–History–War of 1812–Naval operations.
5. United States–History, Naval–To 1900. I. Title.

E353.1.D29 G88 2006
359.0092 B–dc22

 2006046455

First Edition: October 2006

Printed in the United States of America

0 9 8 7 6 5 4 3 2 1

CONTENTS

CONTENTS

PREFACE

The September 11, 2001, attacks on the World Trade Center in New York and the Pentagon were followed by U.S.-led invasions of Afghanistan and Iraq. This drew a reminder from at least one prominent American newspaper that it was not the first conflict between the United States and Islamic extremists. There were two American wars against hostile Muslims in the early nineteenth century, but in each case the enemy were not labeled "terrorists," a word yet to be widely used, but were considered heathen pirates from their practice of seizing non-Islamic ships and crews and holding them for ransom.

They were the Barbary States, domains that stretched across North Africa from the Atlantic to the Red Sea and were ruled by despots whose only earthly homage was to the Sultan of the Ottoman Empire. Their rationale for the "piracy" was that the Mediterranean and other adjacent waters were theirs by holy right. Infidel intruders had to pay annual tribute if they wished to conduct trade in safety. Like most European naval powers, the United States, during its first decades of independence, went along with this Mediterranean protection-money tradition. Then the young republic developed its own navy, modest in size but whose grit and gunnery eventually led to the end of Barbary

7

piracy, even as, along the way, it fought England's Royal Navy boldly, if not always successfully, in the War of 1812.

These events produced an American naval hero. There are twenty-six towns in the United States named Decatur, yet when Stephen Decatur is remembered at all, it is most often in connection with a toast he proposed that rang with a patriotic emotion easily construed from a modern-day perspective as chauvinism. Decatur's love of country was beyond dispute. At the same time, his concept of duty betrayed an appetite for glory. Even the advice of his beautiful wife was more than once brushed aside in deference to what he saw as duty. Duty became synonymous with glory. Decatur was by no means alone in this regard, but his pursuit of glory had a ruthless edge to it.

He was brave, audacious, a superb if sometimes perilously imprudent commander at sea, a gracious gentleman, and loving husband ashore. Thus he would remain until a complex of circumstances brought him to tragedy.

I recognized the elements that made Decatur's life story dramatic when working on an earlier book about the American sailing navy. Later, while engaged in a writing project not altogether connected with the sea, I had the good fortune to meet William M. P. Dunne, whose knowledge of maritime history was extensive, especially in relation to details of ship design and construction. He had begun research for a biography of Stephen Decatur, and he was the most charming man anybody could wish to meet. We were immediately friends, and I turned over to him my own Decatur research files. To the sadness of all who loved Bill Dunne, he was taken from us.

Thanks to the generosity of his son, Dr. William Dunne, of Tennessee, the material Bill had already gathered, combined with what I had and have since added to, enabled me to continue the work we had independently undertaken. It is to the memory of Bill Dunne that this book is respectfully dedicated.

1

*Blazing
Frigate*

The gale that halted the first attempt to steal into Tripoli harbor struck at dawn on February 7, 1807. Even so, the commander of the former Barbary slave ketch now in American hands and christened *Intrepid* by her captors rejected the advice of his Maltese pilot that they dare not venture farther into the rising seas. He bade the pilot and a midshipman take a boat with muffled oars to more closely inspect conditions at the harbor mouth. Only when the boat returned a near wreck with its occupants thoroughly drenched did Lieutenant Stephen Decatur decide to drop anchor and ride out the storm.

One week passed before the winds subsided. All that time, seventy American midshipmen, seamen, and marines crouched or sprawled, retching and coughing, in the hold of a craft that could hardly have been more loaded in its slave-transport days. The seventy-ton *Intrepid* was only sixty feet long, its beam but twelve across, and it was rigged with three square sails on the foremast and a single fore-and-aft sail on the mainmast. Garbed as Arabs, men who were not doubled up behind the bulwarks clung full length to timbers laid upon water casks or huddled below amid hogsheads of combustibles. Wearied by shifts at the pumps whenever the ketch took heavy water, they also hungered for food. Few slept or ate. At Syracuse, Sicily, where they

had weighed anchor the first week of the month, Decatur found that his salt beef was packed in uncleaned fish barrels and had so putrefied that it could be consumed only by the vermin that infested every corner of the *Intrepid*'s hold.

Its tiny cabin was headquarters for Decatur, three other lieutenants, and a ship's surgeon. But throughout those storm-tossed days Decatur was not always on the ketch. At times he could be found aboard the sixteen-gun brig *Syren,* three or four miles astern, where in relative comfort he discussed the task ahead with Lieutenant Charles Stewart, the brig's commander. Given variable winds, uncertain tides, and the probability of enemy attack, plans made on the flagship *Constitution* at Syracuse, the United States Navy's Mediterranean base, might well have to be altered.

Stewart's orders were straightforward. His brig would follow at some distance in the *Intrepid*'s wake but close enough to provide reinforcements when Decatur's party achieved the objective, and then to cover its withdrawal. The target, anchored in captivity with Tripolitan colors at the masthead, was the twelve-hundred-ton frigate *Philadelphia,* whose entire crew, from captain to loblolly boy, languished within Bashaw Yusuf Karamanli's castle. They had been imprisoned there more than one hundred days.

Mediterranean-stationed European diplomats expected the Bashaw to demand up to half a million American dollars for the release of the *Philadelphia*'s people. No ransom had yet been paid. That was for the politicians in Washington to decide. In the meantime, Edward Preble, dyspeptic commodore of the American squadron in the Mediterranean, had developed the idea of a secret mission: set the *Philadelphia* on fire, thus denying the Bashaw a powerful addition to his piratical fleet. And the burning would be done not noisily with newfangled Congreve rockets but through a boarding ruse coupled with reliable combustibles.

Weather had driven the *Intrepid* so far off course it took her four days to regain a position close to Tripoli. Then darkness fell before

Decatur, now on the ketch, could maneuver it sufficiently into the harbor to locate the captive ship. And his boarding party was deteriorating into a tired and famished rabble, muttering mutiny.

Yet their spirits revived each time Decatur addressed them. Unlike many another officer in the American navy who depended on curses and the lash to sustain morale, he preferred mutual respect. He never bullied, seldom swore or raised his voice. He possessed a magnetism that itself grew out of sailors' loyalty to him. Aged twenty-five, at five feet ten inches he was tall for his generation but not overbearingly so. He had wavy brown hair, with darkly piercing eyes set in a face rather aquiline but undoubtedly handsome. And in both attitude and deed he evinced a determination noble when need be and pointedly unsafe to oppose.

On the fifteenth the *Intrepid* with its long-suffering but reinvigorated crew wound its way amid a barrier of rocks and shoals to enter Tripoli harbor, flying English colors. Americans in Maltese dress waited on deck. Decatur waited in the cabin. Tension gripped the ketch's lookouts. The *Syren* now lay five miles astern, farther away than Karamanli's twin-domed palace and white-walled castle. Decatur knew that a fort on the long mole east of the inner harbor was sure to hold the Bashaw's artillery. In fact, it bristled with more than one hundred cannon. And in the spray-misted gloom under a setting moon, no one on the *Intrepid* could guess how many Tripolitan gunboats lurked within the harbor.

One boat appeared, rowed strenuously by six men from the *Syren*. It pulled alongside the *Intrepid,* and the exhausted oarsmen asked for a progress report to take back to Lieutenant Stewart. Decatur told them that all was well and attached them to his boarding party. About then the *Philadelphia* came into sight—huge, gaunt, and skeletal against the darkening sky, pale lantern light glimmering from her open gun ports.

Decatur thought it likely that her thirty-six guns were shotted. So were the *Intrepid*'s four, but he hadn't sailed 250 miles from Syracuse

to bombard the town of Tripoli or the *Philadelphia*. Neither were pistols to be used. His boarders must take the ship with naked steel, and they would not make their move until dusk gave way to nightfall. When a perverse breeze against the lateen sails forced too rapid a headway, Decatur ordered drags out. Spars, a ladder, lumber, lashed together, were quietly dropped over the stern rail. The *Intrepid* slowed.

Huddled out of sight on the ketch, officers mentally rehearsed their moves. First, obviously, was to overcome any resistance with cutlass, sword, and dagger. Native disguise might cause confusion, so Decatur had decided upon a watchword: *Philadelphia*. Men would speed fore and aft to ignite storerooms and selected points along the berth deck, below in the orlop and cockpit. The boarders had familiarized themselves with the frigate's construction under supervision of Commodore Preble, who in his farewell words at Syracuse had told the lieutenant, "The destruction of the *Philadelphia* is an object of great importance."

The *Intrepid* drew nearer the prize. The two vessels were some two hundred yards apart when voices rang out from the frigate. Salvatore Catalano, Decatur's pilot, knew the language. Guards on the *Philadelphia* had sighted the *Intrepid,* ordered her to anchor or be fired on. Poised at the *Intrepid*'s helm with Decatur concealed close by, Catalano shouted back. They were a British trader, robbed of their anchor by the recent storm, now helplessly adrift. Coached by Decatur's whispered dictation, Catalano continued. Might they make fast to the frigate until sunrise? During this dialogue the vessels closed to seventy-five yards . . . then sixty . . . fifty. When they were almost abreast of each other, Decatur ordered the drags hauled in.

Twenty-year-old midshipman Charles Morris, assigned the torching of the *Philadelphia*'s cockpit, would remember the tension. "I kept near Decatur who I supposed would naturally be among the first to board." But would the moment be premature? Once safely secured to the frigate, were they not to wait for the *Syren* to catch up? The

brig and the ketch were supposed to rendezvous at ten o'clock. It was now 9:30. The *Syren*'s additional men and the cover she provided would more likely guarantee success during the imminent hours of darkness.

But Stephen Decatur's instincts allowed no such consideration. In his book, delay was seldom if ever an option. Upon his quiet orders the *Intrepid*'s small boat, manned by turbaned Americans, had already put out with a line they intended to secure to the *Philadelphia*'s forechains. The commander's response to Morris's voiced concerns was, why wait? And few words could have been more characteristic of Decatur than those he next uttered to his hesitant midshipman. "The fewer the number, the greater the honor."

Now the *Intrepid* was attached to the *Philadelphia,* the vessels ten yards apart. Decatur's men hauled on the line, warping the ketch closer. Then it was alongside the frigate's port bow, under her guns, in the shadow of her shrouds. Something alerted the Tripolitans, a glimpse of the lost anchor, or the glint of a cutlass in the dim moonlight. Cries of alarm issued from the frigate. The *Intrepid*'s pilot, Catalano, yelled, "Board, Captain, board!"

But prudence tempered Decatur's impetuosity. He gauged the space between his small craft and the frigate's huge hull as still too wide. Now his voice was heard, stern yet calm. "No order will be obeyed but that of the commanding officer." Scant minutes more of hauling on the line. Then: *"Board!"* Decatur shouted even as he sprang for the frigate's chain plates. Eagerness to be first on the *Philadelphia*'s deck got the better of him. About to grasp a chain plate, he slipped, almost fell, might have drowned or been crushed between the two vessels grinding one against the other. And it was Midshipman Charles Morris who first alighted on the *Philadelphia*'s foredeck.

Decatur was right behind him. Apparently unaware that he was not the first American on board and mistaking Morris for a Tripolitan, he swept his sword upward. *"Philadelphia!"* Morris panted, and

the watchword probably saved his life. The boarding was under way. Surgeon's Mate Lewis Heermann, left with shipmates in the ketch to defend her if need be, would never forget it. "Not a man seen or heard to breathe a moment before. At next, the boarders hung on the ship's side like cluster bees and in another instant every man was swarming on board." Resistance was slight. Only here and there was needed the swoop of a cutlass or a dagger's thrust. Estimates would vary as to the number of Tripolitans manning the *Philadelphia.* None above twenty, several of whom leaped over the starboard rail and swam for the handful of gunboats lying offshore.

Decatur had divided his party into four squads, each man operating with a lighted lantern slung over his shoulder. The men carried short sperm-oil candles with turpentine wicks. They worked without a Tripolitan in sight. Combustibles were hauled aboard and distributed, along with boxes of tar, lint, wood shavings, an assortment of ignitible bric-a-brac. Once on board, at Decatur's direction, the teams moved deftly, lighted their candles from the lanterns, hurried to their assigned locations.

Lieutenant James Lawrence with Midshipman Laws set fire to the berth deck and forward storeroom. Lieutenant Joseph Bainbridge, whose brother William was the highest-ranking officer of the Bashaw's prisoners, attended to the wardroom and steerage. Heading below with eight men to set the cockpit alight, Midshipman Morris ran into Decatur and again had to hastily avoid the commander's ready blade. Morris was still in trouble. His combustibles were late coming down. His party waited in the cockpit while much of the ship was already burning. By the time they started their own fire, flames had crept above their heads. Morris had to lead his men struggling through smoke and sparks to reach the forward hatch and rejoin their shipmates.

They were going over the side fast. Decatur and sixteen men stationed along the upper deck as lookouts had spotted three of Karamanli's gunboats emerging from the inner harbor. "I remained on

deck," Decatur would report, "until flames had issued from the spar deck, hatchways and ports." Not quite the first to set foot on the *Philadelphia* with arson in mind, he was certainly the last to leave her. His ketch was already backing off as he jumped for the shrouds, briefly losing grip before sliding down the rigging to a safe landing. He ordered oarsmen to pull harder.

Fire consumed the *Philadelphia* so rapidly it imperiled the *Intrepid*. In the words of Surgeon's Mate Heermann, "Flames rushed from every gun port and scupper hole to within a few feet of the ketch's cotton sails. It shoved off with long sweeps, and the jib hoisted. But the jib took the wrong way and the ketch fell to again." Even as the oarsmen, four to a side, pulled with all their muscle, the *Philadelphia* seemed determined not to let her destroyers escape. The *Intrepid*'s long boom fouled her blazing quarter gallery. Swords hacked it free, pikes and the sweeps finally pushing the ketch clear of collapsing yards and lines.

The fire had reached the *Philadelphia*'s standing rigging, spiraled up well-tarred ropes to envelop her eighty-foot-high tops. A fortuitous breeze helped carry the *Intrepid* clear. Men delighted with the bonfire they had created broke into cheers. Decatur silenced them. They were not yet out of danger. The Bashaw's flotilla had closed to within gunshot. And his shore batteries thundered into action. Their aim was bad. But the gunboats scored a hit, a ball piercing the *Intrepid*'s topgallant sails. The ketch was otherwise undamaged, only one American wounded.

Now the raiders were at a safe distance from the once proud *Philadelphia*. Her scorched cables had parted. Erect at the *Intrepid*'s hold, Stephen Decatur stared out at a spectacular floating inferno. Its glare illuminated the two-mile-wide harbor, in its wake a wall of smoke and the stench of burning tar and timber. The receding crackle of flames, the hiss of blazing fragments striking water, and the boom of cannon fire from ashore, might now have been joined by hurrahs from the *Intrepid*'s officers and men. There was instead a sudden

awed silence as they watched the American-built frigate cease its fiery drift and blow up at the very foot of Bashaw Yusuf Karamanli's castle.

On the *Constitution* anchored in Syracuse harbor Commodore Preble had anxiously waited for two weeks. Days had elapsed since the anticipated date of the *Intrepid*'s and *Syren*'s return. When at last they were sighted on February 19, signal flags fluttered high. Preble's ten A.M.: "Business or enterprise, have you completed that you were sent on?" Decatur's answer: "Business completed that I was sent on."

In later detail, Decatur was pleased to declare that he had lost not a man. "Every support that could be given I received from my officers." He praised "the brave fellows I have the honour to command, whose coolness and intrepidity was such as I trust will ever characterize the American tars." Salvatore Catalano was not forgotten. In due course he would receive American citizenship and join the United States Navy.

However glorious the deed, what was the gain? At home, in the media of his day, Decatur was a hero. The audacity of destroying the *Philadelphia* under the guns of "barbarians" was universally praised. Even England's Admiral Lord Horatio Nelson was described as impressed. And the Tripolitan Bashaw's demand for ransom had reportedly dwindled to $60,000. Still, at home there were mutterings of discord. Already it had been widely held that Captain William Bainbridge should never have surrendered the *Philadelphia* in the first place. And the war with Tripoli was not yet over. The Bashaw had lost the powerful warship that he had boasted made him the envy of every other ruler of North Africa's Barbary States—the Sultan of Morocco, the Bey of Tunis, the Dey of Algiers. He would undoubtedly take out his frustration on the Americans locked within his fortress.

On a different level, when Preble recommended to Robert Smith, secretary of the navy, that Decatur was "of too much value to be neg-

lected" and deserved a captaincy, the Navy Department's chief clerk privately suggested to the commodore that Decatur be persuaded to say no thanks. His elevation over the heads of lieutenants his senior was sure to cause resentment. It did, notwithstanding Secretary Smith's stated belief that Decatur's promotion for a "brilliant achievement" would prove an inspiration to every other officer in the young service. Preble had ignored the chief clerk's suggestion, and Decatur was soon a captain. Resentful lieutenants included Andrew Sterrett, who two years earlier had displayed his own capacity for brilliant achievements by capturing a fully manned Tripolitan cruiser. Although the secretary promised him a special sword for the deed, Sterrett couldn't be mollified and resigned from the navy.

But this was Decatur's hour. Before burning the *Philadelphia* he had refused to wait for the *Syren* to catch up. That brig's commander, Charles Stewart, may have been among the naval officers disaffected by Decatur's sudden celebrity. Many of his peers were envious of him. To officers of the fledgling American fleet, *honor* was synonymous with glory. The fewer the men, the greater the glory. There could hardly have been an officer more instinctively bound to this tenet than Stephen Decatur, who could not foresee that what glory he pursued and won would in the end exact a fearful price.

2

*The
Midshipman*

Berlin is a modestly sized Maryland town close to the Atlantic shore. Its tree-lined sidewalks and notable Victorian homes have more or less resisted the encroachment of big-city commercialism, and it is bypassed unseen by the millions who drive every summer from Washington and Baltimore to Ocean City. The name has no relation to Germany but is derived from the Burleigh Inn, a bygone stopping place on the old Philadelphia post road. Two or three blocks off Main Street is Stephen Decatur Park, adjacent to a street named Tripoli.

Eight miles east of Berlin, Assateague Island stretches ribbonlike along the coastline. Where it widens forms Sinepuxent Bay. The bay itself narrows northward, and here, during the last years of the War of Independence, might have been seen an armed galley named *Retaliation* returning from the latest of her several privateering strikes at British merchantmen. After crossing Sinepuxent Bay and Newport Bay, her captain, twenty-seven-year-old Stephen Decatur Sr., anchored his vessel at the mouth of Trapp Creek. With handshakes and good wishes he dismissed his crew and assured them of their share in prize money. He then rowed alone upstream to within two miles of a cypress-walled and shingled two-room farmhouse measuring only

twenty-five feet by seventeen feet. To this seafarer with a wife, infant daughter, and baby son, this was home.

He was born in 1752 to a lieutenant in the French navy named Étienne who, following naval service, had come to America, first settling in Rhode Island, where he married an Irish girl, Priscilla Hill. The couple moved to Philadelphia, where Étienne Decatur died, leaving his wife and son in near poverty. Stephen followed his father's calling and went to sea, first as master of a merchant ship.

The American Revolution had begun. After *Retaliation,* Decatur's next command was the *Comet,* a ten-gun sloop carrying messages between the Continental Congress and the new states. It was also a privateer and in the fall of 1779 took three British cargo ships. On January 5 of that same year Decatur's wife, Ann Pine Decatur, of Scots-Irish descent, had produced the first of three sons. The parents named him Stephen, after his father. The senior Decatur saw very little of the infant. He was too busy at sea, so successful a master of the *Comet* that he secured command of a sturdier ship, *Fair American,* a one-hundred-ton brig manned by three hundred seamen.

In spring 1780 Decatur captured four English ships single-handedly, five more in company with other American privateers. His list of prizes grew. He seized a four-hundred-ton merchantman bound from England to New York and after convoying it to a New Jersey port sailed farther north. Off Sandy Hook he spotted a strange sail, which proved to be an enemy schooner loaded with precious European chinaware. Its capture sealed Stephen Decatur's reputation as one of the Revolutionary War's busiest and most successful privateersman.

In August the *Fair American* challenged the *Mercury,* a Scots-built vessel armed with sixteen 6-pound and four 18-pound carronades, named after the Scots town where they were first cast and nicknamed "smashers" for their shattering firepower. Also on board were seven women, British garrison wives hoping to join their husbands in New York. Decatur was unaware of this when, as one of his men wrote, "we ran alongside, gave her a broadside, they returned

fire but at our second broadside struck her colours." At that moment "we could hear ladies screeching." Decatur allowed them to remain on the ship, and from Philadelphia they sailed on to New York under flag of truce. "Had it not been for the ladies on board," the *Mercury*'s captain said, "I would not have struck so soon."

If the younger Decatur had grown from babyhood, tales like these told at the fireside each time his father returned to shore might well have stirred his blood. But he was still a child when his parents, enriched by prize money, left their humble Berlin home and moved to Philadelphia following the British evacuation. Decatur invested in a three-story brick house at 261 Front Street, providing his family, now increased to four by the arrival of a daughter christened Ann, with the first home of their own. And Decatur had a new backer, General Francis Gurney, a partner with Daniel Smith in a Philadelphia mercantile firm on Union Street. A politically potent figure, Gurney became Decatur's personal friend as well as business associate.

He provided him with a magnificent flush-decked 310-ton sloop of war, *Royal Louis.* Armed with twenty-two guns and a crew of two hundred, she was victor in the most significant engagement of Decatur's Revolutionary War career. His prize this time was no cargo ship but the Royal Navy brig *Active,* taken off Cape Henlopen. This was one of the rare occasions when a privately armed vessel captured a ship commissioned by the British Admiralty. And even when the *Royal Louis* was herself overhauled and outgunned by the HMS *Amphion,* Decatur's good fortune prevailed. Following a brief imprisonment in New York, he was pardoned by the British, perhaps because of his respectful treatment of the *Mercury*'s female passengers. At any rate, he was soon at sea again, master of the *Rising Sun,* harassing English traders along European coasts.

Although his spells at home had become longer, Decatur was still more often at sea than with his family. A second daughter, born in July 1784, lived less than a year. Two boys were added to the household,

John Pine and James Bruce. Stephen was the only child to bear no middle name. And it was doubtless the father's prolonged absences at sea, denying his offspring the benefits of paternal authority, that encouraged the emergence of young Stephen's combative nature.

When the war ended, his father was wealthy enough to provide his wife and children with a reasonably high standard of living. His capital was held in gold and silver specie, not the worthless Continental Congress paper currency. His last two privateering successes brought him command of the Gurney and Smith ship *Ariel,* with which he made business voyages to France. On one of these he took Stephen along. The boy suffered whooping cough and it was hoped the cruise would improve his health. It evidently did. This was the first and only instance where father and son were alone together for any appreciable length of time. Yet, as events would show soon enough, whatever disciplinary lecturing the lad might have received from his father proved little effect.

However unruly, the young Decatur would never lack in courage or audacity. Boyhood friends remembered, "We used to bathe in the Delaware River near a bank called Old Fort [near] the navy yard. Once, while the boys were swimming about, a few made for a ship moored to a wharf at hand, that they might dive from her sides. One of them ran up the bowsprit quite out to the tip from which he plunged foremost into the stream. It was Decatur. Shouts rose from the boys, and the very sailors may have been amazed, as the ship was large and the height seemed fearful." A natural swimmer, Decatur would be unusual among his naval comrades, many of whom were unable to swim a stroke.

In 1793 when Decatur was fourteen, news reached Philadelphia that the French Republic had declared war on England. Philadelphians were quick to support either cause. Colorful cockades adorning their hats identified the wearer's loyalty, red for France, blue for England. One day in May, Stephen and friends headed south from the city on a fishing expedition to Hollander's Creek. As they passed

Buck's Head Tavern a crowd sporting red cockades blocked their path. These were celebrating the arrival in America of the quixotic French minister Edmond Charles Genet. Since Decatur and his fishing companions wore blue cockades, they were quickly surrounded and ordered to change colors. Decatur's friends were nervous. Not so Decatur, who refused to obey and, according to an eyewitness, declared that "he did not interfere with their cockades and claimed for himself the privilege of wearing that of his country."

One Francophile grabbed at Decatur's cockade. He struck back hard. This emboldened his companions, and the brawl that erupted only ended when a group of seamen, several of whom had sailed with Decatur's father, came out of the Buck's Head Tavern to break it up. Battered and bruised, Stephen had managed to retain his blue symbol, which he waved aloft in triumph.

That same year, returning from another fishing outing, Decatur reached Front Street and saw his mother gather up his brother John from the pavement. It looked as if the child had been knocked down by a drunk hovering nearby. John had mocked the man or played some prank on him and been roughly handled in consequence. Ann Decatur had rushed from the house to rebuke the drunk, who reacted by cursing her. Stephen sped to the scene, confronted the man, and rapped out, "That is my mother. She must be treated with respect." The drunk swung wildly, unsteady on his feet. Sturdily built at fourteen, Stephen punched back with such force that the man fell and was, according to reports, badly injured.

Decatur was well educated. At first he was tutored by a Mrs. Gordon, widow of a shipmaster lost at sea. She maintained a frugal livelihood teaching students before they entered the local grammar school. Decatur would never forget her, even helping her financially when he was old enough to earn a wage. His parents next entered him into the new Academy of the Protestant Church, which stood on Fourth Street between Market and Chestnut and administered separate "schools," for Latin, Greek, English, French, and mathematics.

School days opened and closed with prayers and readings from the Scriptures. The school week was six days, with special Saturday hours set aside for instruction in Episcopal catechism. Classes ran eight A.M. through noon and two to four P.M. Holidays included New Year's Day, four days at Christmas and Easter, ten days in August. The academy's regimen perfectly suited the Decaturs' belief that a religious and classical education would improve their son's behavior. He began his studies in the English school during the academy's first quarter session of 1787. He was no bully but never retreated from a fight; indeed, he appeared to relish the opportunity. A fellow student recalled that "I never knew a boy so fond of a bout at fisticuffs."

When the Episcopal academy, short of funds, closed its doors in 1790, he was enrolled in the Academy of Philadelphia, a prep school for entry into the University of Pennsylvania. His name is on the academy's roll book for four weeks, but there is no record showing attendance at the university. At seventeen he began work as a junior clerk in Gurney and Smith's waterfront offices. But having a steady job seems not to have moderated his impulsive pugnacity.

This was certainly the case, if one believes a story that appeared in Delaware's *Wilmington Daily Commercial* on December 22, 1874. Bylined "Special Correspondent in Berlin, Maryland," and signed "Occasional," it describes Decatur as "in youth self-willed, high-spirited, dissipated and reckless. He was persuaded to enter a certain well-known merchant house, but grew worse and worse until, being greatly incensed at the conduct of a woman of doubtful integrity, he dealt her a blow which resulted in her instant death. For this he was arrested and tried for his life but through the skillful management of his case by two prominent lawyers, Bedford and Sergeant, he was acquitted. About this time Commodore [John] Barry was ordered to the Straits of Gibraltar and Decatur was urged to apply for some position abroad, which he did."

This grave charge, published some seventy-six years after the alleged incident, would merit scant attention but for the naming of two

lawyers who were indeed Philadelphians, at least one of them, John Sergeant, a longtime friend of the Decatur family. Even so, in the absence of court records, "Occasional"'s column must be considered guardedly.

Whatever the truth of it, the young Stephen Decatur's seagoing career began under John Barry's command. He was recommended for a midshipman's warrant, and his father engaged Talbot Hamilton, a former British naval officer, to tutor him in nautical science. In May 1798 he was assigned as midshipman to the *United States,* a forty-four-gun frigate just built at Philadelphia and ready for the high seas. She was the first of six such ships whose construction was authorized by Congress in March 1794 to resist piracies committed by cruisers of the Barbary States upon American commerce. The costly program was slowed or stopped when the crisis with Algeria that had necessitated it ended with a million dollars' tribute paid the Dey. But when John Adams became president in 1797, interest in the formation of a navy had revived and Congress appropriated $172,000 for the building of three warships. In April 1798 the Navy Department was established, and by then France had replaced Algiers as a threat to American shipping.

The principal designer of the new vessels was Joshua Humphreys, a Quaker who had never been to sea but studied everything published on marine architecture and who owned a Philadelphia shipyard. The *United States* was built there, and on May 10 crowds swarmed down Chestnut Street on foot or by carriage to see the 1,600-ton, 175-foot-long vessel descend her launching way. Due to a technical hitch the operation was perilously fast, but the spectators were unaware of this and loudly cheered. Neither did they know that because of work layoffs resulting from the previous year's yellow fever epidemic, the new ship's captain, fifty-four-year-old John Barry, was forced to supervise hasty repairs. Seams in the frigate's decks and topsides had split wide open. Six of her eight 12-pounder guns under test had burst the first day.

But outwardly at least, the *United States* was a handsome craft and Midshipman Stephen Decatur proud to be a member of her crew.

This was equally true of his fellow reefers who crowded the steerage forward of the wardroom and strutted the decks in their buff and blue. Later that summer the young Decatur had additional cause for pride. Angered by French privateering assaults on American commerce, the U.S. Congress had passed the Act to Provide for a Naval Armament. On July 8 President Adams appointed the first secretary of the navy, Benjamin Stoddert, who ordered his commanders in home waters or the high seas "to subdue, seize and take any armed vessel or vessels sailing under the authority or pretense of authority, from the French Republic." Thus began a half-war, a quasi war. And the first American ship to strike back at the French by chasing and overpowering an enemy-armed schooner, *La Croyable,* was the converted merchantman *Delaware,* commanded by Stephen's father.

The senior Decatur's last two privateer commands in the Revolutionary War, particularly the capture of a royal mail packet and a Royal Navy brig, had given him sufficient prestige to merit a captain's commission in the United States Navy. He brought his French prize in triumph up Delaware Bay to Newcastle while citizens lined the water's edge cheering and church bells rang. In those same summer weeks the *United States* had dropped downstream to Newcastle, where, on July 4, John Barry came on board. At dawn four days later, from the quarterdeck of his victorious *Delaware,* Captain Stephen Decatur hailed the southbound frigate. Barry's officers gathered on deck shouting hurrahs, and as his father's ship and prize glided by, few might have been more emotionally moved than Midshipman Decatur.

That much can be imagined. Other emotions, normal enough, were much awake within the nineteen-year-old midshipman. This is evident from a spirited letter, long concealed, that also suggests that he did not enter the navy willingly. The letter is addressed to a Sarah or Sally Mason, living on Vine Street, Philadelphia, and was written in July 1798. Ashore at Newcastle he had met a girl with "a mouth precisely like yours . . . I have been endeavouring to persuade her to permit me to kiss her lips but . . . she has offered me her cheek." It

wasn't like Sally's, "therefore I will kiss her lips or not kiss her at all." The letter goes on about "a report that I had got marryed [sic] & had resigned. I wish to god that the report had been true." He signed as "Yours, solely and everlastingly."

John Barry, who felt privileged to call himself commodore although that title would formally be conferred on an officer commanding more than a single ship, reported from the *United States* to the Navy Department that her people were quartered and the great guns ready for exercise. Barry thereupon received the order that he and his crew of four hundred had awaited. "The *United States* under your command being equipped, manned and armed, you will proceed to sea with the first fair wind." In full sail, with a figurehead representing the Goddess of Liberty, the forty-four-gun warship made course for the Caribbean.

By all accounts those West Indian waters were infested with French privateers. Yet although he was under department orders for a mission of offense, it appeared as if Barry was too enamored of his vessel to risk her in seas prone to windstorms. Secretary Stoddert had to advise him that "the hurricanes, I understand, are not so dangerous as they are generally believed." But Barry turned back for New Jersey. Stoddert repeated his order. The commodore again wore southward. And this time he ran into the weather he had feared.

A huge wave carried away part of his ship's figurehead. The gusts strengthened and split her foresail. She sprang her bowsprit. Some of the crew climbed aloft to reduce sail, but the ship still pitched heavily. Warm air currents had softened the tar-coated rigging. Fore, main, and mizzen topmasts, eighty to one hundred feet tall, shifted in their steps and threatened to go by the board. The crew, officers included, were much at a loss. An exception was James Barron, third lieutenant, who gained the commodore's consent to try and tauten the rigging himself. Running before the wind, the ship rolled incessantly. Even so, Barron succeeded in getting the lanyards secured and the rigging once more firm.

The frigate stabilized. By midnight the storm had abated. Barry wore his beloved ship homeward. Midshipman Decatur had witnessed Lieutenant Barron's action with as much relief and admiration as had any of his shipmates. Not remotely could he have had any inkling of how, just two decades hence, destiny would force him and Barron into tragic confrontation.

Secretary Stoddert, dismayed by the *United States*'s second return empty-handed, and uneasy lest it imply a weakness of his pioneer fleet, wrote to Barry that "we have nothing to fear but inactivity." The situation was made all the more distressing to Stoddert by the surrender back to the French of the first vessel taken from them. *La Croyable,* captured at the outset of the Quasi-War by Captain Stephen Decatur, had been refitted as a fourteen-gun American schooner renamed *Retaliation,* her captain William Bainbridge. On November 20, 1798, she came under the thirty-six guns of the fast French warship *Insurgente.* Bainbridge took her to be British. He realized his mistake too late. While personally brave, he was an experienced officer who never believed in risking death for himself or his crew when engaged against a more powerful foe. Without firing a shot he struck his flag and was taken as a prisoner of war to French-held Guadeloupe. That outcome forever fettered Bainbridge's reputation of being the first captain of the national navy to surrender his ship. For this proud and patriotic officer the future held further misfortune, which would warp his character to a morbid, even lethal, degree.

It was not an auspicious debut for the United States Navy. Thomas Truxtun relieved things. Possessed of an arrogant personality that made him a bane to his shore-based superiors, he was at the same time the fledgling fleet's most truculent commander. In February 1799 as captain of the frigate *Constellation,* he patrolled among the Leeward Islands and met Bainbridge's nemesis, the *Insurgente.* During a savage battle in rough seas he reduced her to a floating wreck with a series of broadsides that killed so many that his first lieutenant,

John Rodgers, gloated that never had he felt more joy than to see "seventy French pirates wallowing in their gore."

But the course of the *Constellation*'s sister ship, *United States,* continued uneventful. In the same month when Truxtun shattered the *Insurgente,* one of Commodore Barry's lieutenants (not Barron) reported only "indifferent cruising" and the capture of a single ten-gun French schooner. This prolonged lull gave James Barron ample opportunity to share his extensive nautical knowledge among the midshipmen, not with any attitude of superiority but from a genuine, even paternal, concern for their professional advancement. Though six feet tall and broad-shouldered, he never gave an impression of bullying, nor did he mock the youngsters or treat them as merely shipboard messenger boys, as did other senior officers. Barron had begun service in the Virginia State Navy before he was twelve. Years of merchant voyaging had made him a highly skilled mariner. His seamanship and resourcefulness were on vivid display during the Atlantic storm that might have dismasted the *United States* but for his prompt intervention.

Stephen Decatur was to spend more time at sea with Barron, eleven years his senior, than he ever had with his own father. And at this stage, according to Barron's later words, the lieutenant kept an especially watchful eye on him. Before the *United States* sailed, Decatur's father had told Barron that "his son had given him much uneasiness by his wild and unsettled character" and asked that Barron "give personal attention to his professional advancement." Barron assented, saying he was "kindly disposed" toward the boy. By custom, United States Navy crews were divided into two watches: starboard and larboard. The starboard watch was supervised by the first and third lieutenants, assisted by half the midshipmen. Decatur was assigned to Barron's watch. That he benefited from the association Decatur attested to in later years. "When he took me, a midshipman, under his paternal care he treated me as a son."

3

The
First Duels

What neither James Barron nor anyone else could have done was purge Decatur of his zest for contention. Already his youthful recklessness had gotten him into trouble. He could keep it under control, and at twenty-one he had outgrown juvenile antics. His demeanor was calm, and he could be charmingly polite to ladies and gentlemen alike. But a combative spirit, however concealed, never left him and in peacetime found gratification in the deadly game of dueling.

It was a practice all too prevalent in the early United States Navy, its ostensible purpose to settle issues of insult and honor. Never legalized, it was mostly indulged in among the young and was sometimes conducted with such elaboration as to appear, certainly from future perspectives, as murderous displays of absurdity. The very design and construction of those first frigates encouraged the phenomenon. No serious thought had gone into the subject of equality in living space. The captain's great cabin aft, sealed by removable bulkheads, was elegantly commodious, with curtained windows and mahogany furniture. The lieutenants' quarters, or wardroom, aft on the berth deck, had cabins on either side that might have resembled prison cells. Then came the steerage, crammed with youngsters,

mostly adolescent, some scarcely beyond puberty. Tensions here were inevitable, even more than in the ship's forepart housing older men, the common crew, where differences might be resolved by fist-fights more likely to end with handshakes than with pistols.

At first, aboard the *United States* as she leisurely patrolled the At-lantic coast, contentment ruled. Competence was duly rewarded. When Secretary Stoddert asked Commodore Barry to recommend officers deserving promotion, Barry replied, "My third lieutenant, James Barron, is as good an officer and as fit to command as any in the service, and I hope that when you do promote him, you will give him a ship that will do credit to himself and honour to the country." And when Stoddert passed Barry's recommendation to John Adams, the president endorsed it by adding that Barron was not only the choice of his commodore but admired "by every officer in the Navy, with whom I have communicated on the subject, as one of the best of-ficers in the Service."

Barry made other recommendations. The "young gentlemen" Richard Somers and Stephen Decatur should each be elevated in rank to lieutenant. Barry was ailing, asthmatic. His fame established as the first commandant of the United States Navy, he tended to show less interest in the personal business of his crew and was probably un-aware that both midshipmen had just participated in an "affair of honor" bizarre by any standards.

Decatur had, unintentionally, provided the essential pretext. Somers was his close friend and Decatur was only joking when, during some banter in the gun room, he called him a fool. Decatur was quick with an apology. But half a dozen other midshipmen denounced Somers for accepting the insult and refused to drink with him unless he called Decatur to account. Not disposed to fight with his friend, Somers turned upon his tormenters and challenged all six, one by one. Decatur had enough common sense and strength of personality to have imposed a bloodless settlement. Instead he pronounced him-self Somers's second.

The first exchange of shots left Somers with a wounded arm and the next with a torn thigh. He fainted from loss of blood but recovered enough to grip his pistol for round three. Decatur offered himself as a substitute. Somers refused. Unable to stand upright, he propped himself against Decatur's willing arms. The third fire wounded their opponent, whereupon some scrap of reason prevailed and the bloodletting ended. All agreed that honor was served and Somers's spunk no longer in doubt. Aware at the outset of the odds against his killing or wounding any of the six, Somers had come close to inviting suicide. He did not know that he would die soon enough, blown to bits in a real struggle.

Stephen Decatur was commissioned lieutenant on May 21, 1799. Barron had become Commodore Barry's flag captain. On July 2, before sailing for Europe with an American peace envoy seeking an end to the conflict with France, Captain Barron sent Decatur to Philadelphia in search of recruits. After he had paid bounty to volunteers, some abandoned him for higher amounts offered by the mate of a merchant ship. Decatur boarded the vessel to reclaim them. Harsh words led to his second involvement in a duel within three months. It took place onshore at Newcastle, Delaware. Decatur had several times claimed—not boasted, which would have been out of character—that firing a pistol he could place the ball on an opponent's body wherever he chose. Before this latest encounter he told Lieutenant Charles Stewart, also of the *United States,* that he would wound the ship's mate in the hip. So expert was his marksmanship that he did just that.

In 1800 the *United States,* needing repair, put in at Philadelphia. Not wishing to remain in port, Decatur applied for and received command of the *Norfolk,* a small eighteen-gun brig on a convoy cruise to Haiti. Meanwhile, his mentor, James Barron, was given furlough. He had a wife and ten-year-old daughter at Hampton, near Norfolk. He should have concentrated on rejoining his family. But tactlessness combined with a true interest in the betterment of the navy, both typical of the man, created his first enemy. He would not lack for others.

He interrupted his journey home by pausing at Fell's Point, Baltimore, to examine the *Insurgente,* undergoing refit as an American warship in the charge of Captain Alexander Murray. Barron found fault in Murray's work methods. Instead of keeping his opinions to himself or gently confiding them to Murray, he revealed them to a Virginia congressman, writing that he "would not go to sea in [the *Insurgente*] for all the world." Murray was half deaf, the result of an accidental discharge of a cannon during the Revolutionary War. But he certainly heard of Barron's indiscreet comments on the *Insurgente*'s seaworthiness and was all the more hostile toward him after the ship sailed out in August 1800 and sank in mid-Atlantic.

Barron and Decatur went their separate ways. Barron received command of a twenty-gun ship, the *Warren,* half of whose crew had succumbed to yellow fever. When the *Warren* reached her Caribbean station, Barron was himself stricken. He would recover but for the rest of his life suffer periodic bouts of malarial ague. As for Decatur, life proceeded uneventfully. At twenty-one he had not lost his taste for duels, but opportunities were sparse. Which was just as well. Duels could occur almost routinely. Infinitely greater and bloodier contests awaited Decatur in the Mediterranean.

It had become a historic tradition, the payment of tribute by European powers to the Islamic states of Tunis, Tripoli, Algiers, and Morocco. The payments ensured protection of busy Mediterranean commerce from what were regarded by the non-Islamic world as acts of piracy. All four states were part of the Ottoman Empire and had terrorized merchant shipping for centuries. From their standpoint they were making infidels pay for an exploitation of Arab resources dating back to the Crusades. Merchant vessels could come and go throughout the million square miles of inland sea so long as their governments paid the Bey of Tunis, the Dey of Algiers, the Bashaw of Tripoli, and the Sultan of Morocco what they demanded. Generations of apparent pusillanimity on the part of the great powers of Eu-

rope was simply a conviction that it was cheaper to pay protection money than to deploy expensive naval squadrons.

The American colonies had their own burgeoning overseas trade, but having gained independence, the new nation could no longer look to Britain's Royal Navy as its shield. Like the Europeans, it negotiated with the Barbary States and signed treaties of appeasement. While desultorily fighting the French, America had let its own annual tribute to Barbary fall into three years' arrears. Given the close of the Quasi-War, those payments had to be resumed. In Washington the John Adams administration saw that they were, but with a new look: some show, however small, of naval strength. Send gifts (anything from chinaware to Irish linen) on board a converted merchantman mounting 36 guns and manned by 220 American tars. The ship was the *George Washington,* her captain William Bainbridge.

She sailed from Delaware in August 1800 and dropped anchor forty days later off Algiers. Bainbridge was unhappy assigned to what he considered a degrading mission. He had by no means recovered from the shame of being the first United States naval commander to yield his ship and crew in wartime. That wound was permanent. The Dey of Algiers rubbed salt in it. Bainbridge had rashly anchored the *George Washington* under Algerian shore batteries. The Dey was delighted. He wished to send emissaries and a goodwill cargo to Constantinople for delivery to the Sultan of Turkey. Now the Americans had supplied him with means of not only expressing his devotion to the Ottoman ruler but displaying superiority over his coastal neighbors, Tunis and Tripoli. He would impress the *George Washington* into service.

Bainbridge had to stand by and watch the vessel that bore his country's revered name loaded with a positive zoo of lions, tigers, parrots, horses, sheep, and even an ostrich. The Algerians boarded as well, complete with wives, concubines, and servants. On October 9, 1800, for the second time in his career, William Bainbridge saw the flag of a ship he commanded ignominiously lowered, this time to

be replaced by the crimson colors of Algiers. A midshipman on board wrote, "The pendant of the United States was struck and the flag of Islamic Algiers hoisted on the maintop gallant royal mast-head. Some tears fell at this instance of national humility."

Bainbridge was no mere puppet. Once beyond range of the Dey's batteries he rehoisted American colors. He would write to the Navy Department, "Had we ten or twelve sloops in these seas . . . we should not experience these mortifying depredations." He tried to make the best of the situation. The ship's officers and men were greeted at Constantinople with luxuriant hospitality. And back home the *Boston Gazette* said that there was "nothing peculiar or unprecedented in this affair. The Swedes, Danes, and even the British have been compelled by this petty despot to be the passive bearer of his errands." But while acknowledging that some good might result, Bainbridge told the secretary of the navy, "I hope that I may never again be sent to Algiers with tribute, unless I am authorized to deliver it from the mouth of a cannon."

4

*To the
Mediterranean*

Notable among those appalled by reports that the *George Washington* had been dragooned for the convenience of a heathen potentate was Thomas Jefferson. A pacifist at heart, no believer in standing armies or navies, he nevertheless began his presidency in 1801 by accelerating the navy's growth. He would rather destroy Barbary Coast piracy than subsidize it. On May 15 his cabinet voted unanimously to send three frigates and a twelve-gun schooner to the Mediterranean. The frigates were *Philadelphia, President,* and *Essex,* the smaller vessel *Enterprise.* With Richard Dale, a mild-tempered captain, flying his commodore's broad pennant on the *President,* the first American naval force to attempt an Atlantic crossing cleared the Virginia capes on June 1, 1801.

Two weeks earlier Yusuf Karamanli, the Bashaw of Tripoli, jealous that Algiers was getting greater tribute from the Americans than they paid him, had sent soldiers from his castle to the United States consulate. They broke in and chopped down the American flag. This symbolic declaration of war would become a grim reality to the thousand-plus sailors crossing the Atlantic under American colors. James Barron was Dale's flag captain. Barron's ailing brother, Samuel, commanded the *Philadelphia.* William Bainbridge, who had returned home braced

to face derision for having served as a pirate state's lackey, met no overt criticism and was appointed captain of the *Essex*. Stephen Decatur was his first lieutenant.

Decatur kept no personal diary, hated writing letters. Nothing would survive to reveal what he had thought of Bainbridge's submission to the Dey's whim. And it can only be speculated how he would have reacted had he been in Bainbridge's position. Nor have we any picture of how Bainbridge and Decatur got along on this, their only cruise together, of whether there was the complete mutual respect between captain and first lieutenant so essential to the smooth running of a ship at sea.

But it is clear there was a difference between how each man regarded and treated the common crew. As "Number One" on the *Essex,* Decatur was an officer for whom subordinates felt trust and affection. A nineteenth-century biographer able to interview veteran tars who had known Decatur wrote that immediately upon coming aboard he addressed the crew in this fashion: "The first quality of a good seaman is personal courage–the second, obedience to orders– the third, fortitude under sufferings; to these may be added, an ardent love of country. I need say no more–I am confident you possess them all." The very sight and voice of this twenty-two-year-old, resplendent in lieutenant's uniform, orating from the quarterdeck to almost three hundred men, must indeed have been inspirational.

With William Bainbridge, however, the image darkens. When the *Essex* was less than a week at sea, he spent part of a day "disciplining the crew." Right then, back in America a seaman named John Rea, who had served under Bainbridge on the *George Washington,* was preparing an attack upon him that would be pamphleteered the following year. "Whenever you appeared on deck, terror and disgust pervaded every heart–all mirth was banished!" The writer charged Bainbridge with mismanagement, cruelty, and all but murder. Rea's missive was perhaps overwrought. But Bainbridge's life at sea had begun as a harsh young merchant-ship master; he came from the school

of controlling lowly seamen with the lash or naked fist. He did not enter the navy as a midshipman, and he once wrote that "I believe that never was so depraved a set of mortals as sailors are; under discipline they are peaceable and serviceable—divest them of that and they constitute a perfect rabble." Decatur of course had no inkling of future circumstances that would bind him fatally to his captain on the *Essex*. Throughout their yearlong association on this frigate, they could only have lived in whatever comradeship or intimacy their limited space and private inclinations permitted.

On July 1, off Gibraltar, the *Essex* exchanged a gun salute with the British garrison on the Rock. A week later, positive word of Tripoli's war declaration reached the *Essex*. When she brought to an American brig out of Leghorn, Italy, bound for New York, Bainbridge was handed a circular written by James L. Cathcart, ex-United States consul at Tripoli, announcing that the Barbary power had commenced hostilities.

The *Essex* was damaged from storms on the Atlantic crossing and was undergoing repair. Decatur quickened the work and stepped up the frequency of drills. All hands rushed to and from battle stations. There were other reactions to the outbreak of war. From his flagship *President,* Commodore Dale ordered Captain Samuel Barron on the *Philadelphia* to keep watch outside Gibraltar harbor, where two Tripolitan gunboats were believed hiding. One of them was supposed to be carrying Murad Reis, grand admiral of the Tripolitan Navy, less exaltedly identified as renegade Scots-born Peter Lisle, who had secured the title and the power that went with it by adopting the Islamic faith and marrying the Bashaw's daughter. Barron was ordered to "lay off this port and watch his movements."

The *Enterprise,* under Lieutenant Andrew Sterrett, so disabled a three-masted schooner called *Tripoli* that it had to struggle back into its namesake port, where the Bashaw, humiliated by so early a defeat in his war, had its captain tied backward on a donkey, paraded through the streets, and bastinadoed a hundred times. Commodore Dale

anchored the *President* before Tripoli, in effect a single-ship blockade.

Decatur on the *Essex* yearned for action. To his chagrin, the ship on which he was first lieutenant was put on mere convoy duty. He was denied even the thrill of a duel. On August 3 off Barcelona, returning from a visit into the Catalonian seaport, he was loudly insulted by a Spanish officer standing on a waterfront guard ship. Decatur shouted that he would be back the next morning to call the officer out. At sunrise the offender was nowhere to be seen. Decatur was rowed to the guard ship, where he bellowed at the man on duty, "Then tell him that Lieutenant Decatur of the frigate *Essex* pronounced him a cowardly scoundrel." Also that should they meet onshore, "I will cut off his ears." They never met, despite a citywide search Decatur was said to have made and thanks to the mollifying intervention of the American consul.

Once in the middle of the night the *Essex* had sixteen American merchantmen under convoy. And in daylight a battle seemed imminent when a xebec with lateen sails and the red flag of Islam bore down on the frigate. In his journal, Bainbridge described what ensued. "He crossed our bows with red colours flying. Saw they all had turbans on, ordered him immediately to heave to and lower away his sails. Made every motion possible for him to understand me, which had no effect, fired two guns ahead of him to no purpose. The wind dying away and falling calm, fearful of his getting away, and every reason to believe he was a Tripolitan cruiser, fired into him, which cut away his rigging and mortally wounded one man. Obliged him to haul down his colours, boarded him, found him to be a Moorish vessel."

Of all North African powers, Morocco was friendliest to the United States. Once again mortification was Bainbridge's lot, and his first lieutenant must at least have been embarrassed. So the *Essex* continued her unspectacular cruise. The dull routine seemed interrupted only by an occasional fatality. October 5, 1801: "Jack Suggs, a

lad of 16 years, captain of the Mizzen Top, fell from the cross-jackyard, broke both arms and fractured his skull, died in 30 minutes." Bainbridge's terse eulogy: "He was a very smart active youth." Four days later George Washington Tew died after a lingering illness. A commissioned lieutenant, he rated a somewhat longer tribute than was given young Suggs. Tew was "an excellent officer and fine companion," his death "lamented by all the *Essex*'s crew."

But dueling accounted for at least one other. Lieutenant Decatur's supervision was not enough to dampen ardor for the practice, and given his impatience with the lack of war activity, he may have been tempted to stoke it. On March 26, 1802, he reported in the *Essex* log, without comment, that "Mr. Higginbotham and Mr. Swarthout with several others had permission to go on shore [at Algeciras, Spain] and above gentlemen fought without my knowledge and Mr. Swarthout was brought on board dead."

In Washington the Navy Department had become disenchanted with Commodore Dale's Mediterranean performance. It was particularly unpleasant for Robert Smith, the new navy secretary, to learn that Murad Reis and his Tripolitan crews had taken to rowboats and under cover of darkness stolen across the Straits of Gibraltar to Morocco. Captain Samuel Barron on the *Philadelphia,* enfeebled by sickness, kept vigil at the harbor mouth unaware that he was blockading stripped and unmanned vessels. Barron could have blamed lack of alertness on his malady. But Richard Dale was supreme commander of the American sailors in the Mediterranean and doubtless too much the "man of singular simplicity and moderation" as the naval historian and novelist James Fenimore Cooper described him. Secretary Smith recalled Dale to the United States.

In summer 1802 William Bainbridge was also ordered to bring home his *Essex.* By this time her crew had been so long at sea, some were in an ugly mood. On arrival off Long Island a Sandy Hook pilot took the weatherworn frigate down to the Washington Navy Yard,

where the men were to be discharged. There, some learned, they were to be paid off "on a tobacco plantation," an unflattering reference to the new U.S. capital. Bainbridge "discovered" symptoms of mutiny, a leading dissident underlining "their determination not to proceed." The captain and Decatur acted promptly, shackled eighteen crewmen, took on water and provisions, and got under way for Washington, anchoring there August 9 to await repairs.

Bainbridge spent time with his wife and their five children before assignment to a series of shore duties. Decatur managed to see his father, who might have found opportunity to relate his recent adventures. After command of the *Delaware* off Cuba in 1799 he had been given the then-new *Philadelphia,* with which he took five French prizes. He had returned home in March 1801 and at the close of the Quasi-War was honorably discharged. On this occasion with his eldest son, he lived on an estate, Millsdale, near Frankford, five miles from Philadelphia, where he had established a plant to manufacture gunpowder for the navy.

But the younger Decatur's visit was brief. James Barron had not long returned to Washington with the *President* and the Navy Department honored him with command of the thirty-six-gun frigate *New York.* There were lieutenants senior to Decatur. But the friendly association he and Barron had enjoyed during their shared cruises on the *United States* had prompted Barron to ask Secretary Smith for Decatur as his second in command. Decatur left the *Essex* at the Washington Navy Yard in mid-August and almost immediately boarded the *New York.*

Barron was in the midst of recommissioning his ship. As before, he and Decatur worked in harmony. The *New York* sailed for Norfolk. Bucking a September gale "we lost our foretopgallant and maintopgallant masts, with the loss of only one man." The ship arrived in Hampton Roads on September 14. She was scheduled for the Mediterranean, but there were delays. An outbreak of yellow fever obliged Barron and the ship's surgeon to quarantine part of the crew. Those

stricken were watched over by William Lewis, a midshipman newly on board. Lewis wrote to his family, "I am stationed to take care of a parcel of sick men. . . . Captain Barron is a man of warm passions, but good-natured withal. In the line of his profession, I am told he is extremely clever, and I believe it to be true. No time to form complete opinion, but I like him extremely well as yet, and I hope I shall have cause to increase my esteem." He did, and upon his later separation from service under Barron, he authored a testimonial to the captain that he and fellow midshipmen signed, regretting Barron's transfer to a new command. "We shall lose the benefits which were derived to us, both from your example, and those lessons of instruction which you were so anxious to bestow upon us." Lewis would write slander-ously different words about Barron at that future time when the fates of Barron, William Bainbridge, and Stephen Decatur would so woe-fully intertwine.

But for now all thoughts concentrated on the ship that would be their home throughout the months, years perhaps, that stretched ahead. Decatur conducted a survey of topmasts and determined "from their having been exposed to the sun that they are dry and un-fit for sea service." This was among several faults in need of correc-tion before departure. The ship finally sailed, but with no clear promise of honor and glory. Barron's mission was to pay $30,000 tribute to the Dey of Algiers. And the frigate would join the third United States naval squadron sent to that sea, this time under Dale's successor, Richard Valentine Morris.

While Morris was the most conspicuous naval officer in the Mediterranean, his country's prestige and influence there were hardly more impressive than during Dale's tenure. Morris had political ties to Jefferson's administration, which probably explains why Secretary Smith allowed him to take his wife, son, and a servant with him. His lackluster campaign prompted William Eaton, U.S. consul at Tunis, to scoff that the government "might as well send out Quaker houses

to float about the sea." And when rumors circulated among ships that Morris spent so much time in safe European ports he had forgotten the significance of his mission, the acid-tongued Eaton gibed that the U.S. Navy might next try confronting Tripoli with "a company of co-medians and a seraglio."

The *New York* arrived off Gibraltar on October 14, 1802. Here Decatur learned of the death of his brother-in-law, Captain James McKnight of the U.S. Marine Corps. McKnight had married De-catur's sister, Ann, in 1796, and they had three children, one of them christened Stephen Decatur after their uncle. While serving on the *Constellation* the marine was shot through the head in a duel at Leghorn with the frigate's second lieutenant.

In November while the *New York* still anchored off Gibraltar, a storm swept the straits, lasting eight days. Midshipman Lewis again found cause to admire James Barron. "Tremendous waves . . . wind, rain, thunder. We housed the guns the first evening and the captain, who is one of the most experienced and able men in the sevice, en-deavoured as much as possible to put the ship in a state for riding out the gale." Despite Barron's efforts "we expected to roll away our masts, and were prepared to clear the wreck."

The *New York* survived and shaped course eastward, leaking badly. After calling at Algiers, she entered the British naval base at Port Mahón, Minorca, for repairs. Decatur, by this time a keen and proficient young naval officer, had discovered that the oakum sealing the ship's planking had worked out of the seams in the bends from the gun and spar decks. Moreover, as he reported to Captain Barron two days later, the foremast was "badly sprung from the Partners and unsafe to proceed to sea without being taken out and fished." In non-nautical language, this meant that the fore and aft scantling that sup-ported the opening in each deck through which the masts passed required a temporary repair in the form of timbers lashed to each side of a weakened mast or spar.

The *New York* left Port Mahón in mid-December and joined

Commodore Morris's so far futile attempts to intimidate the Tripolitans. The Americans were now using Malta as their base. Even with a war on, some could not shake off their zest for dueling. Shortly after the *New York* reached Malta, her captain wrote to his brother Samuel Barron of "Mr. Van Dyke—now laying momentarily expecting death to his relief from a most horrid wound which he received in a duel with Mr. [William] Osborne, lieutenant of the marines. Two days will end his life and all for the preference in a single game of billiards." Second Lieutenant Van Dyke died on January 30, 1803. First Lieutenant Decatur was not involved in this duel. His turn, though, was about to come.

5

*Loss of
the*
Philadelphia

Early in 1803 seasonal gales confined Morris's ships to Malta. In February some of their personnel were exploring the culture and social life of Valletta. Decatur was one of a group that attended a carnival ball, probably held at il Teatro Manoel. Midshipman Joseph Bainbridge, William's younger brother, was among his companions. Crossing the lobby, they ran into some locals who tossed jeers at them. A scuffle ensued, resulting in a duel between Bainbridge and a twenty-three-year-old Irishman named John Corcoran, a clerk in the island's government. Decatur at once pronounced himself the midshipman's second.

The meeting took place on February 14 in a ditch outside Valletta. Decatur insisted on four paces instead of the customary ten or twelve. Corcoran's "friend" protested. "This, sir, looks like murder." Decatur argued otherwise. The advantage should go to his man because "your friend is a professional, mine is wholly inexperienced." These stated reasons were open to doubt, but Decatur won his point; the duelists took their stand and fired. Both missed. Honor might have been satisfied, but the seconds decided on another round. For all his alleged marksmanship, Corcoran missed again. Bainbridge didn't. His ball smashed into Corcoran's head. A sergeant in the Maltese Provincial

Regiment witnessed the affair and reported it to authorities. Talk arose of murder charges against the Americans. But Corcoran's second, a fellow clerk named Mills, when examined by a criminal-court judge, refused to make a statement. Sir Alexander Ball, Malta's governor, is said to have demanded the two Americans be arrested and tried for murder. At any rate, they were quickly out of reach. Morris had ordered his ships to set sail on the first fair wind for Tunis, then Gibraltar. He intended to send the dueling pair home.

Decatur was not pleased. He had come out to the Mediterranean expecting glory, not to beat a hasty retreat from English officialdom. He was further angered as a result of a letter to Commodore Morris from the secretary of the navy ordering a shift in the ship's commissioned personnel that meant his assignment to another vessel without the post of first lieutenant. He threatened to quit the navy. In later years James Barron would claim that "by advice and argument I saved [Decatur] from resigning the service of his country in a pet." At that future date Decatur strongly denied this.

Some of Commodore Morris's Mediterranean mishaps were plain bad luck. Once, a fire broke out near his flagship's magazine. Ignoring his order to lower boats, the crew, fearing explosions, fled fore, aft, and aloft. A confused quartermaster, told to signal "Fire on board," ran up "Mutiny on board" instead. Dutiful seamen doused the fire, saving the vessel, but fourteen of their shipmates died of burns.

Morris had done his limited best to force Tripoli into discussing peace terms. His latest attempts having failed, he pressed all sail back to Malta, where his pregnant wife awaited him. He now captained the *New York,* which he took through storms in the Strait of Messina and put into Málaga, to find a letter from the secretary of the navy relieving him of command. Robert Smith felt that Morris had "not done that which ought to have been done." At home a court of inquiry deemed him indolent and incompetent. Spared a court-martial, he was merely told that his services were no longer required.

His successor as commander of the American fleet in the Mediterranean was one whose bold and innovative spirit, however irascibly displayed, was infinitely more compatible with Stephen Decatur's thirst for combat. With his pennant secured to the *Constitution*'s masthead, he was a forty-two-year-old New Englander named Edward Preble.

President Jefferson hoped that Preble would humble the Bashaw of Tripoli as his predecessors Dale and Morris had not. A martinet prone to ulcers, twice the age of most of his officers, Preble openly complained that he had been saddled with "nothing but a pack of boys." He ordered the thirty-eight-gun frigate *Philadelphia,* Captain William Bainbridge, and the fourteen-gun brig *Vixen* to escort traders along the southeast coast of Spain, then make via Malta to Tripoli, at which port they were to "annoy the enemy with all the means in your power."

The two ships were close to Tripoli on October 7, 1803. Bainbridge bore Preble's orders in mind. Even so, he found blockading dull. And the gale season neared. He wrote a letter to the secretary of the navy. "Fervent zeal in the cause of my country, and desirous of giving you satisfaction on my conduct, will induce me to persevere to the last." While extravagant verbiage was not uncommon in those days, Bainbridge's choice of words indicated that he had by no means forgotten his experiences with the *Insurgente* and the *George Washington.* No less than Stephen Decatur, albeit for different reasons, Bainbridge needed action. None appeared imminent; he was confined to "this solitary station, without the good fortune of seeing our enemies except under [their] well fortified works."

So when he received a report from a passing Austrian brig of two Tripolitan cruisers at sea, Bainbridge detached the *Vixen* and sent her looking for them. She sighted no Tripolitans, instead ran into a northwesterly gale and was forced into Malta for repairs. Bainbridge, of course, did not know this and patrolled off Tripoli unescorted.

Meanwhile, after two weeks' furlough with his family in Philadelphia and time no doubt spent with the kissable Sally Mason, Stephen was at Boston seeing to completion of work on the *Argus,* a new sixteen-gun brig, in command of which he was to sail out and join Preble in the Mediterranean. On July 11 Secretary Smith had written Decatur of his confidence that "you will use your utmost strenuous exertions to prepare the *Argus* for sea as soon as possible." On that same day, Decatur was writing to Smith, "I am induced to believe that you expected she would be at sea by now." But more work was required. "Her bottom is now [being prepared] for coppering, which will be effected this week. The builder assures me she will be launched this month. There is wanting a gunner, boatswain, carpenter and sailmaster." Were they to be sent to Boston or enlisted locally? "I had better know for it will take some time to procure persons calculated for those situations."

The secretary responded with appropriate orders and again urged that Decatur make all effort to get the job done. "Much is expected from your zeal and activity." Decatur took the hint and on August 2 notified the secretary that "the *Argus* expects to be ready for sea in ten days." She was launched before the month's end. Easterly gales then intervened. Not until September 8 was the *Argus* under way, Decatur reporting that she sailed well.

More difficulties arose. Decatur, with the *Argus* moored in Nantucket Roads, learned that Preble had contracted with the riggers and other workmen that "they should have fourteen days after launching to complete their work. I have found it impossible to urge them to finish before the time they contracted for." Not only that, but a sailing master and carpenter who examined the *Argus*'s bowsprit pronounced it unfit for the transatlantic passage "or even safe to bring the ship by the wind." And it was "so badly sprung as to make it utterly impossible to secure it in any way for the safety of the foremast." Decatur reacted vigorously, speeding up the labor. On August 27, off Rhode Island Light, he reported the repairs completed. A gratified secretary wrote

back, "Sail with the least possible delay." Decatur already had. The letter was returned from Newport to Washington unopened.

In midocean, full bodied with an attractive sheer, the *Argus* proved a good sailor although, according to her log, "in lying to she pitches remarkably heavy." But after thirty-four days at sea she arrived safely off Gibraltar where Preble, on his flagship *Constitution,* transferred the brig to Lieutenant Isaac Hull's charge and gave Decatur the *Enterprise,* a schooner converted into a fourteen-gun brig. As ordered by Preble, the *Enterprise* sailed on to Syracuse, which ancient Sicilian port had its share of bawdy taverns and fleshpots, providing sailors with ample opportunity for frolicking.

They included men under Decatur's command, and he soon received a sharp reproof from the commodore. "Sir, your men on shore for fitting your rigging were this afternoon mostly drunk." This might have happened because of "the negligent officer" in charge of the shore party. "Inquire into this neglect, as I will certainly take notice—one of your men is in irons on my ship for impertinence to me." The troublemakers might have included the dueling midshipman Joseph Bainbridge. Still under Decatur's command, Bainbridge would in the future have his naval career cut short by drink.

However capable a seaman and inspiring an officer, Decatur was no stern disciplinarian, and during his stay at Syracuse he himself again courted violence. The Americans were often set upon by local thugs. Strolling along a street after dark, Decatur and Midshipman Thomas Macdonough were attacked. They drew their swords. The assailants fled, one so frantically to the top of a house that he fell to his death.

But in general, Commodore Preble was proud of his new command. For example, he had written to the secretary of the navy, upon Decatur's arrival on the *Argus,* that the ship was "without exception the handsomest vessel of her rate that I have ever seen. She is admired by every officer. The order she is in does great credit to her commander." But total dismay was about to shatter Preble's mood.

Decatur got the news early, while convoying American merchant ships and delivering dispatches. The *Philadelphia* had run aground and been captured. Preble, who had sworn when he reached the Mediterranean that "there shall not be an idle vessel in my squadron," learned of the disaster from HMS *Amazon,* one of Lord Nelson's warships. In command of the *Constitution* he had lost to the Tripolitans his only other frigate, with her captain, all twenty-two officers of the quarterdeck, and all her seamen.

Near the end of October, alone off Tripoli, the deep-drafted *Philadelphia* had strayed into waters only eight fathoms deep. But nothing could have stopped a restless William Bainbridge from chasing after a Tripolitan xebec he saw trying to sneak into the harbor. By 11:30 A.M. on the thirty-first, four miles east of the harbor entrance, the frigate was in seas that began to shoal. Still Bainbridge continued the pursuit. His first lieutenant, David Porter, who professed to know these waters, said the ship was not yet in danger. Not all the crew shared his confidence, and some especially feared Porter because of a story that while seeking deserters in a Baltimore slum and jeered at by a saloon keeper, he had run the man through with his sword.

It looked as if the xebec would escape. Bainbridge sent Porter to the mizzen top to survey the harbor. He was halfway up the shrouds when a leadsman called six fathoms. A shallow sandbank, which the Tripolitans called Kaliusa Reef, ran parallel to the shore. The *Philadelphia* struck it. Bainbridge's first shouted orders were intended to force his ship over it. When this proved fruitless he tried to move her off stern first. She refused to budge and listed to starboard. By then Bainbridge could see nine Tripolitan gunboats coming out toward his grounded frigate.

He had to lighten her. He could not count on help from the *Vixen,* now three hundred miles away. Bainbridge was to concede that "had

I not sent the schooner from me the accident might have been prevented." He ordered three anchors and all but four of the *Philadelphia*'s cannon heaved into the sea. The foremast was cut away and went overboard in a tangle of yards, carrying the main-topmast with it. The Tripolitans neared. They were in no danger from the *Philadelphia*'s guns, which pointed skyward. Someone on the frigate suggested that they attempt to kedge her off, but this idea was discounted owing to the proximity of the enemy, and anyway, the frigate was too firmly embedded. Actually, the Tripolitans had halted, as if they knew the big beautiful American vessel was at their mercy.

Bainbridge held a council of officers. Their unanimous opinion, in his words, was that "the ship could not be got off, and to continue our exposed situation would only prove a sacrifice of lives without injuring the Enemy, or serving our country." Just five hours after striking the reef, Bainbridge, for the third time in his naval career, ordered his colors struck. According to William Ray, a marine on board who had joined the corps to get out of debt, when the man at the halyards refused to pull them down, a midshipman had to do it. As a humiliating final touch, the Tripolitans seemed unable to believe what they saw and Bainbridge sent out his first lieutenant in a rowboat to tell them that the Americans really meant it. They had surrendered the *Philadelphia*.

The Tripolitans swarmed aboard her, gloating and looting. Her people were forced to row themselves ashore, fated for some eighteen months' imprisonment. The officers would be occasionally well treated, dining in Yusuf Karamanli's palace, thanks to the Danish consul Nicholas C. Nissen and the *Philadelphia* surgeon's attention to the Bashaw's family. The common crew would have to work and suffer hunger and brutality.

An anguished Bainbridge wrote to Preble. "I cannot prevent sad reflections; my character; my loss of services to my country! And my Family, are painful subjects to contemplate. . . . In spite of every

effort, misfortune has attended me throughout my Naval life." He would also write, "Some fanatics may say blowing up the ship would have been the proper step [but] I thought such conduct would not be acquitted before God or man. I never presumed to think that I had the liberty of putting to death 306 souls because they were placed under my command." And to his wife, he confessed that fears of the censure of his countrymen "act as a corroding canker to my heart . . . it would have been a merciful dispensation of Providence if my head had been shot off . . . while our vessel lay rolling on the rocks."

Preble read Bainbridge's lamentable report in Malta. He wrote back a sympathetic letter, which Nissen delivered. He had "not the smallest doubt but that you have all done everything to get the ship off . . . in me you have a friend." To the secretary of the navy, Preble revealed deeper feelings. "Would to God that the officers and crew of the Philadelphia had, one and all, determined to prefer death to slavery. I sent the Vixen of sixteen 18-pounders, carronades, and wholly under the control of Captain Bainbridge, but he sent her to look out off the island of Lampedusa. If he would have kept her with him it is probable he would have saved his ship."

Because Stephen Decatur abhorred writing letters and disdained diarizing, it can only be assumed, but safely so, that had he run his ship aground he would have acted more defiantly, or recklessly, than did Bainbridge. Certainly fate, acting through the disaster on Kaliosa Reef and Bainbridge's choice of surrender rather than bloodshed, set the stage for Decatur's leap to glory.

Two days before Christmas the *Constitution,* flying British colors off Tripoli, sighted a ketch-rigged craft. Preble hoisted the American flag and took the ketch as a prize of war. Meanwhile, from the Bashaw's castle Bainbridge could see the *Philadelphia.* Within forty hours of her grounding, the Tripolitans, favored by a shift in the wind, had freed the frigate and floated her off the sandbar. Thus visible onshore, the ship was a constant reminder, as if Bainbridge needed any, of the ordeal his blunder had brought upon himself and those he had

commanded. He had good reason to wish that the frigate were out of his sight.

Equally though, he realized that better the ship be destroyed than serve the enemy. So in letters Nissen was allowed to take out of Tripoli on his behalf, Bainbridge inserted suggestions penned in "invisible ink," lemon juice diluted with water, that became legible when scorched over hot coals. "Though it will be impossible to remove her from her anchorage and thus restore this beautiful vessel to our navy . . . yet an important end will be gained by her destruction." The idea had already formed in Preble's mind. He named the ketch *Intrepid,* hired a Maltese pilot named Catalano, and by the close of January at Syracuse the ketch was being prepared under Lieutenant Decatur's supervision for a "secret mission," destination Tripoli harbor.

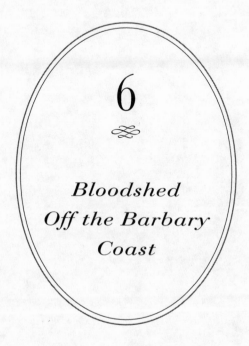

6

*Bloodshed
Off the Barbary
Coast*

In the weeks following Decatur's destruction of the *Philadelphia*, Commodore Preble planned an all-out attack on the town. With his present force, he expected failure. As he informed Secretary Robert Smith, from what intelligence he had gathered, the Bashaw's firepower consisted of more than a hundred cannon onshore, and in the harbor two 8-gun schooners, an armed brig, and nineteen gunboats. Each gunboat mounted a heavy cannon in the bow and two brass howitzers on the quarter and was manned by some three dozen warriors. Many craft were deployed among rocks and shoals, certainly unassailable for the deep-draft *Constitution*.

Preble was not a man to concede defeat prematurely. Without authority from Washington for buying, hiring, or borrowing vessels, he secured on loan from Ferdinand, King of the Two Sicilies, a couple of bomb ketches and six gunboats, with ninety-six Neapolitan sailors, a small contribution from a kingdom that was itself considered to be within Tripoli's armed orbit. The gunboats were flat-bottomed barges, each with a single twenty-five-pound gun, and were designed for coastal defense, not head-on asssault, which is what Preble had in mind. He formed two divisions, one under Richard Somers, the other under Somers's close friend Stephen Decatur. Each division would

be made up of three gunboats and augmented by the pair of bomb ketches.

On August 3, 1804, Preble's armada, consisting of his flagship *Constitution,* brigs *Syren, Argus,* and *Scourge,* and schooners *Nautilus, Vixen,* and *Enterprise,* with the gunboats and ketches in tow, poised at the western entrance of Tripoli harbor. Visible through the commodore's glass as he stood on the quarterdeck were flags flying above Karamanli's castle, soldiers and spectators stationed or moving along the centuries-old fortification and terraces. More ominously visible were the enemy's preparations for defense. Fourteen of the Bashaw's gunboats were creeping out of the inner harbor.

Preble signaled the attack to begin. Cast off from the *Enterprise* and *Nautilus,* Decatur's and Somers's seaborne bombards drove southwestward under sweeps. They were met by a barrage from the Bashaw's fort. None were hit and immediately the mother ship's aft opened fire. It was difficult to see what damage they did to Murad Reis's vessels, but the fighting gathered momentum. Round shot struck the *Constitution*'s mainmast and a quarterdeck gun, but she kept firing, as did even the Sicilian bomb ketches she had towed. They used thirteen-inch brass sea mortars.

Then Preble's gunboats were in the thick of it. Among the first to be hit was Lieutenant Joseph Bainbridge's gunboat number five, a Tripolitan ball carrying his lateen yards over the side. Decatur's number four stood in toward the enemy defense line, four craft in his wake. The moment Decatur closed to within range, his crew opened with round shot that sent the nearest enemy boats hurrying for the shelter of rocks.

Hissing spray from gunshot striking water obscured much of the engagement. Confusion took over. Glancing over his shoulder from gunboat number four, Decatur saw not only Bainbridge's number five and Lieutenant John Trippe's number six but also number two, commanded by his younger brother James, who had followed him into the navy. Then the gunboats, American and Tripolitan, each

carrying up to forty men, were at close quarters, combat a matter of boarding; hand-to-hand struggling, cutlass steel against iron pike; tomahawk cleaving; and point-blank musketry. Blood flew.

Decatur shouted orders almost surely drowned out by the thunder and crackle of gunfire but audible enough for his gunboats to move as one upon a dozen Tripolitans moored beneath the Molehead Battery. Gunwales touched. Decatur boarded with fifteen whooping shipmates, slashing and chopping with a variety of weapons. The Bashaw's finest fought back hard but could never have experienced such offensive fury. In the fading afternoon, spray and rolling waves crimsoned. There were decapitation and dismemberment, all on the Tripolitan side, with thirty-one of them killed or wounded in one encounter, and three Americans bloodied. "I found hand to hand combat no child's play," Decatur would write to purser Keith Spence, a friend and one of the Bashaw's prisoners. Carnage never is. But this, at last, was what he had looked forward to in the Mediterranean. And after hauling down its Tripolitan colors, he took a gore-drenched prize in tow, exhilarated.

Then his intoxication turned murderous. Gunboat number two had come alongside, and his brother lay prone and covered on its deck. Someone told Decatur what had just happened. A Tripolitan had feigned surrender. James had boarded and was felled at once by a musket ball in the brain. Stephen left his prize in a midshipman's hands and with nine men at the oars began a search for the treacherous foe. The giant he found may not have been the man, but that mattered nothing to a Decatur mad for vengeance.

The two grappled in a rocking gunboat amid lifeless or writhing victims of the American attack. Decatur's cutlass clashed with the Tripolitan's spontoon, an axe-headed boarding pike, and its blade flew off the hilt into the spray. The Tripolitan raised his pike. A seaman later claimed (but not proven) to be Daniel Frazier lunged forward, and his arm took the blow. Decatur and the Tripolitan fell to the body-strewn deck. From his waistband the big Tripolitan

whipped a yataghan, a short sword with a double-curved blade, but failed to slice Decatur's squirming body, and then he tried throttling. Both his hands were at Decatur's throat. Decatur wrenched one hand free and groped in his vest pocket for a pistol. He swung it around and shot a ball into his foe's broad back.

The other gunboats were busy. John Trippe and ten shipmates fought while stranded on an enemy boat and outnumbered three to one. They killed fourteen Tripolitans before getting away safely. Somers, in gunboat number two, found himself surrounded by Tripolitans but drove them off with grape and round shot. Preble saw more Tripolitans coming out and hoisted a warning signal. *Nautilus, Enterprise, Argus, Syren,* and *Vixen* stood in close to cover the withdrawal of the gunboats, hurling broadsides at Karamanli's castle and the Molehead Battery.

Yet Preble was less than satisfied with the battle's outcome. It had lasted under an hour. None of his "boys" had been killed outright; only a few, the Decatur brothers included, suffered wounds. Three enemy boats captured, albeit with crews wiped out, still left Murad Reis's piratical flotilla intact. The war had not been won. Edward Preble, of course, could not foresee that naval historians would define those gunnery duels in Tripoli harbor, with what there was of tactical maneuvering, as beginning elements of an American naval tradition rooted in expert seamanship and bold courage.

Slightly injured in the arm by a sword and the breast from a pike, Stephen Decatur spent the night on the *Constitution* at his brother's deathbed. Midshipman Morris heard him say, "I would rather see him thus than living with any cloud on his conduct." And Decatur watched as the body, in its heavily shotted shroud, received the due burial at sea. Preble wrote the official epitaph. "His conduct in action was highly honourable and he died nobly."

Preble hadn't finished with the Tripolitans. With his squadron assembled three miles outside the harbor he planned a second attack. It occurred on August 7 and was directed at the Bashaw's shore batteries,

but it silenced only six of his hundred cannon. That same day the frigate *John Adams* arrived with news that Jefferson had decided to send out a stronger squadron. The homeland had not yet heard of Preble's prowess in seamanship and command. But his days in the Mediterranean were now numbered—he would be outranked when those ships arrived. He informed the Navy Department that with one more frigate he could have ended the war, released Captain Bainbridge and his people from Yusuf Karamanli's clutches.

When days passed without sign of the promised four frigates, Preble renewed the assault. On August 24 his ships again stood in for Tripoli, hurled cannonballs at the castle while Decatur, with eight gunboats, engaged thirteen enemy galleys, sinking one and scattering the rest. And as summer waned, Preble approved a plan even more of a gamble than the burning of the *Philadephia*. As on that occasion, the vessel employed would be the converted slave ship Preble had named *Intrepid.*

It would function as a floating bomb. Rigged like a Tripolitan, it would be steered to its target, a cluster of enemy vessels, by Richard Somers and a dozen other volunteers. It was stacked with 100 barrels of gunpowder and 150 charged shells and had a fuse timed to give Somers and his party fifteen minutes to pull away in rowboats before the ketch exploded.

This proved a suicide mission. Perhaps the fuse malfunctioned. Tripolitan sailors may have caught on to the scheme and fired on the *Intrepid.* Somers had vowed that he would blow himself up, crew and ketch, rather than fall with his men into enemy hands. To his best friend, Decatur, he had left a memento, a ring, or portion of one, inscribed R.S. TO S.D. 1804. The two young men had been closer than brothers.

At nine P.M. on September 3 the *Intrepid* made for the harbor's western entrance, accompanied by the *Argus, Vixen,* and *Nautilus.* A midshipman on one of the vessels recalled that as the thirteen volunteers passed over the side into the ketch, "all took their leave in the

most cheerful manner with a shake of hands, some shouting 'Mind, boys, when you get home, give a good account of us.'" Darkness swallowed the ketch. Just forty-five minutes elapsed before it blew up with a glare that illumined the harbor. In his report to the navy secretary, Preble claimed as if proven that "the gallant Somers and heroes of his party, preferring death to slavery, put a match to the train leading to the magazine." The Bashaw's prize prisoner, William Bainbridge, who had made no such choice when his ship ran aground, was permitted to examine American bodies washed ashore, but most were dissevered beyond recognition.

The American navy's Mediterranean debut had a more favorable impact than Commodore Preble could have anticipated. His campaign had made the Bashaw of Tripoli contemplate an end to the war and the release of the *Philadelphia*'s officers and seamen. Neutral onlookers were impressed. Sir Alexander Ball, Malta's governor, had fought as an admiral alongside Nelson in Britain's naval battles with Bonaparte's French. Ball wrote to Preble that his campaign against Tripoli had been worthy of "a great and rising nation."

Preble's career in foreign waters ended September 9, 1804. He left for home dispirited and ailing but carrying a written declaration from his officers regretting his departure and professing pride at having served under his command. The list of fifty-three signatures was headed by that of Decatur, to whom Preble had recently written, "May you ever continue in the pursuit of glory and be crowned with success." Proud of his own qualities of command, Preble told the secretary of the navy that since arriving in the Mediterranean his tenure had been marked by no court-martial or duel. Fortunately for the peace of mind his naval service merited, Preble did not know that on the very day he reported this to the navy secretary, two midshipmen of the *Syren* dueled, and as noted in the brig's log, "At 6 P.M. Mr. Nicholson's corpse was brought on board." (Nicholson's equally young killer was returned to America, court-martialed, and acquitted.)

Preble was succeeded as commander of the American navy's

Mediterranean fleet by Samuel Barron, who had fought bravely in the Revolutionary War but whose health declined. For much of his time in the region he was hospitalized ashore at Malta. Yet he stubbornly clung to command, angering John Rodgers, an officer too often frustrated by lack of opportunity to vent an apparently unappeasable belligerence. Bribery, the threat of sea power, and some diplomatic double-dealing finally settled the Tripolitan War. A peace treaty was signed on June 4, 1805. But three more months passed before Commodore Barron became so enfeebled that control of the United States fleet off the Barbary Coast at last reached Rodgers's eager hands.

Meanwhile, William Bainbridge, newly freed, anxiously awaited the official inquiry into the loss of his frigate. One was speedily arranged and conducted in the great cabin of the *President,* anchored off Syracuse. Neither James Barron, who presided over the court, nor members Stephen Decatur and Captain Hugh Campbell appeared disposed to ask awkward questions, perhaps out of compassion for a fellow officer who, however culpable, had been punished enough. Bainbridge based his surrender on a stated belief that "where there is no possibility of a successful defense and all means of escape have been tried, the flag may be struck without injuring the captain's honour." Kedging? He had thought of this, but "the enemy had the ground." The court skipped over his folly in sending the *Vixen* away, sat for four hours, and concluded that "Captain Bainbridge acted with fortitude and good conduct, and no degree of censure should attach itself to him."

Quarrels grew from the idleness of peace. Decatur's comrades in the Mediterranean included Lieutenant Charles Ridgley, a Baltimorean whose real name was Goodwin. He had taken the surname Ridgley to secure an inheritance from an uncle of that name. On January 23, ashore in Messina, Sicily, he had quarreled drunkenly with the mate of an English transport and killed him. Decatur championed Ridgley when he was indicted under civilian murder charges. Tried and acquitted, Ridgley had remained in the Mediterranean,

a good friend of Decatur's, until he returned home at his own request.

As for John Rodgers, the Tripolitan War had ended too soon. He had gained no glory, and he took out his ire on the Barron brothers. The peace negotiations Samuel Barron had attempted with the Bashaw should damn his reputation forever. And James had striven to keep command in his brother's weakening grip while pretending otherwise. Thus Rodgers blustered. Like Bainbridge, he had begun his maritime career as a rough-hewn merchant skipper. Now he was all for a duel and had told the newly released Bainbridge that he was ready to meet either Barron at any time, and if no call came from those brothers when he returned home, "I shall impute it to a want of what no gentleman wearing a uniform should be deficient." No duel ensued, but the time was not far off when James Barron would give the truculent Rodgers a chance to trumpet, "I told you so."

Decatur too would soon be involved in James Barron's affairs. But at present he was enjoying a period sweetened by the fruits of his Mediterranean fame. On November 5, 1805, Gould Francis Leckie, Britain's honorary consul at Syracuse, hosted a dinner party for him at his residence, an idyllic villa overlooking the bay. Decatur himself appears to have presided over what Samuel Taylor Coleridge called "a grand entertainment."

The celebrated English poet, serving temporarily as aide to Sir Alexander Ball, was in the region chiefly to escape a wrecked marriage and in hopes of restoring health ruined by opium addiction. He had achieved fame with the publication of "The Rime of the Ancient Mariner" but found little happiness since. Decatur met him at some social event on the island, possibly at Ball's palatial Valletta residence. That the moody and mystical thirty-two-year-old poet and the twenty-five-year-old American naval hero formed a friendship upon their first meeting is certain. But neither left enough behind to document its depth or duration.

There is a glimpse of Decatur's stated political views in Coleridge's

personal writings. "An American commander who has deserved and received the highest honour which his grateful country can bestow on him [almost certainly Decatur] once said to me with a sigh, 'In an evil hour for my country did the French and Spaniards abandon Louisiana to the United States. We were not sufficiently a country before, and should we be mad enough to drive the English from Canada we shall cease to be a country at all.' "

The association with Coleridge is best indicated in one of Decatur's rare personal letters, a farewell dated July 11, 1805, when he was about to leave Valletta as captain of the frigate *Congress.* "I am extremely near the shore, and I have not time to be lengthy, and I have only to beg that you believe me [when] I assure you that there is no man's good opinion upon whom I would set a value. P.S. Should you come out, make a sign and I shall heave to immediately." Two months later Decatur was returning to the United States on the *Congress* with the most exotic diplomatic party any American warship was ever likely to carry.

His passengers were the new Tunisian ambassador, Sidi Solimar Melimeli, a personal entourage of eleven, and a band of Italian musicians. A good deal of the frigate's cargo consisted of ornaments of ivory, gold, and silver, with incense, silks, and tapestries, gifts from Tunis to President Jefferson. The *Congress* dropped anchor off Old Point, Virginia, on November 5. Luke Wheeler, mayor of Norfolk, went on board to personally greet Decatur and his colorful party, and on Friday morning, the eighth, the ambassador returned the mayor's visit. It was uncertain when the Tunisians would leave for Washington, the *Congress* awaiting a fair wind.

The frigate received another visitor. James Barron had read of the ship's arrival while at his Hampton home, named Little England. In view of what lay ahead it was not the most felicitous of names. But now he was engaged in designing a prototype for the gunboats President Jefferson hoped would prove a fleet strong enough to defend America's coast. Barron knew that Decatur had become his equal in

rank, and he visited the *Congress* to congratulate him and to offer the hospitality of Little England.

Decatur would recall the occasion but in an otherwise caustic letter that would bring the two men one step closer to tragedy. The only time he was at Barron's home "was on my arrival in the *Congress.* You came on board and dined with me and invited the Tunisian ambassador and myself to spend the evening with you at Hampton. I accepted."

And another visitation to the *Congress* would affect the course of Decatur's life. When a schooner returning to Norfolk anchored near the vessel, several in the group wanted to see the North African curiosities they had heard were on display in the captain's cabin. What then caught many a female eye had nothing to do with Tunis. It was an Italian miniature, a 3×3 ½ inch watercolor on ivory done probably in 1805 by Olivio Sezzi. Even more certainly, no lady among the visitors was more captivated by the miniature than a petitely graceful, dark-eyed beauty named Susan Wheeler, daughter of Norfolk's mayor.

As for the miniaturist's handsome subject, he would be remembered by Dr. Philip Barraud, a physician whose Hampton home, Little Scotland, lay near the Barron family estate. The *Congress* still lay at anchor in Hampton Roads. One morning at breakfast time Decatur came uninvited to Barraud's house, where James Barron happened to be visiting. Decatur apologized for the early visit but said he had come to see Barron. According to the doctor, Decatur declared that Barron was "a man he had cause to love as a father. 'He promoted me, gave me my first command, he has never lost sight of me since. If I profess talents or merit in my profession, I owe them to James Barron—in truth, sir, he has been more than a father to me and I can never cease to love him as such.' "

Friendly and grateful words were what Barron would have appreciated just then. He was depressed by his brother's lingering illness, pursued by a bellicose John Rodgers, and concerned for the navy's

future. "My brother's health is so bad" he had written Edward Preble on September 29, explaining a failure to write sooner. "I was continuously encompassed in gloom. . . . I have spent much misery and more ahead . . . the Navy has almost ruined me." Besides his attention to gunboats, Barron, gifted with an inventive mind, was considering the design of a new mill, which, he later described, would grind one hundred bushels of corn in twenty-four hours and cost "little more than a common pigeon house. If that fails, God only knows what landfall will bring me up. The Navy wants so many reforms that my hopes are sinking fast to despair." Married to Elizabeth Armistead, who came from a respected Norfolk mercantile family, and blessed with a loving fifteen-year-old daughter, James Barron should have been a happier man. Certainly he had no conception of the heartache that yet lay in store for him.

7

Stephen
and
Susan

Not much is known of Luke Marbury Wheeler, seventy-third mayor of Norfolk, and still less of his daughter Susan. There is reason to believe that her mother was a mulatto Wheeler took as his wife while he managed an ironworks at Elk Ridge, Maryland. He was was born in that state in 1754, and his itinerary thereafter is difficult to trace. After Susan's birth, presumably at Elk Ridge, he appears in Petersburg, Virginia, where by 1793 he is a justice of the peace and a director of the Dismal Swamp Canal Company. The record shows nothing of a wife or a daughter until the turn of the century when he is first a merchant on Main Street, Norfolk, charter member of the chamber of commerce, and in 1805 city mayor. Susan was then thirty and, quadroon or not, among the city's most charming belles.

That she was cultured, sang and played the harp at social events, is clear enough. She was evidently away from her father for several years and was a close friend of Catherine "Kitty" Harper, daughter of Charles Carroll of Carrollton, a Maryland signer of the Declaration of Independence. Susan Wheeler may have been educated with Kitty Harper in Belgium. Stories more substantial than mere tavern gossip place her in Baltimore with members of the Carroll family, where she was wooed, or pursued, by Vice President Aaron Burr and Napoleon

Bonaparte's hedonistic young brother, Jérôme. Reportedly she turned them, and others, down. Certainly her most recent interest was ardently focused on a gallant and handsome, genuinely American, naval hero four years her junior.

At twenty-six, Decatur cut a superb figure, especially when in full uniform with its gold lace and brilliant braid, as he must have appeared on November 8, 1805, when he and the Tunisian ambassador dined at Luke Wheeler's table, also at the ball that followed the feasting and was attended by the most glittering of Norfolk society. Decatur met Susan for the first time. A nineteenth-century tittle-tattler would write that she made advances toward him. The two may at least be pictured dancing together. She was dainty yet self-possessed. As for the fiancée that Decatur was said to have in Philadelphia, the embarrassment of losing him to an enigmatic Norfolk beauty must have been acute, and might explain why her name was not advertised. Very likely she was the Sally Mason to whom Decatur wrote such a warm letter when he was nineteen. At any rate, certainly in Decatur's heart she could never have been much of a match for Susan Wheeler.

Decatur left Norfolk on November 23 to take the *Congress* and the Tunisian delegation to Washington. Knowing of Susan's love for music, he asked a friend, Master Commandant Isaac Chauncey of the brig *Hornet,* bound for Hampton Roads, to deliver some sheet music he had bought for her. In due course Chauncey sailed, and he wrote Decatur from Norfolk that he had delivered the gift but Susan "appeared a little jealous." She had heard that Decatur would marry someone in Philadelphia. Chauncey had scoffed at the report as "premature, for I did not believe you had an idea of marrying any person in Philadelphia."

Chauncey also told Decatur that his gift had "wrought miracles . . . been Music to her soul, for Joy beamed in her Eyes and her every gesture was heavenly." Chauncey must have come close to swooning. "I *may* adopt the language that Milton has put in the Mouth of Adam 'Grace was in all her steps, Heaven in her Eye.' "

Chauncey crowned the letter with another Miltonian quote, one that Decatur may not have altogether appreciated. "You will return this winter and act your part well [and] if I mistake not, you may say with Adam, 'To the Nuptial *Bed* I led her blushing like the Morn, all Heaven and happy Constellations, on that hour shed their choicest influence.'" And that was where Chauncey would leave him, "to make the best of use of your time."

Before hurrying back to Norfolk and his sweetheart, Decatur spent Christmas with his parents at Frankford. The senior Decatur was still in the gunpowder business. Having just heard that the government had a large amount of saltpeter in need of refining, he offered his services, claiming to have "the largest and I believe the most complete works for this business on the continent." But he and Ann mourned the loss of their son James, whose final hours Stephen described to them. During a dinner at the Shakespeare Tavern in Philadelphia, the elder Decatur, replying to a toast in honor of "the gallant father of a gallant son," added perhaps sadly that "our children are our country's property."

Decatur's courtship of Susan Wheeler was made pleasantly easy for him through his assignment to the Norfolk area as commander of a gunboat flotilla under construction. The gunboats would be about seventy feet long and eighteen feet in the beam, of shallow draft, sloop or ketch rigged, and armed with two guns on pivots. Heavier armament would have capsized them on discharge. When Decatur became involved in gunboats, Congress had just approved the funding of fifty additional ones. But if Jefferson and other politicians liked gunboats, most naval officers considered them all but useless. Gunfire recoil during exercises sank one of Decatur's in six fathoms. He wrote of this to William Bainbridge and wondered, "What would be the real national loss if all the gunboats were sunk in 100 fathoms of water?"

But his thoughts at this time were colored by love and hopes for a successful marriage. To achieve this, he determined to acquire as

polished an education as Susan was so obviously blessed with. Early in 1806, while visiting his parents, he talked with his boyhood friend Richard Rush, who had become a prominent physician. "I have risen fast in my profession," he told him, "but my rank is ahead of my acquirements. For professional knowledge I hope to get along. But for other kinds of knowledge, I feel my deficiencies, and I want your friendly aid. List books, historical and others of standard nature as you think will best answer my purpose that I may devote myself at all intervals to peruse them." Rush understood his friend's concern and promised to help all he could.

Thus encouraged, Decatur had returned to Norfolk. His courtship of the mayor's daughter was an open secret except, it seemed, to James Barron. Otherwise he would surely not have made so indiscreet a public remark as he did when, one February morning, he met Decatur with a group who were teasing him about the attraction that so frequently brought him to the town. Barron scolded the teasers to the effect that Decatur could have no romantic interest in Norfolk for it lay elsewhere. The precise words uttered during that wintry-morning street encounter are unknown. But the older man's penchant for unsolicited intrusion, on this occasion, irreparably damaged whatever father-son relationship the two had shared at sea. "From that day," Barron would bitterly recall, "Decatur was an altered man to me."

The following month, on March 8, Decatur and Susan were married by the Reverend Benjamin P. Grigsby, pastor of the Norfolk Presbyterian Church. Edward Preble, in declining health at his home in Maine, congratulated the couple. The gossipy essayist Benjamin Ogle Tayloe wrote that the union was regarded by many as "a blot on [Decatur's] escutcheon." Had Decatur known this, he could not have cared less. Replying to Preble, he wrote, "If a fine-minded, highly cultivated nature, added to more than a common share of good sense and amiability, will ensure happiness, I think I am not over sanguine in calculating on more than falls the lot of men in general."

The only problem was the Southern climate, which "does not accord with Mrs. D's constitution." Decatur thought of moving northward. "Tell me what it will cost to live in Portland, not to cut a dash but live snug and handsomely." The Decaturs did not move that far north, but wherever Susan accompanied Stephen, she was always ready to help the men under his command. To some she became known as "the sailors' friend." Decatur would often be absent at sea, but he never lost his fondness for the sophisticated while solicitous woman he had married. Whatever Susan's origins, and whether her husband knew of them, made no difference. Theirs was a genuine affair of the heart, a childless union, a love story destined for a sorrowful conclusion.

Denied opportunity for glory in the Mediterranean, Commodore John Rodgers came home in the summer still seeking a duel with the Barrons. Ill health put Samuel beyond reach. So Rodgers set his sights on James, sent him word that he was ready to take the field in defense of his maligned integrity. "I hold myself ready to account to you at any time from the present." Considering Rodgers's additional references to "engagements with any other persons," and the lack of evidence that either of the Barrons had vilified him, Commodore Rodgers might well have been suspected as paranoid. But the affair never reached pistol consummation. As William Eaton, American consul in Tunis, summarized things, "Rodgers and the Barrons have been reconnoitering each other but cannot fix on a battleground."

At first Decatur had little or no interest in this business. He was ordered to supervise gunboat building at Newport, Rhode Island; Susan had joined him there and probably accompanied him to Boston, where he sat for the painter Gilbert Stuart, who had painted Susan's portrait at Washington in 1803. Typical of the popularity they quickly won among Newport's elite was a reception in his honor held, according to a local scribe, "at Mr. Townsend's Coffee House. We understand that Captain Decatur intends spending the season at New-

port with his lady." But by this time Decatur had taken enough notice of the Rodgers-Barron affair to at least imply a view unfavorable to the captain he had once "loved as a father." This is clear from a letter Edward Preble wrote Decatur on September 14 reminding him of something he had said in connection with Barron's apparent avoidance of a showdown with Rodgers. With a touch of humor, Preble ended his letter, "It is to be hoped that we, with whom [Rodgers] is determined to war, shall at least be able to stand our ground."

The following month Secretary of the Navy Smith told Decatur to leave his gunboats, meet Preble in Philadelphia without delay, and come with him to the capital. Smith ordered each officer to "tell no one you are coming to Washington." This mysterious directive was followed by another stating that information just obtained rendered the earlier order unnecessary, so "consider [it] suspended until further notice." But on December 17 the secretary wrote Decatur of "circumstances . . . arisen that render your immediate presence at Norfolk necessary. Come here [Washington] without delay, call at the office for instructions and be prepared to proceed at once to Norfolk."

These letters had to do with the crisis precipitated in Washington by the discovery that Aaron Burr, the former vice president and duelist—he had shot and killed a political foe, Alexander Hamilton—allegedly conspired to form a new confederacy, with himself as head, composed of western states and even Mexico. At cabinet meetings in October, President Jefferson had decided to warn governors and district attorneys that Burr must be watched, and arrested the moment he committed any "overt act." It was also agreed that the U.S. Navy be employed to prevent any move Burr made in New Orleans. Preble and Decatur were the officers selected to command, using the brig *Argus* and nine gunboats. Thus Smith's first letter. When news came that there was no hint of subversion or insurrection along the Ohio and Mississippi Rivers, that order was countermanded.

The navy was already involved in the Burr proceedings. One of Burr's oldest friends was Thomas Truxtun, known to bear a grudge

against Jefferson, who, the captain believed, had tricked him into resigning from the service. Burr had wanted Truxtun to be admiral of the fleet that he intended to create once he had taken over Mexico. Burr had also approached Decatur, who, after Burr's arrest, wondered if he would be called to testify at the trial. Decatur wanted to get his story across before receiving a summons. On August 22 he had written to Caesar Rodney, United States attorney general, "As my name has been mentioned in the affair, I should have been better satisfied to have been summoned." Decatur gave Rodney his version of events. Sometime in December 1805 "Colonel Burr told me in confidence that he intended an expedition against Mexico, that people there were ripe for revolt and only wanted a rallying point to enable them to shake off their subjugation to the Spanish." Asked to join Burr's scheme, he had refused, after which Burr never came near him again.

Decatur did receive a formal summons to serve as a witness for the prosecution at Burr's trial in Richmond. He was not called upon to testify before open court, as were Captain Truxtun and other officers, all of whom stated that when solicited by Burr they had refused him. Decatur did, however, in due course appear before a grand jury. There is an ambiguity about this affair. Truxtun wrote privately to Captain James Biddle that Decatur would not have voluntarily told the government of Burr's overtures "until subpoenaed to do so . . . though before a Grand Jury oath was made by him that he was to go to New Providence after a fleet and join me for Jamaica." All in all, a murky business, leaving open the possibility that both Decatur and Truxtun knew more of Burr's plans than they cared to admit and may even have pondered a role in them.

Construction of gunboats at Norfolk's navy yard had proceeded desultorily. In the manner of what later generations would call troubleshooter, Decatur was brought back to supervise. He found that while the boats and bomb vessels were ready for service, muskets and pistols were unfit and would have to be supplied from Washington.

And "so many articles are wanted for equipment. The fact is, stores have been broken open three times." Their contents had been looted. And the rigging of the craft, which the secretary had specifically directed him to examine, afforded Decatur an opportunity to affirm his command quality. He had marched into the supply clerk's office. "I told him it would displease you in having retarded the public business three days unnecessarily, and requested that he would suffer the men attached to each boat to examine their rigging and go to work on it." When the clerk refused, Decatur threatened to "execute [the secretary's] order by force."

He ended this report to Smith with carefully chosen words. No doubt it would be said "I have assumed a power I had no right to . . . but I am confident you will approve the steps I took." He promised that the gunboats could be ready for action within four days. And Secretary Smith's response was not unexpected. "Consider these boats and bomb vessels . . . and all the affairs attached to them as under your command."

It was about this time that the secretary of the navy sent orders to Master Commandant Charles Gordon, a self-indulgent officer in his early twenties who had been inactive for a year and was "heartily tired of an idle life." The orders put Gordon on the frigate *Chesapeake,* being prepared at Norfolk to relieve the *Constitution* on the Mediterranean squadron. That same week the secretary assigned Captain James Barron to the ship's command, and he would henceforth carry the courtesy title of commodore. This was all very well, but Gordon wanted to know who exactly would be the frigate's captain. He had influential connections. Three uncles were active Jeffersonian Republicans. He was related to Albert Gallatin, secretary of the treasury. Gordon was hastily advised that although nominally under the command of Commodore Barron he should consider himself captain of the *Chesapeake.*

Gordon had served under Barron on the *President* when that frigate was Richard Dale's flagship in the Mediterranean. Barron now

recalled him as too pleasure-loving an officer for the challenge of running a man-of-war. As soon as he heard of Gordon's appointment, he asked to be relieved of his own. Smith refused. And as if this was not enough to dismay James Barron, the lieutenants to go on the *Chesapeake* were without exception known cronies of Commodore John Rodgers, especially William Henry Allen, who would come on board, Barron feared, poisoned against him "by all the prejudices his friend Rodgers could inculcate."

But the trouble about to overwhelm Barron had nothing to do with John Rodgers. There were British warships in Hampton Roads. John Hamilton, a well-liked British consul in Norfolk, had written Decatur a politely worded request that he arrange the surrender of four seamen of His Britannic Majesty's ship *Melampus,* who had run off in the captain's gig to Norfolk and at the enlistment rendezvous signed up for service in the American navy. This was a matter for the recruiting officer onshore, Lieutenant Arthur Sinclair, to whom Decatur forwarded Hamilton's letter.

There was no war talk yet. Decatur had just been told by the secretary of the navy that "the gunboats under your command which you were told to prepare for service must be dismasted and laid up in a secure place where you can keep an eye on them. The men must be discharged." Decatur had been working conscientiously on the gunboat program, albeit with little faith in it. On April 9, 1807, he warned the secretary that "the season is now approaching when the worm so destructive to uncoppered vessels will begin to bite. The vessels must be moored in fresh water." Two weeks later, when he had received Smith's order to lay up the gunboats, he advised that sheds be built for their shelter. He had also checked on the *Chesapeake* to the extent of his authority and learned that with the exception of 106 shells, which he was keeping in the navy yard, her condition for sea was satisfactory. Meanwhile, onshore Lieutenant Sinclair had responded to Consul Hamilton's request for surrender of the deserters in an ambiguous, or negative, tone, which drew from the

Briton a note of "regret that you do not feel justified in giving up the men."

On May 15 Secretary Smith sent Barron final sailing orders. "Being at peace with all the world, our principal object in sending vessels of war into the Mediterranean is to protect our commerce and seamen against the predatory dispositions of the Barbary powers." At the same time, "Our interest as well as good faith requires that we should continuously avoid whatever may have a tendency to bring us into collision with any other power." Barron had also received a letter from the president. Thomas Jefferson wished him to contact a Mr. Higgins at Malta and "ask him to send back a pipe of Marsala Madeira if conveyance is available." Either at that moment or, more likely, in later years, Barron scribbled an endorsement on the request: "From that infamous Hypocrite, T. Jefferson."

At Halifax, Nova Scotia, Vice Admiral Sir George Cranfield Berkeley, commander-in-chief of his Majesty's ships on the North American Station, was also writing letters. He had recently complained to the Lords of the Admiralty in London that more than ten thousand Englishmen had joined the American navy. Berkeley knew of the impasse at Norfolk. Commodore Barron had examined four suspected British deserters on the *Chesapeake*'s spar deck and declared them to be positively American. It mattered little. Even as Barron notified the secretary of the navy that his flag captain, Gordon, reported the *Chesapeake* ready for sea, a message from Admiral Berkeley was on its way south to his captains in Hampton Roads.

The four *Melampus* deserters had signed on as members of the *Chesapeake*'s crew and "openly paraded in the streets of Norfolk, in sight of their officers, under the American flag. His Majesty's ships that meet the *Chesapeake* outside the limits of the United States must show this order and search for the men." The admiral's directive was in the hands of Salisbury Pryce Humphreys, captain of the fifty-six-gun warship *Leopard*.

8

Chesapeake
and
Leopard

The thirteen-hundred-ton frigate *Chesapeake* was fast, handsome, and haunted by misfortune. Her passage down the Potomac and Chesapeake Bay had seldom been trouble-free. Hardly two miles from the river's eastern bank, almost still within sight of her original anchorage at the Washington Navy Yard, she grounded on Greenleaf Point, and Captain Gordon had to order all hands to heave her clear. The following Sunday morning, while undergoing carpentry off Alexandria, her fore-topgallant yard came unhitched and the thirty-six-foot spar crashed to the foredeck, killing a seaman and a boy. Eleven days after leaving the navy yard, the ship lay abreast of Mount Vernon, and when Gordon prepared to fire a salute in honor of George Washington, he found half his cartridges were too large to be forced into the muzzles of some of her forty-four guns. Gordon immediately ordered the arrest of Gunner William Hook, who was, however, soon reinstated because no better gunner could be found. And a seaman fell overboard and drowned.

On June 4 the ship dropped anchor in Hampton Roads, and on the sixth Commodore Barron boarded, hoisted his broad pennant, and stayed but three hours. When he made another visit four days later, he found arrangements afoot for a party Gordon planned to give friends.

Gordon's lieutenants threw a second party a week later. Further delay Gordon would blame on pious Hampton suppliers who refused to work on Sundays. Barron boarded for departure on Sunday, June 21, and the next day at seven A.M. the *Chesapeake* stood for the Atlantic.

She was well armed, with twenty-eight 18-pounders on the gun deck and twelve 32-pound carronades on the quarterdeck. But of her 339 men and boys, many had never laid eyes on a ship's gun. The frigate also carried a marine contingent of fifty-two, commanded by Captain John Hall, whose bride of six months was with him. Another passenger, accompanied by his wife and three children, was Dr. John Bullus, newly appointed U.S. naval agent in the Mediterranean. Baggage and furniture belonging to the Halls and the Bulluses were piled on the gun deck. The U.S. Marine Corps had recruited twelve musicians in the Mediterranean. In the United States they had failed to please and were ordered back to Sicily. They too were on the *Chesapeake,* belowdecks, complete with instruments and families.

At nine Monday morning the frigate passed Lynnhaven Bay, where four British warships lay at anchor. Two of them signaled to each other, then to a third, which backed south, preceding the *Chesapeake* into the Atlantic. This was HMS *Leopard.* By 3:30 P.M. she had rounded up on the *Chesapeake*'s windward quarter and approached to within fifty yards. Her captain hailed, identified himself and his ship, and called across the water that he carried dispatches for the *Chesapeake*'s commander.

Barron allowed a British lieutenant to come on board. He carried Admiral Berkeley's directive. Barron's response was that no British deserters were on his ship and he could not muster the crew to search for any. The lieutenant returned to the *Leopard.* Again Humphreys hailed, motivated as he would say by "an ardent desire to prevent bloodshed." On the *Chesapeake*'s quarterdeck Barron told Captain Gordon to clear the gun deck—a tall order given its lumbered state. To Humphreys's repeated hailing Barron shouted back through his speaking trumpet that he couldn't hear clearly. Humphreys's next

words were ominously to the point. "Captain Barron, you must be aware of the necessity I am under of complying with orders."

Barron again turned to Gordon: hurry the men to quarters secretly. No drumbeat, no piping. Barron had Secretary Smith's warning in mind, to avoid friction with foreign ships. His officers knew nothing of this and interpreted their commodore's hesitant reaction to Humphreys's demand as timidity. Twenty-three-year-old Lieutenant Allen, for instance, thought that were the men properly beat to quarters the *Chesapeake* would be quite ready to fight. Allen was one of two lieutenants who sped to a forward division, cursing when they found it crammed with an armorer's forge and anvil, carpenter's workbench, a grindstone, casks, and meat barrels. Allen had them shoved aside and the guns cast loose. His fellow officers were equally busy, clearing their divisions of impedimenta. The magazine below was locked. Gunner Hook hadn't reached it with his key when the *Leopard* opened fire.

No mere warning shot, it was an attack. The first balls flew across the *Chesapeake*'s bow and stern. Then two dozen British guns hurled shot and canister, which cut the frigate's skysail in two, shredded the mainmast, hammered the hull. Below in the cockpit Captain Hall's wife and the Bulluses clung fearfully to one another. Hall's marines had scant time to draw and load their muskets. Men rushing fore and aft included Midshipman Jesse Duncan Elliott, undistinguished at this moment, by no means so in future years.

Though gun divisions were no longer obstructed, the guns were mute without powder, lighted match, or hot iron loggerhead. Elliott sent a man to the magazine. He crawled back with multiple wounds, the loggerhead he still stubbornly clutched grown cold. A ball that struck Allen's second division left it like a slaughterhouse: two of his men had each lost an arm, another's leg was torn off, a fourth died at the lieutenant's feet. Blood-spattered but unhurt, Allen primed three guns himself but his loggerhead had cooled. He raced along the gun deck to the galley and plucked a burning coal from the stove. Acrid smoke, blind confusion, and cries of agony obscured any accurate

impression of how that fiery nub reached the gun, leaving legend to place it in Allen's bare hand. The eighteen-pounder fired. A ball flew to the *Leopard,* pierced its hull to crash into her wardroom.

Barron had leaned against a quarterdeck gun as Sailing Master Sam Brook bound wounds left in the commodore's right leg by the *Leopard*'s opening fire. "Is it possible," Barron had cried, "that we cannot get a gun to fire?" Someone had heard him call "For God's sake, will nobody do his duty?" Then he had addressed Gordon. At least one gun should be fired for the honor of the ship because "I mean to strike." Lieutenant Allen's single shot had obliged him. From the open gangway Barron hailed Humphreys. His words, hardly audible in the general clamor, ended, "We will send our boat on board of you." And someone aft, not the commodore, was heard to shout, "God damn you, haul down the colors!"

The American flag and commodore's broad pennant descended even as the *Leopard* hurled her sixth or seventh broadside—no one was keeping count. And with dozens wounded added to the sixty seamen already sick in hammocks when the attack began, untended now because the ship's surgeon was among the casualties, Barron braced against the fife rail and dictated a melancholy note. "Sir, I consider the frigate your prize and am ready to deliver her to an officer authorized to receive her."

Lieutenant Benjamin Smith was ordered to carry the missive to the British. Ill luck marred even this act of surrender. Lowering the ship's boat a seaman got his hand jammed in the block. With his other hand he took a knife to sever the tackle. Smith bellowed up at him, "If you cut this boat's fall, I will cut your throat." The boat was lowered and the message delivered. Soon an English officer stood on the *Chesapeake*'s bloodied deck. He refused to take Barron's proffered sword and asked that all hands be called on deck. They were; three were "identified" as British. A fourth had hidden in the *Chesapeake*'s coal hole. He was discovered and hauled away with the others; within weeks he would hang from the yardarm of a Royal Navy sloop.

Captain Humphreys rejected Barron's offer of the *Chesapeake* as a prize of war, made sail, and stood to the north. By way of farewell he wrote Barron that he had "nothing more to desire" and deplored the violence caused by "the execution of a service which might have been adjusted more amicably." Wearied, in mental and physical pain, Barron probably paid the words little heed. Instead, slumped in the frigate's great cabin, he listened to his officers' expressions of blame and shame. Gordon said that while continued bloodshed had been averted, "a few broadsides would have been more to our credit." Lieutenant William Crane said bluntly, "It had been better if the *Chesapeake* had been blown from under us than be thus dishonored." During this distressing postmortem, the torn and battered frigate crept through rain squalls back to Hampton Roads.

She dropped anchor at half past meridian on June 23. By then, in the ship's wardroom and urged by Allen, her five lieutenants and sailing master had composed and signed a letter addressed to the secretary of the navy, lamenting their sense of disgrace and requesting that Commodore Barron be arrested on two charges amounting to failure of command and neglect of duty. Dr. Bullus and Captain Gordon carried it from Norfolk to Washington in the *Chesapeake*'s pilot boat. The letter, which contained no reference to Gordon, appeared in newspapers almost immediately. Secretary Smith replied to the signers, "It does you honour. It will be attended to. I have ordered Captain Decatur to take command of the *Chesapeake*."

Barron wrote the secretary that he was prepared to refute the officers' accusations before a court of inquiry but could not travel any distance yet because of his wounds. He received no word of sympathy from Robert Smith, who merely ordered him to hand over the ship's papers to Decatur, who would have the same status as had Barron, "with Mr. Gordon as captain under you."

On July 1 Decatur boarded the frigate and from his onetime mentor and father figure received the ship's papers. Then Barron climbed to the quarterdeck. Officers had assembled to witness his departure.

He limped past them in what surely was an agony of spirit and at the gangway seemed almost to stumble. He recovered and climbed down the ladder to a waiting cutter. At four P.M. James Barron quit the *Chesapeake.*

Three days later on, of all dates, July 4, Decatur reported that he had relieved Barron of his command. He was seeing to the *Chesapeake*'s repairs and reinvigorating the crew when a boatload of Virginia militiamen passing the ship received no expected gun salute. One of them wondered why. Answer was given that according to naval tradition a ship without honor could confer none on others. "We heard the explanation with a sigh," wrote a militiaman, but he added, "If Barron has disgraced you, Decatur will retrieve your honour."

That same midsummer week, bedridden and almost incoherent, Barron wrote to Dr. Bullus. "I have attached no blame to you . . . [but] the officers were on that day the greatest cowards that ever stood on a ship's deck . . . my worst wound is what you would call shocking but to me that have known so many darts in the heart . . . shot by my countrymen without knowing the merits of my case, it is scarcely felt except when dressing. The two Smiths [Benjamin and Sidney] on the quarterdeck were as useful to me as if they had been in the infernal region, where they will go if an abominable degree of cowardice will send a man there. . . . Allen is the most vindictive rascal of them all . . . and I am induced to believe that the reports in circulation prejudiced to me have originated with him. I only ask people to suspend their opinion for the present, let the true story come out . . . had I been prepared and supported I would never have hauled down the *Chesapeake*'s colours."

Once news of the *Leopard*'s attack reached shore, outraged Norfolk citizens formed a committee to plan protest and retaliation. It included Decatur's father-in-law, Luke Wheeler, now ex-mayor, and James Barron's brother-in-law Theodore Armistead. Henceforth, the British squadron would be considered hostile. So would anybody

carrying messages or supplies to the British sailors. Citizens of neighboring Hampton destroyed water casks intended for the British ships. While Jefferson's government and the British minister in Washington tried to talk their way out of the near war crisis, Consul Hamilton in Norfolk was unable to communicate with his shipboard compatriots.

On the *Chesapeake,* Stephen Decatur relished the prospect of action. Even before taking command he had advised the navy secretary that the people of Norfolk were calling on him for gunboat assistance. He believed that the British intended to seize his ship. "I have no doubt we shall have a fight."

There were good grounds for such apprehension. The British ships were seen to be lightening their loads. A Norfolk pilot swore that he had heard a lieutenant of the *Bellona* report that his vessel was under orders to blockade Norfolk. The *Bellona* was lightened by transfer of forty guns to an escort schooner, and with the same purpose HMS *Triumph* had shifted her ballast from aft forward. Captain John Douglas of the *Bellona* wrote Norfolk's mayor, Richard Evers Lee, a highly provocative letter boasting of his "power to obstruct the whole trade of the Chesapeake." He penned these words on the eve of July 4, a coincidence the mayor promptly exploited by warning Douglas that the date should remind him that Americans were no longer vulnerable to threats of force, even when concealed by false friendship. "That delusive security is passed for ever."

At the same time Secretary Smith sent Decatur a positive banquet of encomiums as to his "sound judgement . . . patriotism and valour," with the government's faith that if war comes, "the honour of the nation will not suffer from its having been committed to your hands." Decatur's report to the secretary, also composed on the Fourth, brimmed with self-confidence. The *Chesapeake*'s hull could be repaired in four days, the foremast and mainsail within seven days, the whole ship made ready for sea in three weeks. He would move her closer to town, so that combined with the nine 18-pounders mounted on Fort Norfolk, they could resist any British invasion attempt. At

the same time, he was seeing to the Jefferson gunboats, in good condition though needing crews. "Give me men who will be subject to the articles of war, men who if not disposed to see their duty I can force them to do it."

An Englishman whose position might have become uncomfortable was one Mr. Petty, assigned by Robert Smith as Decatur's secretary. How this came about is not clear, but Petty's service on the frigate was short-lived. "I have no particular reason to distrust his integrity," Smith wrote to Decatur, "yet under existing circumstances it would subject me to just censure if I were to continue him in the station he now holds." Decatur put Mr. Petty onshore. Then there were the *Chesapeake*'s marines. "They were," Decatur told Smith, "the worst detachment I have ever seen. Our marines, sir, we have ever considered as our sheet anchor men." He believed that the shore barracks had better personnel. "I have been told that they have selected the worst for us."

And his gunboats were still short on crews. Enough men had arrived from Baltimore, Washington, and Philadelphia to man only half of the sixteen he had fitted for service. Still, the British gave no additional signs of trouble. Admiral Berkeley, in fact, had been scolded by the Lords of the Admiralty and recalled to London. And in due course the squadron off Norfolk sailed out of Hampton Roads.

Despite the absence of any further hostile moves by British ships, Decatur remained active and alert. He deployed the gunboats into more effectively defensive positions while they still awaited men. He calculated that thirty were needed to man each boat. "Should the British return again to Hampton Roads and we have men, we will convince them that our boats are superior to their ships." Two of his gunboats came upon a pair of well-armed schooners suspiciously close to shore. They turned out to be tenders belonging to the British squadron, blown inshore by strong easterlies. Unmoved by this explanation, Decatur ordered them back out to sea. In August he shifted the *Chesapeake* into the bight of Craney Island to prevent desertion

and keep the crew healthy, neither of which he could have done with the frigate lying in Norfolk harbor. He had charged two of her people with desertion, insolence, and mutinous conduct. They were court-martialed and dismissed from the service. Otherwise conditions were, as Decatur put it, "tranquil," which enabled him to spend more time living at Luke Wheeler's home with Susan, whose beauty and sophistication were still objects of admiration and envy among Norfolk society.

The official court of inquiry into Commodore Barron's surrender of the *Chesapeake* was pending. The secretary of the navy had ordered Commodore Preble to preside over it. But Barron's pleas of indisposition forced one adjournment after another until the appointed judge advocate, Littleton Waller Tazewell, a gifted young Norfolk attorney and close friend of Decatur, became impatient. "Events might at any time deprive the court of valuable disclosure." Tazewell meant not only the possibility of war with England. Preble died, as did one of the *Chesapeake*'s lieutenants, Benjamin Smith, of "bilious fever."

The court got down to business in October, and Barron's spirits could hardly have risen when he heard that its president would be Captain Alexander Murray, a cousin of Charles Gordon and an officer unlikely to have forgotten Barron's criticism of the methods Murray had used to recondition the *Insurgente*. The court met daily on the *Chesapeake,* with Decatur one of its members. Barron had just written to the *Norfolk Public Ledger* protesting against published stories "calculated to injure my character." He had not responded to them, relying on the court to collect the true facts. But whatever optimism Barron clung to soon evaporated.

Still physically weakened, he attended only the first week's hearing, having secured permission to be represented by counsel. Robert Barraud Taylor was a Norfolk attorney of considerable experience and respectability, but hardly a match for Tazewell. From Marine Captain John Hall and several midshipmen, including Jesse Elliott, Taylor drew agreement that throughout the *Leopard*'s attack Barron

was "calm . . . showed no agitation . . . acted bravely." But Tazewell, partly coached in advance by Lieutenant Allen, summoned officers only too eager to contradict. Captain Gordon said it had been Barron's intention all along to surrender the frigate. His lieutenants, especially Allen, portrayed him as fearful, confused, and irresolute. Even Sailing Master Brook was "doubtful of his courage."

Taylor evidently thought officers of the court would recognize prejudice when they heard it and said little of pivotal significance. In early November the court adjourned with a damning report. It appeared that Barron had visited the *Chesapeake* only twice when she lay in Hampton Roads, and on neither occasion did he examine her. The guns were never exercised before she proceeded to sea, the crew called to quarters no more than three times. Barron knew of English deserters on board, had seen the *Leopard*'s menacing movements, the tompions out of her guns while the *Chesapeake*'s "lower deck ports were all triced up." After the British lieutenant had left the *Chesapeake* with Barron's rejection of Captain Humphreys's ultimatum, "his first order was merely to clear his gun deck, and the second, after some lapse of time, to get his men to quarters secretly, without beat of drum. He manifested great disposition to negotiate rather than a determination bravely to defend his ship." He used language within the crew's earshot "calculated to dispirit . . . by ordering them to keep down, that they would all be cut to pieces."

Secretary Smith may not have bothered to study the court's full report. As summarized by its president, Alexander Murray, the record was "prolix and elaborate." The gist was that Barron "struck his colours without consulting a single officer, thereby disgracing the flag of the United States." Tazewell also wrote to Smith. The *Chesapeake*'s ordeal was caused by Barron's failure to prepare for an attack he had ample reason to expect. None of these documents referred to Charles Gordon's responsibility as captain of the frigate. Court-martials were now inevitable, Barron the principal defendant.

9

Barron's
Trial

National anger over the *Chesapeake-Leopard* affair had subsided, except in Norfolk, where passions still ran hot and touched off duels. Following a meeting between two *Chesapeake* midshipmen named Broom and Crump, which left the latter wounded in the thigh, Secretary Smith wrote anxiously to Decatur of hearing "with great pain" of the gunplay in Norfolk. This sort of thing exposed naval officers, especially those of the *Chesapeake,* to harsh criticism. Smith urged Decatur to "prevent the practice by all the means in your power." The secretary had only weeks before reminded John Rodgers, still in pursuit of the Barrons, that under the Articles of War "no person in the Navy shall quarrel with any other person in the Navy, nor use provoking or reproachful words, gestures or measures, on pain of such punishment as a court martial shall adjudge."

Such legalism had no effect on the most sensational duel of that late fall. There were in fact two duels, both involving Charles Gordon. Decatur kept the secretary informed. Two young Norfolkians "said to be connections of Commodore Barron" had made insulting comments regarding Gordon's conduct on the *Chesapeake.* From their standing in society they were "not entitled to [his] notice, one is a

counting house clerk." Decatur promised he would do all that he could to head off bloodshed.

His efforts, such as they were, proved futile. One of Gordon's meetings was with a Dr. Stark and a Norfolk citizen named Mc-Connico. Both were friends of Barron. Arrangements for the meeting with Stark stipulated that should either man fire too soon, the other's second could shoot him. Six shots were fired. At word for the seventh, Stark fired prematurely, whereupon Gordon's second, Lieutenant William Crane, shot at the doctor, wounding him in the arm. Further gunfire left both Gordon and Stark wounded. On November 19 Decatur was "happy to inform" the navy secretary that "all differences between the officers and gentlemen at this place I am informed are adjusted . . . Captain Gordon has entirely recovered from his wound." But Gordon had not fought his last *Chesapeake* duel.

In Washington just then, Congress had reassembled, and as a marked result of the *Chesapeake-Leopard* affair national defense was high on the agenda. But since the British warships had left American waters, fear of war had ebbed, and following debates and cabinet meetings all that remained of the active navy were Thomas Jefferson's gunboats, with the frigates laid up in port "as receptacles for enlisting seamen to fill the gunboats occasionally." Decatur was still commander of the *Chesapeake* with little to occupy his mind other than the ship's maintenance, the crew's discipline, and the gunboats. But then he had something else to think about, a decision to be made. The week before Christmas, the secretary of the navy had sent Commodore John Rodgers to Norfolk with orders to arrest Commodore Barron, Captain Gordon, Gunner Hook, and Captain John Hall of the marines. Their court-martials were imminent.

Commodore Rodgers left the gunboats whose construction he had supervised at New York and hastened south. He had lost none of his grudges against the Barrons; indeed, they had probably intensified after James Barron's surrender of his ship. Rodgers's animus was no secret. Even so, Secretary Smith named him president of the court, and

Rodgers obeyed without demur. But Decatur's conscience dictated otherwise. He had lost none of his zest for a show of strength. The captain of a French warship, *Patriot,* had recently demanded the surrender of a deserter from his crew who allegedly had enlisted in Decatur's gunboat flotilla. Decatur replied in characteristic terms that "after having men placed under my command, I cannot authorize (nor am I disposed to) that they be taken from me. . . . Every respect due your flag, sir, I shall most scrupulously and cheerfully obey, but at the same time must tenaciously guard from insult that under which I have the honour to serve." But when directed by the secretary of the navy to join the court that would try the man he had once venerated on charges of negligence and implied cowardice, he hesitated. He wrote back to Smith on December 17, "I cannot, in justice to Commodore Barron, and my own feelings, sit on the court."

It was no outright refusal. Certainly no disobedience. It was an appeal for which Decatur was obliged to state his reasons. "When the unfortunate affair of 22nd of June occurred, I formed and expressed an opinion that Commodore Barron had not done his duty–during the court of inquiry I was present when the evidence of the officers was given–I have since seen the opinion of the Court, which I think was lenient. It is probable that I am prejudiced against Commodore Barron, and view his conduct in the case more severely than it deserves–prior to his sailing, my opinion of him as a soldier was not favourable. Although, sir, I hope and trust I should most conscientiously decide on Commd. Barron's case, still, sir, there is no circumstance that should occasion me so much regret, as to be compelled to serve on a court martial that tries him–I have therefore to solicit that I may be excused from this duty."

Obeying the dictates of his conscience was certainly the right thing for Decatur to do. Yet there are questions. Why was his opinion of Barron "as a soldier" before the *Chesapeake-Leopard* affair unfavorable? Did he feel that Barron had employed craven tactics to dodge a meeting with John Rodgers? But Decatur had no particular liking

for Rodgers. Was there, behind his words, some unshakable memory, still rankling, of Barron's hapless interference in the ribbing Decatur took on a Norfolk street concerning his interest in Susan Wheeler? And was his appeal to the secretary all that commendable? How could he have honorably remained silent since he had expressed his prejudice against Barron, presumably to fellow officers?

He sent a copy of his letter to Robert Taylor, Barron's counsel, who could thereby have protested Smith's choice of Decatur for a seat on the court. The lawyer could have made a particular case against the appointment of John Rodgers as its president. But Taylor's peculiar reasoning was that officers known to be prejudiced against the accused would serve to emphasize the vindication that, he tried to assure his friend, was bound to be the final outcome.

Decatur could not have been surprised by the secretary's response. "It does you honour. . . . I have no doubt you will do justice to the accused and to the country." There had been other such applications. "I cannot excuse any of you. Already there are fewer captains on the court than I could have wished." Besides Rodgers and Decatur, they included William Bainbridge, who more than once had surrendered his ship without a fight. The court was completed by four lieutenants and two masters commandant. It assembled in the *Chesapeake*'s great cabin on January 4, 1808, its formal opening signaled by a discharge from a quarterdeck gun.

Commodore James Barron, to give him the rank that had been his on the *Chesapeake* and would never be again on any ship, was accused of (a) neglecting to sufficiently visit and examine the *Chesapeake* before sailing; (b) neglecting, on the probability of an engagement, to clear his ship for action; (c) failing to encourage, in his own person, his officers and men to fight courageously; and (d) not doing his utmost to take or destroy the *Leopard,* which vessel it was his duty to encounter. Under Article Four, *Rules for the Better Government of the United States Navy, 1801,* a conviction on any but the first of those

charges meant a death sentence "or such punishment as a court-martial shall adjudge."

Every member of the court that would try Barron, except its president, was his junior. Bainbridge had only recently returned from a prolonged furlough he had obtained for overseas trading. The now accused Barron had presided over the court that had so glowingly acquitted him of responsibility for surrendering the *Philadelphia*. But no such acquittal could have freed Bainbridge from the lingering hurt he would miss no opportunity of escaping. In the immediate wake of the *Chesapeake-Leopard* affair he had assured the Navy Department of his readiness for action, should war come with England. "When the imperious voice of my country calls, I shall not think any sacrifice too great to be made of it."

On the court's second day, the *Chesapeake* received an unexpected caller, Richard H. Bromley, captain of the Royal Navy warship *Statira*. A week earlier she had arrived in Hampton Roads with a British peace envoy, George Henry Rose. The consul in Norfolk, John Hamilton, had notified Decatur of Rose's mission and asked whether the *Statira* would be "received here on the same footing as the national ships of any other country in amity with the United States." Decatur had curtly but politely referred Hamilton to Norfolk's port collector. The *Statira*'s captain came alongside in a pilot boat and, Decatur wrote, "came on board before I was informed." Barron's court-martial was under way. Decatur told Bromley that therefore he could not be invited. But all the visitor wished was to pay his respects, which were politely acknowledged. And as if to let Secretary Smith know that the *Statira*'s captain was duly impressed, Decatur wrote that at this time "the *Chesapeake* could not have been in better order."

The smartly uniformed officers of Barron's court-martial sat solemnly around a table dominated at one end by a glowering John Rodgers. At the other end, to the right of Littleton Tazewell, stood two chairs, one for the accused and one for his counsel. Witnesses would be seated in a chair at Tazewell's left. Wintry light filtered

through the ports. Lieutenant William Crane was first called. Decatur asked him if he considered it a commander's duty to consult officers on whether to surrender. Crane said it was. When Barron's counsel, Robert Taylor, wondered aloud under what circumstances was a commander excepted from so doing, Crane had a ready answer: after he had made a gallant defense.

Taylor tried to show that his client had no cause to expect an attack. Crane convincingly countered each question. Was it not usual for a two-decker to have her lower ports triced up? Possibly in a calm, Crane said, but at the time "there was so much sea [the *Leopard*'s] lower ports were dripping before she came alongside of us." And while the *Chesapeake* had no reasonable hope of taking the *Leopard*, "she might have fought her a long time."

William Allen succeeded Crane in the witness chair. So intense was this young lieutenant's sense of shame, it had induced him to regard himself as on trial. If Barron was exonerated, then he, Allen, was guilty. He had written his father, "If I am honourably acquitted, you may see me again. If not, never." Allen was given no opportunity for melodramatic exclamation at the trial, but questions put to him by Stephen Decatur were as suitably incisive as the lieutenant might have wished. Did he hear Commodore Barron hail the *Leopard* during the attack?

"I did not."

"What resistance was made by the *Chesapeake* to the attack of the *Leopard*?

"None whatever, except the firing of one gun."

"What were the *Chesapeake*'s injuries, and those of her crew, when you first knew her colours were hauled down?"

"Thirteen round shot in her hull, of which about two were above the surface of the water. . . . Her foremast wounded . . . mainmast shot through in three places . . . shrouds cut away. Three seamen, two in the first division and one in the second, killed. Twenty wounded."

"Were the ship's injuries such as to make a surrender of her necessary?"

"No, sir."

The same question was asked of Lieutenant John Orde Creighton. Had the *Chesapeake*'s damage and casualties warranted surrender? This time the questioner was William Bainbridge, whose ship had suffered neither damage nor casualties when he had surrendered her off Tripoli. Creighton's answer, like Allen's, was no. After this, Bainbridge contributed little to the proceedings beyond a question prompted perhaps by sympathy for an officer who, like himself, knew the pain of ignominy. It was whether Barron, during the attack, had displayed any conduct of a character unbecoming that of an American officer. Creighton's answer was noncommittal. "I did not see him during the attack. He was on the upper deck, I on the gun deck."

Lieutenant David Porter, who had personally handed over the *Philadelphia* to an enemy when directed by Bainbridge, was not so reticent as his former commander. He asked scores of questions, one to Lieutenant Sidney Smith. Did any aspect of Barron's conduct indicate a lack of determination to defend the *Chesapeake?* Smith cited two examples: Barron's failure to order the crew to quarters and to have the gun deck cleared during the forty minutes the British lieutenant was on board.

Tazewell picked up the thread. Anything in Barron's behavior seem caused by fear? "He appeared much agitated," Smith said, "as if not knowing what order to give."

Barron's counsel intervened. "You believe the agitation produced by fear?"

"I thought it was."

Robert Taylor pressed further for detail. Smith could add nothing and was about to rise from the witness chair when Taylor checked him with "Were you ever in an engagement before?"

Smith said no and left the cabin.

Guided by Robert Taylor, Midshipman Jesse Duncan Elliott gave

testimony favorable to the accused. He had heard Barron hail down the hatchway, for the firing of a gun, three times. Marine Captain John Hall also spoke well of the commodore. He was not agitated, gave firm and distinct orders, encouraged the men. Not that Hall expected his words to count for much among the array of naval gold lace and blue cloth that he, a lowly marine, confronted. It was about this stage in the trial when Barron, whose thinking distorted by bitterness would blame Jefferson's administration for the *Leopard*'s attack, asked that Secretary of State James Madison be subpoenaed for questioning on the matter of British deserters serving under American colors. Barron insisted that before sailing he understood that it had been settled to the satisfaction of both governments. Tazewell wrote an appropriate letter, to which Madison replied from Washington that, sorry, he could recall no circumstance that would be of importance to the court-martial.

Alleged deserters on the *Chesapeake* was the subject of a mild verbal war Stephen Decatur was waging just then with Captain Bromley of the *Statira*. Seeing to the running of the *Chesapeake,* its repair and crew discipline, prevented him from attending every session of Barron's trial, but he spent considerable time writing letters to Bromley. Responding to charges that American deserters sheltered on British ships, a reversal of the issue that had precipitated the *Chesapeake-Leopard* crisis, Bromley had asked Consul Hamilton to assure Decatur and other American naval commanders that he would always be ready to surrender any men on British vessels if given proof of their American citizenship. This, however, on condition that three British subjects said to be on the *Chesapeake* and wishing to return to their native colors be permitted to do so.

Hamilton relayed this to Decatur, who wrote back that he had questioned the men and "I find they all deny having applied or wished to be placed under the British flag." Bromley had declared that his overtures as to a fair exchange of British and American nationals were in accordance with a proclamation made by his monarch

in England granting pardons to English black sheep who returned to the fold. This failed to impress Decatur, who wrote that he was not bound in any way by a proclamation of King George III.

Bromley addressed Decatur directly on January 17, 1808. "It does not rest with me to lay down particular laws for distinguishing the subjects of our respective nations," and he added the names of four more men, not necessarily on the frigate but serving on Decatur's gunboats. He also referred to "others" detained on the *Chesapeake*. Decatur grew snappish. Bromley had "no right even to enquire about any person on my ship." And he turned his attention back to Barron's trial. Owing to the frigid weather, the court had adjourned to a well-heated lodging house onshore. By then, Charles Gordon occupied the witness chair, with damning testimony to the effect that Barron had failed to encourage his men to fight. And when Barron's counsel asked was it not a fact that deficiencies in the gun department had prevented firing a salute off Mount Vernon before Barron came on board, Gordon refused to answer. Tazewell had advised him that with the approach of his own trial he was permitted to avoid self-incrimination. Further questions drew the same response. "I must decline to answer and claim the privilege which the court has granted me."

He likewise avoided discussion of a letter addressed to Barron dated June 19, 1807, describing the *Chesapeake* as in good order. Taylor forced him to acknowledge that it bore his signature. Gordon had also to concede that with the *Leopard*'s preparations for attack in plain view, he had not checked the gun deck for readiness. "I considered it my duty to be on the quarterdeck." But did not his admitted suspicion of trouble induce him to even grill Gunner Hook about the state of the ship's magazine? Again, "I must decline to answer."

Taylor countered Gordon's tactic by asking the court's permission to examine the judge advocate. Tazewell raised no objection. He took his seat in the witness chair, and after Rodgers had administered the oath, the two Norfolk attorneys confronted each other. Taylor

first directed Tazewell to read aloud Gordon's original sworn state-
ment at the court of inquiry, that neither he nor Barron had expected
trouble from British ships. Gordon had told the present court that he
had been informed that a British demand would be made for alleged
British deserters. This move of Robert Taylor's carried the implica-
tion that Gordon had committed perjury. The court did not pursue it.
And presumably with a resigned shrug, neither did Barron's counsel.

Barron was not called to testify. Taylor read his closing plea,
whose theme was that blame for the frigate's unpreparedness when
under the *Leopard*'s guns rested on Gordon's shoulders, since he was
captain. Taylor quoted from Naval Regulations. "A captain, whether
sailing alone or in a squadron, is responsible for the whole conduct
and good government of the ship." Gordon had neglected to have the
Chesapeake ready for action, and as a result Barron had no option
other than to surrender.

The court went into private session in its warm lodging house.
Three of the four charges foundered. Barron had not neglected his
duty. He was not to blame for omitting to call his crew to quarters be-
fore reading Captain Humphreys's letter. He had shown coolness and
personal courage under severe circumstances and did right by strik-
ing his flag. It was on the second charge that Barron was condemned.
He received from the commanding officer of the *Leopard* "a commu-
nication that clearly intimated that if certain men were not delivered
up he would proceed to use force." Yet Barron had not even then
cleared his ship for action. The punishment? "Suspension from all
commands without pay or official emoluments of any kind for the
term of five years."

10

The
Captain
Reprimanded

Charles Gordon's trial before the same court lasted less than a week. Tazewell read his defense, which was a surprising admission that while in sole command of the *Chesapeake* from May 1 until June 6, he had never ordered his gunners to make a regular report on the ship's armament, had not once exercised his guns, nor had he called his crew to quarters more than three times. But his men were too sick, or busy, and from his experience on other ships, guns were never exercised until in midocean. He had known nothing of badly mounted guns. "I might as well be responsible for not succeeding with a torpedo in blowing up the *Leopard*."

Midshipman Elliott testified that after the *Leopard*'s attack, the third-division guns were found defectively mounted and he had ordered their carriages sawn down to make them fit. This brought a rare comment from Decatur. The fault Elliott described was a minor one, the remedy he had adopted clumsy and unnecessary. Decatur went on to question the ship's carpenter, to show that all Elliott needed to do to secure the guns was knock down the clamps with a maul. Memory of this aspersion upon his competence may well have been among the elements that, in coming years, would make Jesse

Duncan Elliott, in the widowed Susan Decatur's uncompromising judgment, one of two men who had murdered her husband.

On February 13, at Gordon's request, Decatur was sworn in as a witness. Gordon's purpose was to show that the *Chesapeake* was not all that unprepared when the *Leopard* approached. He asked, "Were the sponges and breechings of the *Chesapeake,* when you took command of her, sufficient for the ship in action?"

He got the reply he wanted. "I think they would have answered," Decatur said. "After I took command of this ship, I had the men exercised to their guns very frequently, twice a day sometimes. In so doing I used the same sponges and breechings which I found on board when I took command."

Barron was also summoned as a witness. He had yet to hear the conclusions of his own court-martial and was still in physical pain. Convinced that "there was an influence in the cabinet which protected Captain Gordon," he endured Gordon's cross-examination with an apathy that bespoke resignation to the adverse verdict he expected.

Gordon: Did I not state to you in Hampton, at your home, the deficiencies I had discovered coming down the Potomac?

Barron: I presume you did. I do not recollect the particulars.

Gordon: Is it customary in the American navy to exercise the men on the guns while coming down the Potomac, with all your guns not yet aboard and your crew not complete?

Barron: I do not believe it is.

Gordon: Was I to blame for the lumbered state of the ship?

Barron: No. The government had organized a number of passengers in the ship. Their luggage could not be moved without offending them.

The court accepted Gordon's arguments and held him largely blameless. His offense was "a very slight one." His penalty was a private reprimand by the secretary of the navy, the court openly stating that this was the lightest it could impose. Captain John Hall also got off with a reprimand but took the opportunity of publicly hoping that

it would not become the rule for a marine to be tried before an all-navy court. Gunner Hook, who had served seven years under the colors and was one of Decatur's party that burned the *Philadelphia,* was dismissed from the navy. So ended the judicial scenario of the *Chesa-peake-Leopard* affair. And if Decatur suspected that secret manipulation from Washington preserved Gordon's reputation at the expense of Barron's, he left nothing in writing to show it.

Decatur was still sparring verbally with the *Statira*'s Captain Bromley. On February 16 he wrote, "In my first communication, I told you I should not retain in United States service any British subject and deserter after having been satisfied of their being such." But he would insist on "full and satisfactory proof [and] I have to tell you I shall not deviate from this determination unless my government so directs." And when Bromley persisted in his demands for British seamen said to be on the *Chesapeake,* Decatur wrote testily, "I have to repeat to you a third time that I shall not discharge from United States service anyone not proven foreign deserters . . . the mere furnishing a list of names stating where the persons were born . . . I will not admit as proof." Citing the case of a man Bromley asked about, Decatur rapped back, "You are greatly in error, sir . . . I shall give no answer . . . I do not admit your right to make the enquiry."

The exchange dragged on into March. "I have tried to be as explicit as possible," Decatur told Bromley, and he complained to Secretary Smith that "Captain Bromley has not shown me much delicacy. I have answered him in a manner I think he deserved. I had hoped the correspondence had closed, but I now fear he will continue it . . . I have viewed [his letters] presumptuous and insolent, and only a fear of increasing the difficulties that exist between the two countries and thereby exposing myself to censure prevents my telling him so."

But no more was heard from Bromley. And Decatur had known all along that by no means was the *Chesapeake*'s crew wholly American. Fifty-nine foreigners had died or deserted. Decatur discharged 175 others, mostly British, but he denied Bromley the benefit of their

services by having them transported up Chesapeake Bay in gunboats and put ashore at Baltimore.

Other matters preoccupied Decatur. Several of his young officers were frequenting Norfolk gambling houses. More disturbing was the discovery that the ship's purser accompanied them. Decatur warned him against risking public money and extracted a promise that such conduct would be discontinued. But the purser added drinking to his transgressions. Decatur put him ashore and left it up to the navy secretary as to what action should be taken. The *Chesapeake* soon had a new purser.

Susan Decatur had been living with her father, but by the middle of 1808 she and her husband resided in a sedate Norfolk home of their own at 517 Warren Street. Someone who met her twice said she did not mix much with other ladies. Nor did she see much of Stephen, whose command still included gunboats. He was eager to return to sea. On July 12 he reported the *Chesapeake* ready to sail, even without a boatswain, a habitual drunk he had dumped off the frigate onto a gunboat.

The previous December the United States Congress had passed an act laying an embargo on all foreign vessels entering American ports. Popular reaction was divided. The legislation, declared the *National Intelligencer* of Washington, proceeded from a surge of patriotism ignited by the attack on the *Chesapeake.* Anti-British feeling was as strong in Norfolk as elsewhere, but the city's *Gazette* foresaw the embargo as "sure to bring ruin to thousands of industrious citizens." Under Navy Department orders, the *Chesapeake* set sail northward, and on August 2, patrolling off Nantucket and Martha's Vineyard, Decatur assured Secretary Smith that "I will do all in my power to prevent violations of the Embargo."

Late in the fall Decatur anchored off Long Island. He went into New York and learned to his grief that just four days after the remarriage of his sister, Ann, their father had died. Decatur hurried to

Philadelphia for the burial at St. Peter's Church but was soon back on a ship's deck, where he appears always to have been happiest. Heavy weather had limited his coastal patrols and provided him with little action beyond interception of cargo ships to make sure they were not violating the embargo.

Early the following year he was appointed commander of the frigate *United States,* on which he had been a midshipman ten years before. The *Chesapeake* was placed in ordinary and thus idled until given to Charles Gordon, who would have preferred never setting eyes on her. He had again fallen victim to one of the duels in her melancholy wake. Visiting relatives in Annapolis he read an article by Alexander Contee Hanson of the *Federalist Republican* attacking his reputation. He and Hanson met with pistols just outside Washington on January 10, 1810. Gordon was shot in the stomach. He was taken to the home of the secretary of the treasury, Albert Gallatin, whose wife nursed him until he had sufficient strength to take charge of "that *unfortunate, unhappy* ship on board of which all my *wretchedness and misery* commenced."

Decatur felt more at home on the *United States.* Younger officers, even those not directly under his command, viewed him with admiration and respect. George Rodgers, related to the irascible John, wrote that while he was in Baltimore recruiting volunteers, Decatur had treated him "like a brother and appears interested in my welfare. My conduct will be such as to merit his esteem and confidence." There were exceptions. A physician named William Barton wanted badly to serve on the *United States* under Decatur. This was arranged, but within a year Decatur had the doctor court-martialed for "scandalous conduct in striking Sailing Master John Gallagher on the quarterdeck."

In 1809 President James Madison had appointed Paul Hamilton to succeed Robert Smith as secretary of the navy. A South Carolina planter and former state governor, Hamilton overcame a weakness

for liquor sufficiently to introduce programs to improve the navy's image. But he could do little to enhance its strength while a frugal Congress held the purse strings. There was more verve than realistic appraisal behind the letter he sent to John Rodgers and Stephen Decatur resenting the "injuries and insults heaped on us" by the warring English and French. "You must submit to not even a menace or threats from a force not materially your superior." Decatur wrote back that "no new indignity will pass with impunity." He had in mind not only the *Chesapeake-Leopard* clash but an 1810 incident when a British brig of war fired two shots into the American schooner *Vixen* off the Bahama Banks. The British captain apologized for what he called his mistake. The *Vixen*'s captain, John Trippe, demanded the apology in writing, which was fair enough, Decatur thought, but by not shooting back, Trippe had "lost a glorious opportunity to cancel the blot under which our flag suffers." (Secretary Hamilton recalled Trippe to face a court of inquiry, but his letter never reached the captain, who, succumbing to yellow fever, died off Havana, in Hamilton's words "at a most unseasonable moment.")

The following spring, John Rodgers found opportunity for action. The British frigate *Guerrière* was reported as harassing American shipping off Sandy Hook, New Jersey. Immediately Rodgers sailed out of Annapolis in command of the forty-four-gun frigate *President*. The *Richmond Inquirer* bade him good luck. "May the wounds of the *Chesapeake* and *Vixen* now be washed away." On May 16 Rodgers had all hands at battle stations when a strange ship was sighted in the falling dusk. The *President*'s people eagerly told themselves it must be the *Guerrière*. The stranger fired first, damaging the *President*'s mainmast and severing a boy's arm. American guns thundered back with broadsides. The next morning Rodgers discovered to his chagrin that he had thoroughly disabled a twenty-two-gun British sloop *Little Belt*, killing a dozen of her crew.

As a result, it was Rodgers's turn to face a court of inquiry, the United States being technically at peace with England. Decatur was

appointed court president. He arrived in New York and sent Rodgers an encouraging letter giving him the choice of time and place for the hearing. Decatur was in a pleasant mood, anticipating an early meeting with Susan. His letter to Rodgers carried a postscript: "I do not know what I have written above. I am in such haste to see my little wife." And he would have welcomed what solace Susan's arms could provide, for he had lost his mother. She had died at the close of March in Philadelphia and was buried beside her husband in St. Peter's churchyard. Decatur's grief can only be imagined, so reluctant was he to betray his emotions in writing. That lively postscript to Rodgers was a rare exception.

The court of inquiry into Rodgers's attack on the *Little Belt* consisted of Decatur and Captains Charles Stewart and Isaac Chauncey. It decided wholeheartedly in Rodgers's favor. But Decatur was not pleased with at least one consequence of the *Little Belt* affair. Secretary Hamilton had written Rodgers to ask that, "as a war now appears inevitable," he draft a plan of operations that, "in your judgement will enable our little navy to annoy to the utmost extent the trade of Great Britain." Decatur was unaware of Hamilton's request but soon faced the result of a second letter that Hamilton, on May 28, wrote Rodgers. What the secretary called "the chastizement which you have properly inflicted"–meaning the attack on the *Little Belt*–"will cause you to be marked for British vengeance. When you put to sea, you will look for Commodore Decatur, take him with you, have him remain with you until further orders." A letter of the same date from Hamilton directed Decatur to discontinue coastal patrols with his *United States* and stay close to Rodgers.

Escorting an overrated commodore was not to Decatur's liking. But he wanted the chance to "whip an Englishman," virtually every American navy captain's dream at this point, and he could hardly wait for official hostilities to begin. On June 9 two small British warships, the *Eurydice* and *Atlanta,* stood down for the United States off the Virginia coast. Their captains satisfied Decatur that they were on

a peaceful mission carrying dispatches for the American government. But when they stood off again, a cannonball from one of the *United States*'s long twenty-fours flew after them. "An accidental firing" was Decatur's straight-faced explanation.

Uncertain how to deploy his small navy, Hamilton had solicited the opinions of his senior officers. Decatur's advice to Hamilton typified his predilection for lone-wolf foraging: send out the ships well stocked with provisions, "distant from our coasts and singly, or not more than two frigates in company, without specific instructions, relying on the enterprise of the officers." It was about now that the thirty-eight-gun British frigate *Macedonian* anchored off Norfolk for an innocently formal visit, and despite a still smoldering hostility in that seaport her officers were greeted politely. The British consul John Hamilton arranged entertainments. British and American officers mingled. Decatur and the *Macedonian*'s captain, John Surman Carden, most likely met, under decidedly different circumstances than they would meet later.

11

Love
and
Glory

In May 1812 the *National Intelligencer* had headlined, DECLARE WAR
NOW. WHAT ARE WE WAITING FOR? Madison's government obliged on
June 18. Three days earlier former president John Adams had written
with picturesque exaggeration, "Our Navy is so Lilliputian that Her-
cules after a hasty dinner would sink it by putting his foot on it. I had
like to say that Gulliver might bury it in the deep by making water on
it." Analogized differently, it was certainly a David versus Goliath sit-
uation. Britain had almost seven hundred warships at sea, one third
of them ships of the line and frigates. But most were blockading
Bonaparte's navy or on convoy duty, and the Lords of the Admiralty
assessed the American fleet as hardly worth the expense of sending
ships across the Atlantic. It was enough, they felt, to leave one ship of
the line and a modest assortment of frigates, sloops, and brigs on the
North American Station.

Secretary Hamilton divided his "little navy" into two squadrons,
one under John Rodgers patrolling north of the Virginia capes, De-
catur commanding another southward from Sandy Hook, New Jer-
sey. Their zones overlapped at the approaches to the Delaware Bay,
and Chesapeake Bay. The United States Navy groped into the War of
1812 with less than a score of seaworthy ships, manned by crews of

adolescent greenhorns and seasoned mariners, proud, patriotic, and prone to golden dreams of prize money. Even Charles Gordon, with a suppurating side wound, savored hopes of avenging the *Leopard*'s attack. He wrote on September 19, 1812, that as "a poor helpless invalid" he had been assigned to Baltimore, "major domo of ten gunboats." But he had applied for command of a corvette fitting out at Washington. "I must have some hand in the war if I live through next year."

No sooner was war declared than the commodores Decatur and Rodgers met on the latter's flagship, *President,* with the *United States, Congress,* the sloop of war *Hornet,* and the brig *Argus* nearby. They formally agreed to "share and share alike in all prizes whatsoever which they should capture, their wives and children to receive in the event of either officer's capture, wounding or death." Then both squadrons stood for the Atlantic.

Rodgers had learned of a Liverpool-bound enemy convoy out of Jamaica. He abandoned pursuit of it to go after HMS *Belvidera.* Within a half-mile range upon smooth sea, the warships opened fire. The *Belvidera*'s stern chasers roared first, but what killed or wounded sixteen Americans, Rodgers included with a broken leg, and half wrecked his forecastle was the explosion of one of the *President*'s own guns, a starboard bow chaser. Limping painfully, Rodgers shouted for broadsides. This meant yawing, which increased the distance between the two vessels. With the margin too wide and torn shrouds, the *President* could not be maneuvered into any attack position for her superior gunpower to bear. The *Belvidera* fled for Halifax, casting away her two anchors to gain speed. The *President* fell astern, with twenty-two casualties, few caused by the enemy. Rodgers tacked to resume chase of the convoy, but scraps of debris left in its wake were about all he saw. Near the mouth of the English Channel in mid-July he wheeled his squadron southward, by which time his whereabouts had become something of a mystery at home.

While the *Chesapeake-Leopard* affair had continued to rankle among American naval officers, James Barron had been largely forgotten. But Lieutenant William Lewis, who had helped Decatur enforce the embargo, saw to it that the Navy Department would be furnished fresh evidence to show that Barron was "vindictive, not only a coward but a traitor." Lewis had been furloughed from the United States in 1811, to command an Indiaman that sailed in South American waters trading in opium. Later that summer Lewis's ship, the *Pennsylvania Packet,* anchored at Pernambuco, and from this Brazilian port he sent a letter to Charles W. Goldsborough, chief clerk of the Navy Department. Its gist was that a Baltimore merchant at Pernambuco had heard Barron revile his own government while in company with the British consul. Barron was alleged to have said that the United States president knew there were English deserters on the *Chesapeake,* and that the Royal Navy intended to take them.

Lewis had obtained this information from Thomas D. Goodwin, brother of Decatur's old friend Lieutenant Charles Ridgley. Goodwin had talked with the British consul. Lewis's hearsay-filled letter would be filed away for eight years until Goodwin, at the Navy Department's request, confirmed its contents as accurate. All that time, Barron would know nothing of it. Following the court-martial, he had struggled to make a living as master of a merchant brig. His brother had died, and his wife was chronically ill. Although he drew strength from the loyalty of his eldest daughter, he wrote, "God knows what I am to witness in a world of torment." But President Madison's repeal of the embargo had improved trade prospects. Barron's brother-in-law Theodore Armistead gave him command of the 170-ton *Portia,* to trade between Copenhagen and Lisbon. On April 5, 1812, Barron had sailed out of Hampton Roads, bound for Europe.

First blood in the naval War of 1812 went to Isaac Hull, a captain with a penchant for business enterprise, ashore and afloat. When

in command of the *Constitution,* he had used her as an English Channel ferry charging twenty-five guineas per head, also as a cargo ship laden with French merchandise for sale at home. The outbreak of war saved Hull from a court-martial. In the middle of August he found himself struggling to escape a seven-ship British squadron, all vessels trapped in a sultry calm. Hull's boats were out for strenuous kedging, likewise the British. The labor was brutally slow, but Hull was not about to yield a frigate he had commanded for six years. When dusk fell, Hull sent men to the yards with buckets of seawater to spill down the sails so they would hold more of the wind. The arduous kedging continued, and at last the British fell astern.

Hull made for the Bermudas. His lookouts sighted HMS *Guerrière,* captain James Dacres, on the afternoon of August 19. Now the wind had freshened, the sea rose. For an hour the two ships maneuvered about each other, seeking the best position to rake. Hull stood cool, his ship exposed to the enemy's gun divisions, but he would not fire until sure of maximum effect. He gave the word when the range had narrowed to one hundred yards. For fifteen minutes the two ships battered each other with broadsides. The *Constitution*'s last fire shattered Dacres's gun deck, brought down her mizzenmast. The ships collided, bowsprits locked, and their crews prepared to board. Musket fire and hand-to-hand struggle replaced use of heavy guns. Lieutenant Charles Morris jumped to the *Guerrière*'s taffrail with the agility that had landed him on the *Philadelphia* before Decatur. A musket ball struck him in the stomach. Though out of action, he would survive. Not so Hull's marine commander, shot in the brain. The ferocious battle subsided. Dacres, like most of his crew, was wounded. He was carried to the *Constitution,* where Hull chivalrously refused his proffered sword. Once abandoned, the *Guerrière* was set afire and sunk.

The victorious Hull reached Boston the day after a mortified John Rodgers arrived to report a cruise "barren of action." He doubtless envied Hull, to whom Secretary Hamilton wrote, "We know not what

most to applaud, your gallantry or your skill." Decatur was also in Boston, on hand to greet the war's first naval hero. Hull's was an achievement Decatur had yearned for, to be "first in the race for renown." But he considered Hull a friend and felt no rancor or jealousy. And he was now determined to break the link with Rodgers and sail alone. To Littleton Tazewell, his fiscal agent, he wrote, "We have lost the *Belvidera,* which ought to have been ours. We have crossed the Atlantic twice, which I believe never ship sailed before. We captured and sent in four vessels, burned two and recaptured one. I boarded. The Golden Opportunity has passed."

Golden Opportunity. He might have meant prize money or glory, probably both. But the gold was still out there, best gained by oneself. Again, the fewer the number, the greater the glory. He was accommodated by a shift in Paul Hamilton's strategic planning. American ships would henceforth go out divided into three small squadrons, commanded by Rodgers, Decatur, and William Bainbridge. Rodgers's and Decatur's ships sailed together from Boston on October 8. The *United States* was escorted by the well-worn brig *Argus.* After an uneventful fortnight's scouring among British East India trade routes, Decatur detached the brig and cruised alone. He shaped course for the Canary Islands and was in the Sargasso Sea, fifty miles south of the Azores, when his topmen sighted a large sail about a dozen leagues to windward and steadily approaching. Not for a moment could Decatur have suspected that the captain was an Englishman he had once befriended.

His Majesty's ship *Macedonian,* a thirty-eight-gun frigate, had left the Devon coast convoying India-bound merchantmen. She was only two years old, built of the best English oak, and but four months out of Plymouth dockyard. Her captain, John Surman Carden, was the son of an English army major killed in the American Revolution. Carden was forty-one, eight years older than Decatur. He had served twenty-four years in the British navy and, although steady

and brave under fire, had achieved no great distinction. Nor did he pamper his crew, preserving discipline through excessive use of the lash. At least once he had sentenced a man to be flogged through the fleet.

Carden's bane while commanding the *Macedonian* was his first lieutenant, a Scot named David Hope who had lost two brothers in outposts of the British Empire. Hope had seen more high-seas battle action than had Carden, whom he regarded as a less-than-competent officer. Carden was aware of Hope's antipathy and before leaving England had appealed to the Admiralty for a different first lieutenant. "It was impossible for him and me to sail together. I trusted the Admiralty would remove one or other of us from the ship." The Admiralty had made no such change. From this shipboard tension Carden may have found relief in the music provided by a group of French instrumentalists he had located on a hulk at Lisbon and who had volunteered to form a band for him.

Decatur had no music on the *United States,* at least none worthy of record. Unlike Carden, he did have a loyal first lieutenant, William Henry Allen, who had idolized him ever since their service together on the *Chesapeake.* Allen had shown his devotion by rigorously enforcing gunnery practice. At daybreak on October 25 the two stood side by side on their frigate's quarterdeck, eyeing through telescopes the oncoming stranger. Then she wasn't so strange, her British ensign seen flying. Decatur lost no time in beating his ship to quarters.

His first impulse was to wear the *United States* to windward of the enemy, hoping to seize the weather gauge from her. In naval warfare under sail, the vessel lying closer to the wind had two distinct advantages. By holding "the weather gauge" a ship could choose whether or not to engage. If she chose to engage, and sailed down to her leeward opponent, when the two ships came broadside to broadside the windward ship exposed no area below her waterline while the leeward ship sailed with part of her underbody out of the water and more vulnerable to her enemy's fire.

As the distance between the two vessels narrowed, the sea rose to a heavy swell. The *Macedonian,* while noted for speed, was the inferior ship, deficient in manpower and mounting five guns fewer than the American, which, though rated a forty-four carried fifty-five. Carden had no intention of losing the weather gauge, even if it meant leaving gunnery range. He discussed options with his sailing master and first lieutenant. The sailing master thought Carden too obsessed with keeping to windward of his opponent. He favored closing by going under the American's stern and hauling up to leeward. No surprise to the captain, Lieutenant Hope also disagreed and thought they should try crossing the enemy's bows.

The crews of both ships had just finished breakfast, had been preparing for Sunday service read by their respective captains, who wore full dress for the occasion. The ships' approximate position was latitude 29° north, longitude 30° west. By skillful seamanship Decatur evaded each of the *Macedonian*'s attempts to hold the weather gauge, until both vessels found themselves on nearly parallel lines, sailing in opposite directions.

Roused by the drumroll and fife, Decatur's people had rushed to battle quarters. His thoughts were concentrated on the imminent contest when twelve-year-old John Cremar came up and asked if his name could be put on the frigate's muster roll. Allowed on board as an apprentice midshipman but too young to be a formal member of the crew, he wanted a share of the prize money should his ship take the enemy. Decatur nodded assent, probably with a friendly smile, and the lad sped back to the gun division he was serving as a powder monkey.

As the two ships passed each other on opposite tacks, Decatur ordered open fire. Her first shots from the main-deck twenty-four-pounders fell short. The *Macedonian* was still beyond range. Carden, whose ship was faster and now had the advantage, could have decreased the range, enabling him to effectively use his powerful short-range carronades. His first lieutenant impatiently urged him to close in. Carden refused, fearing the raking shot he might be exposed to if he did.

Decatur was eager to engage. From his quarterdeck he watched the *Macedonian* come about and take up a pursuing position astern, on the port side. He watched until she was within a half mile distant. Then he attacked with main-deck battery and spar-deck carronades. He strode past gun divisions, calling orders and voicing encouragement. Of the eight or ten hands that made up each division, many were stripped to the waist, heads bound with handkerchiefs to shield their eyes from the sun.

The speed with which they moved paid tribute to Lieutenant Allen's passion for gunnery exercises. The tompions had been swiftly removed, guns cast loose, loaded with balls or bags of langrage thrust into muzzles and rammed fully the length of each barrel. Priming took split seconds, powder sprinkled into the touchhole of each cannon's breech. At the command *Fire*, crouching cannoneers touched their long matches or loggerheads to powder. Each discharge shot the two- or three-ton gun backward, a recoil checked by thick ropes. This was Decatur's first real sea fight, and he rejoiced in its smoke, stench, and thunder.

Astonishment may have mentally paralyzed the *Macedonian*'s people. The American's broadsides became incessant, gunports flashing so rapidly some thought their attacker had caught fire. Struck repeatedly, the *Macedonian*'s mizzenmast went first, collapsing half over the side with its topmen. Her maintop followed the mizzen. Other shots from Decatur's long twenty-fours hammered the *Macedonian*'s hull, came close to decapitating Alexander the Great, whose bust was the warship's figurehead. Samuel Leech of the British crew would tell of a nearby gunner who lost an arm and of a lieutenant who while trying to bind the man's shoulder stump was hurled to the deck by American fire. Of fifty-two officers and men stationed with Carden on the quarterdeck, only nine, himself included, escaped injury or death. So many maimed seamen crawled or staggered into the cockpit, the surgeon and his mates moved with their blood-soaked burdens to the midshipmen's steerage, then finally to

the wardroom, where they sponged wounds and performed amputations on the dining table with rum their only anesthetic. Men killed were heaved overboard without ceremony.

The broadsides kept flying, grapeshot and canister. No shelter protected anyone on the *Macedonian.* The grommet from a hammock clew struck Lieutenant Hope in the head. After being helped below, he shortly reappeared on the quarterdeck, scalp bandaged, to resume arguing with his captain, urging more desperately now that they get closer to the American, attack at short range even if it meant sinking alongside of her.

It was too late for suicidal valor. Carden faced grim reality. Thirty-six of his crew were killed, his boatswain among them, and his seventy wounded included the first and third lieutenants. The *United States*'s broadsides had knocked gun carriages from their trunnions; the six foremost carronades on Carden's quarterdeck were useless, buried under rigging and spars. The smoke-filled air rang with the cries of bleeding men. Carden ordered his colors lowered and Hope sullenly agreed. The American broadsides ceased. The *United States* was not entirely unscathed. What shooting the *Macedonian* had managed with her carronades killed two seamen, a boy, and two marines. Five were badly wounded, among them Lieutenant James Funk, like Decatur a Philadelphian and one of his favorite officers. Funk died on board.

Decatur felt the loss but had no time to mourn. So mauled was the *Macedonian,* having lost all her yards and sails save for a portion of her foresail, and with debris piled on deck and dragging over the side, she was more a misshapen hulk than a ship of war, what Carden himself would call "an unmanageable log." Crossing her bow, Decatur mercifully refrained from raking. He sent Lieutenant John B. Nicholson on board to bring Carden before him. Officially enemies, they still shared a spirit of friendship. So it was more than just chivalry when, upon the Englishman offering his sword, Decatur refused it, saying, "I cannot receive the sword of a man who has so bravely

defended his ship, but I will receive your hand." He took Carden to the great cabin for refreshments and relieved his feelings somewhat by telling him that his was not the first British warship to surrender in this war. Carden had not heard of the *Guerrière*'s fate. He later acknowledged Decatur's "generous and gentlemanly treatment of myself, my officers and crew . . . if ever we should turn the tables, we will endeavour if possible to improve on your unusual goodness."

Aided and supervised by Lieutenant Allen, the rest of the *Macedonian*'s officers, except the surgeon and his mates, were brought on board the *United States.* Allen organized still-upright English sailors into cleansing-and-repair teams. Some Americans were detailed to help patch sails, reassemble spars. Hot vinegar removed bloodstains. Jury-rigged, the *Macedonian* could still float, effectively a bark with square sails on her fore and main-topmasts. Allen took command of her with a prize crew on board. Decatur suspended his cruise, and the two ships, victor and vanquished, sailed in company northwest across the Atlantic, a voyage of forty days.

Fog separated the ships upon their arrival in American waters, but they reunited to sail together through Long Island Sound guided by the "two damn good Hell Gate pilots" Decatur had demanded; in the same letter describing his prize as "a beauty, a look at her will be good for sore eyes." From his cabin on the *United States* he drafted his report to the Navy Department. It was characteristically terse, devoid of boasting, and ascribed his victory in large part to "the obvious superiority of our gunnery." This in turn he attributed to Lieutenant William Allen's "unremitted exertions" in disciplining the crew.

He wrote his wife what was for him a wordy letter, which incidentally showed his regard for Captain Carden as more a friend than a beaten foe:

My beloved Susan,

I have had the good fortune to capture His Britannic Majesty's Frigate Macedonian, Captain Carden, by which I

have gained a small sprig of laurel, which I shall hasten to lay at your feet. I tried burning on a former occasion, which might do for a very young man; but now that I have a precious little wife, I wish to have something more substantial to offer in case she should become weary of love and glory. One half of the satisfaction arising from the victory is destroyed in seeing the distress of poor Carden, who deserved success as much as we did, who had the good fortune to obtain it. I do all I can to console him. Do not be anxious about me, my beloved, I shall soon press you to my heart.

<div style="text-align: right">
Your devoted,

S. Decatur.
</div>

P.S. Love turns aside the balls which round me fly
 Lest precious tears should drop from Susan's eye.

December 16, the two frigates were anchored off Rikers Island, at the Hell Gate. Decatur selected Archibald Hamilton, one of his lieutenants and a son of the secretary of the navy, to hurry south for Washington, bearing the *Macedonian*'s flag. Decatur's feat was, after all, something special in the honor roll of this war's naval exploits. A grimly proud Hull wrote after capturing HMS *Guerrière,* the British "are not now fighting Frenchmen or Spaniards." Jacob Jones on the sloop *Wasp* had dismasted HMS *Frolic* with firepower that destroyed or disabled half her crew. But the *Guerrière,* originally a British prize in the war with France, was so badly damaged she had been blown up. The *Frolic* was recaptured by an enemy ship of the line. Decatur's British prize was intact and moored where Americans could feast their eyes on her. They might also have caught a glimpse of the commodore, who at least once bounded up the *Macedonian*'s gangplank wearing a faded straw hat and commonplace street clothes. He may have had in his pocket the holiday greetings sent him on Christmas Day by the captain he had defeated. Carden sought his influence with

the State Department to speed the departure of the cartel carrying him home to the consolation of his wife. In the same spirit the Englishman wished Decatur "and your Good Wife the Embrace and Passage to those Happy Regions where Wars and Bloodshed are not known."

New York outdid itself in a red-carpet welcome for the returning naval heroes. Officers of the *Constitution, Wasp,* and *United States* were hosted at a banquet in the City Hotel on Broadway between Cedar and Thames Streets. Decatur and Hull were the special guests of honor. The hotel was elaborately decorated with masts, sails, flags, and sea-fight scenes painted on backlighted transparencies.

The ships themselves remained at their moorings under Lieutenant Allen's control. Their formal appearance in New York harbor was scheduled for New Year's Day following a ball the previous night graced by three hundred ladies. On the first day of 1813, aided by a light northerly breeze, the ships sailed down the East River. An anchor accidentally dropped from the *United States* into the seabed, and had its cable not been cut the *Macedonian* might have rammed into her stern. This mishap in no way chilled the spirit of celebration. Both vessels halted off Peck's Slip, where seventy years later would loom the Brooklyn Bridge. Shore artillery greeted them with twenty-one guns, and the *United States* thundered back in response.

The New York celebration climaxed on January 7, first with a parade of some four hundred officers and seamen, all in their best uniform and marching to the beat of the French band Decatur had liberated from the *Macedonian.* Cheering crowds thronged Pearl Street, Wall Street, Broadway. Again the City Hotel was the setting for feasting, drinking, and bursts of patriotic oratory. Some were aptly phrased, for instance, Alderman John Vanderbilt's "Remember, ye gallant Tars, that you were rocked in Freedom's cradle, enlisted voluntarily under your country's banner, not torn by a merciless press gang from your wives and children." How Decatur reacted to the speechifying might be imagined. But he undoubtedly savored the

adulation, the freedom of New York, the gifts of swords and metals. And while many of the countless toasts were on the level of "To all the pretty girls who like Tars," what must have moved him was memory of the words first uttered by his father and now engraved on the gold-handled sword presented him by his beloved city of Philadelphia: "Our Children Are the Property of Their Country."

From New York in the midst of all the jollity, Decatur wrote to a downcast Commodore John Rodgers, who had returned home from a seventy-day cruise with little to show. Decatur's reference to the defeat of the *Macedonian* could hardly have raised Rodgers's spirits. "Our fellows did as I always knew they would, they fired straight and fast. I always told you I could settle one of their best in 20 minutes. I have changed my opinion. I think it would be all over in 15." Decatur did not think, however, that prize money would amount to much. The government was parsimonious. It had bought the *Alert,* a British ship captured the previous August by Captain David Porter, for a measly $8,000, "not half her value. Hull will get nothing." And given Rodgers's sorry performance, Decatur wished to end their share-and-share-alike partnership. "As in our recent cruise we have made enough to keep the wolf from the doors, if you have no objection I would prefer going on our own accounts for the remainder of the war."

William Bainbridge, meanwhile, had replaced Hull as commander of the *Constitution.* He took the ship on her third cruise of the war and on December 12 in mid-Atlantic had fallen in with the *Java,* a refitted French ship the British had armed with forty-seven guns. Her captain was Henry Lambert, and the vessel was bound for Bombay, carrying a British army general and 350 soldiers. The ships were soon at close range exchanging barrages. Each captain became a casualty. Shot in the head by an American marine, Lambert died. Bainbridge was struck in the thigh but, though limping, retained control. His gunners brought down the *Java*'s mainmast, and with upward of one hundred dead or wounded, she surrendered. The *Constitution* was badly damaged, the *Java*'s first broadside having carried away her wheel.

But she had outmaneuvered the British craft and ruined her as a warship. Bainbridge had every reason to feel proud. Ignoring his wound, he had driven his gun divisions to maximum effort.

The sea fight was, in fact, among the War of 1812's briefest and most brutal. Bainbridge took off the *Java*'s people, blew her up, then made landfall at San Salvador, thanks to his ingenious method of steering by tackles attached to the tiller, rigged with ropes, and operated manually below. All this was to Bainbridge's credit. Yet his safe arrival at Boston on February 4 met with no great joy. He learned that his victory over England's navy was by no means the first, and his nation had so exhausted itself in celebrating the deeds of Hull, Jones, and especially Decatur that in the public prints his destruction of the *Java* received less applause than it deserved.

A cause for uncertainty and considerable discontent during the naval struggle was the disposition of prize money. For example, Secretary Hamilton could not at first decide how to compensate Decatur for capturing the *Macedonian*. Ship's weight and gunnery were necessary considerations in the assessment of how much, if anything, should be awarded to victorious captains and crews. Were the *Macedonian* of equal or greater force than Decatur's frigate, the United States Congress might have decided the whole of her value as prize money owed the Americans. But the *United States* was larger, heavier, carried more guns and a bigger crew. Hamilton had written Decatur that the *Macedonian*'s relative power must be promptly established. He nominated Captain Jacob Lewis as one "referee," Decatur to name another, "and if they disagree a third's opinion will be got and his decision conclusive."

This was among the last letters Hamilton wrote as navy secretary. Under presidential pressure to resign, in part because of insobriety, he was succeeded by William Jones, a Philadelphia merchant to whom Decatur lost no time in communicating his thoughts as a thirty-four-year-old veteran sea warrior. "Hitherto, whatever may

have been the talents of the gentlemen filling that office, their deficiency in practical nautical knowledge was such as to increase the expense of our establishment infinitely beyond what it ought to have been." Aware that Jones had early sea experience–he had served as a privateer under Thomas Truxtun–Decatur registered optimism that the navy was at last in capable hands.

He expected improvements in the allotment of prize money. Decatur had two business agents, his father-in-law, Luke Wheeler, and the clever Norfolk lawyer Littleton Tazewell. But neither of them made much headway against naval bureaucracy. In March 1814 they were still trying to settle the matter for Decatur and his crew. On the twenty-second Wheeler wrote uncomfortably to Tazewell that after several postponed appointments, including with the secretary, "I hope for an early audience tomorrow and will settle things without another day's delay." Privately, Wheeler believed that the sum Decatur wanted was too large. And he was tiring of his enforced stay in Washington attending to Decatur's business. "The thoughts of not seeing my dear daughter and her husband before he again puts to sea stagger me . . . we are indeed in bad luck." Even a belated meeting with Secretary Jones proved unproductive and drew from Luke Wheeler an unusually stern letter to him concerning "the prize money due the captors of the *Macedonian.* If after the delay of so many days I should be at last compelled to go without it, you cannot imagine the discontent resulting. To the worthy commander, the mortification of not being able to redeem the pledge to his gallant crew that 'they should receive the fruits of one cruise before they sail on another' is little in comparison with that he would experience in perceiving the reluctance with which the govt. yield that pecuniary pittance." This had the desired effect. Referees estimated the *Macedonian* to be worth $200,000. Decatur's share was $30,000, a sizeable fortune in those days. The rest was divided among his officers and crew, with $200 going to the bold young powder monkey John Cremar.

12

Blockaded

By early 1813, Britain having unexpectedly lost five valuable frigates and sloops to the American navy, the Lords of the Admiralty retaliated by imposing a blockade on ports along the United States seaboard. It only partly impeded America's ocean commerce because many New England merchants, preferring business as usual, traded with the enemy as much as they dared. But it did prevent any significant movement of American warships. Decatur, under Navy Department orders, began organizing a naval force powerful enough, he hoped, to break through the blockade and resume the ocean war.

"We are driving the repairs of the [eighteen-gun sloop] *Hornet* as fast as possible," he wrote Secretary Jones on April 12. Some of the crew's term of service had expired, but "a rendezvous is now open for men and I apprehend little difficulty or delay in completing her complement." And the *United States* was repaired and ready for sea. New York was totally blockaded. "There has been a force off this harbour for the past ten days. But it will not be in their power to keep us very long, the first blow from the southward to the northward will give us opportunity to pass out."

Fretting against the virtual imprisonment to which the British

subjected him, Decatur was prepared to consider any plan, however unheard of, which might free him from it. Frustration as much as anything brought him into contact with Robert Fulton. It was not Decatur's first acquaintance with the inventor. Once he might have been among those who scoffed at Fulton's dreams. An American diplomat would recall describing to him the advantage of a single steamship to act as auxiliary for battle squadrons. Decatur had appeared to listen approvingly, "but when I ventured to say one such ship could destroy a whole fleet of sailing vessels, his man-of-war notions prevailed and ripping out an oath he said, 'God damn you, you are just like Fulton, always imagining impossible things.'"

Like most pioneers Fulton knew the pain of derision and discouragement, yet as early as 1800, when he was thirty-five, he had already created useful mechanical devices for carpentry, canal navigation, and sawing marble, and he crowned these efforts with the development of a submarine. He turned his attention to the potential of steam. The year when the *Leopard* attacked the *Chesapeake* he launched the first successful steamboat, on the Hudson River. He won Thomas Jefferson's sympathetic ear, and it was largely through the former president's influence that in 1810 Congress subsidized his torpedo experiments. When they failed, he sought to improve his submarine designs. John Rodgers was among the naval officers who continued to jeer, but an increasing number showed interest, and few if any more keenly than Stephen Decatur.

Early in May 1813 Decatur added the sloop *Argus* to his command of the *United States* and *Hornet.* Once at sea, the *Hornet* would be detached for a cruise to the Gulf of St. Lawrence where she might intercept British transports leaving and entering Canada. Decatur's target area would be the South Atlantic. Such were the orders. But a British frigate and a ship of the line were sighted at the entrance to the Narrows. Decatur was daring but no longer an officer prone to court foolhardy risks, and he decided to wait. It was about then that he began consulting with Robert Fulton.

On May 6 he wrote, "Should Fulton's efforts prove, as he hopes they will, 36 or 42lb shot can be fired from 15 to 20 feet through water . . . with such force as to pass through a ship of the line." No vessel could withstand broadsides of this nature. "The water would rush in with a rapidity that could not be cleared by the pumps and she would sink in a few minutes." After a single broadside the attacker could retreat without risk. "This new mode of warfare must annihilate the present system by rendering small vessels equal to large ones." Decatur felt it his duty "to solicit the government to prosecute these experiments . . . to their utmost extent."

Fulton sent a copy of Decatur's statement to Jefferson, who passed it on to President Madison. Optimistically, Decatur and Fulton signed an agreement to share expenses and any ensuing profits from experiments proving that "guns and cannon can be fired under water."

Near the end of spring, Decatur's little force, still blockaded, had grown. Retaining the same name, his prize *Macedonian* had been repaired, commissioned as an American warship, and, flying Captain Jacob Jones's colors, was attached to Decatur's squadron. Still Decatur made no movement. Actually, the seventy-four-gun *Valiant* and consort *Acosta* were the only British ships on direct blockade duty, and their joint gunpower was inferior to Decatur's. But he believed more enemy ships lurked out of sight below the horizon, false information based in part on stories from *Acosta* deserters who said the ships intended to attack New York with Congreve rockets.

On May 24 Decatur decided to hazard a breakout. He ordered his captains to make sail northeastward along the Long Island shore. But in close company they were still short of Oyster Point when struck by a violent thunderstorm. Lightning hit the mainmast of the *United States,* the bolt severing the commodore's broad pennant and sweeping down dangerously near the magazine scuttle before flashing overboard. The ships continued sailing but not for long. About midnight on the twenty-seventh, thick fog forced them to seek safe anchorage

near Block Island. A gale swept the fog clear but so pounded the *United States* that she dragged her anchor only yards off rocks. Fatigued and furious but very much in control, Decatur hustled his crew from their hammocks to haul on the anchor cable until its flukes once more gripped the seabed. And before they could return to their quarters he had the men strengthening rigging and drilling at the guns.

On the month's last day he summoned his ships' officers to a war council aboard the *United States.* It adjourned indecisively. Neither Captain James Biddle of the *Hornet* nor Jacob Jones of the *Macedonian* had much to offer regarding the British force beyond Hell Gate. Decatur's latest information was that the seventy-four-gun *Ramillies* and the frigate *Orpheus* hovered somewhere off Block Island. He did not know the identities of two other British sails his lookouts had sighted. They were in fact the *Valiant* and *Acosta.* But now he determined to make a break for the ocean the next morning, June 1.

It dawned peacefully, with a cloudless sky, no enemy vessel in sight except the seventy-four and the frigate, and they a long way off. Decatur felt increasingly confident. His ships were to windward of the blockaders. Then he made an abrupt decision he could not know would be deemed by some of his countrymen as timidity. His own words would offer no explanation. "As we approached Block Island we discovered two men of war under it, finding the ships were in chase of us to leeward, hauling their wind to cut us off from New London, and three in Block Island channel . . . we hauled our wind and beat back."

Throughout his life thus far, *retreat* was a word not easily found in Decatur's personal lexicon. His fame was founded on audacity. Perhaps he preferred to wait for a chance to break the British blockade alone on the *United States,* rather than in company with three other stout warships. "The fewer the number, the greater the honour." That could account for what became, in American naval historiography, something of a mystery. A charitable view is that the boldness that had made him a national hero could, as he aged, be tempered by prudence and concern for the welfare of those under his command.

Still, there was gunfire on that June 1, not entirely to Decatur's credit. The *Acosta* had approached the *United States* to within range of the American guns. She fired one of her own, a challenging shot to which the *United States* might have tacked about and replied with her superior gunnery. Instead, Decatur apparently satisfied himself with a simple parting shot from his stern chasers and kept going for the shelter of well-fortified New London. Neither could the *Macedonian* nor *Hornet* have punished the *Acosta,* for Biddle and Jones had run their ships aground at the mouth of the Thames River.

Was it just a mistake on Decatur's part, his belief that the British force was too powerful to take on? He wrote a somewhat ambiguous report implying that there were five or seven Royal Navy warships blocking his attempted breakout. Jacob Jones seemed to have counted three. Biddle saw three, two of them ships of the line. "This induced us to haul our wind to return to our former anchorage, but we were chased into this harbour by the 74 and the frigate."

When Decatur and his captains were able to catch up with news of the war's progress, on land, the Great Lakes, and elsewhere at sea, it was possible to perceive that unlike nineteen years earlier when Britain's naval hero Horatio Nelson defeated a French fleet of twenty-six ships, this was no "Glorious First of June" for the American navy. Even as Decatur's handful of ships tried to break from their entrapment, thirty miles east of Boston Light HMS *Shannon* had thoroughly shattered the ill-fated *Chesapeake,* killing sixty-one of her officers and crew, her dying captain James Lawrence's words "Don't give up the ship" enshrined in naval annals but of no avail at all on the occasion.

By midsummer the British fleet blockading the New England coast numbered seven ships of the line and frigates. Their commander-in-chief was the formidable Admiral Sir Thomas Masterman Hardy, Nelson's flag captain at Trafalgar. Hardy was determined to keep the Americans bottled up. In this northeastern region of the United

States Mr. Madison's war had never been popular, and the U.S. Navy's apparent reluctance to confront the British generated an ill feeling in private and public against even the commodore whose heroism six months earlier had been universally toasted throughout the country. With limited force at his disposal Decatur could do little but seethe, confined to home waters. Not far off was the sound of iron stakes and ring bolts hammered into the bedrock on either side of the Thames for the suspension of a heavy chain across the river to prevent any attempted British incursions.

13

Decatur
and
Fulton

Susan was staying with her sister-in-law at Millsdale, the former residence and factory site of Stephen's late father near Philadelphia. Like many wives of the blockaded American tars, she was worried. To John Bullus, whose career had gone from surgeon to diplomat to naval agent in New York, she wrote asking if he could forward a letter she had written to her husband, whom she had not heard from. "The rumors concerning the state of things at New England have made me extremely uneasy."

Admiral Hardy's blockaders had their own problems: a decline in shipboard morale, breakdowns in discipline wrought by tedium, inadequate or inedible food, and a variety of sicknesses including syphilis contracted by seamen who regularly sneaked ashore. Some of Hardy's ships moved from outside New London harbor to a position near Long Island. On July 2 Decatur had communicated to the navy secretary what he believed was the reason. "This change of position has resulted from several torpedo and submarine experiments prepared at this place." For days an anxious Admiral Hardy had his flagship *Ramillies*'s bottom swept with a cable every two hours. "The night before last a Captain [Silas Clowden] Halsey left the harbor in a submarine boat and from a description I have heard of it the enemy, had

they not been apprised of the precise moment of the attack, would have been in danger. Halsey had not left the harbor five minutes when a signal from the shore (gunfire answered by a ship) was made. Halsey, I believe, has not been heard of since."

Decatur had by no means abandoned hope of breaking through the blockade with aid from the innovative Robert Fulton, who wrote to him on July 29 that a New London company had been trying to work up a "torpedo expedition." Fulton mentioned Halsey as "the submarine boatman . . . [who] could work under the bottom of a vessel, attached his Torpedo by piercing the copper [with] a small spear, which he drove in with a mallet." According to Fulton, Halsey could "sink his boat [i.e., submarine] by admitting water, and raise it again by discharging it with a pump." Fulton wished that Decatur could have met him. But Halsey had vanished, never to be seen again.

Summer passed. The longer hours of darkness and the descent of autumn storms gave Decatur fresh hope of running the blockade. In October he wrote the secretary that "the enemy off here keep a vigilant lookout for us but I indulge a hope that we shall soon be able to avoid them and get to sea." The hope remained unfulfilled. From newspapers he learned of Oliver Hazard Perry's victory against the British on Lake Erie, with no hint yet of Jesse Duncan Elliott's controversial conduct as a commander in that American fleet. The stories were of courage and carnage, thirty killed on Perry's *Lawrence,* forty on the Royal Navy's *Queen Charlotte,* and Perry's penciled message to General William Harrison onshore awaiting a chance to rout the British: "We have met the enemy and they are ours." Sad tidings too for Decatur: word of Lieutenant William Henry Allen's death in a Plymouth prison hospital after a battle off the Welsh coast.

Decatur wondered about the possibility of steam-driven vessels on the Great Lakes. Again he turned to Fulton, who acknowledged their practicability for harbor defense but thought lake waters could be as turbulent as the ocean. Even so, he would "reflect on the kind of [steam vessel] which would be useful on the lakes" and was "almost

finishing the model of one to carry not more than 1 or 2 guns of heavy metal and to apply torpedoes . . . she may be made shot-proof." He promised Decatur more positive word soon. The two men continued their postal contact. By the end of the year Decatur enthused over Fulton's latest design of steamboats for coastal defense. "The advantages of this plan are so numerous and so self-evident . . ." Decatur had added an idea of his own, for the boats' protection from boarders: "an iron rail of 2 inches diameter to run around the vessel, supported from its sides by iron braces and thrown off, say, 8 or 10 feet . . . no boat could then get alongside." He enclosed a sketch of the anti-boarding contraption, six braces jutting out from the steamboat. And Decatur concluded with, as Susan especially knew only too well, "By the by, of all things in this world that I most detest, writing is the most abhorrent."

The Fulton-Decatur attempts to fund their plans for submarine cannon and torpedo attacks came to naught. Fulton intensified his research in steam navigation. In 1815 would be launched the first steam-driven warship, yet even this would fail to stir naval bureaucracy or excite naval commanders senior to Decatur, and that same year Fulton died.

On December 1, 1813, opposite Market Wharf in New London harbor, Decatur secretly planned a breakout for a moonless Sunday night, the twelfth. The tide was favorable and he prepared to weigh anchor. But word of his intention reached shore. "That evening," he informed the secretary angrily, "two blue lights burned on both sides of the harbour's mouth as signals to the enemy." In disgust he had abandoned the attempt. "These signals have been repeated, seen by 20 persons at least in this squadron." Not everybody believed the report of treasonable lights. Locals attested that they were fishermen's lanterns. The *New London Gazette* vouched that blue lights were raised on the heights flanking the harbor. The *Rhode Island American* refused to believe New Englanders could be so traitorous

and said the lights were from British ships. Whatever the truth, as the new year dawned, the *United States* and the *Macedonian* were ignominiously laid upriver side by side behind the chain barrier. "Here we are," Decatur wrote to John Bullus, perhaps with a deliberate play on words, "John Bull and us, all of a lump. [The British] want to be at something . . . whatever they intend to do will soon be done."

On January 17, 1814, he wrote a letter to Admiral Hardy. The master of a sloop briefly in British hands had just told him that while questioned on board HMS *Ramillies* he was asked by Hardy's flag captain, Henry Hope, whether the blockaded American commodore would avoid an action if challenged. According to the sloop skipper, Hardy joined the interrogation to say that he had heard that Decatur wanted to match his *Macedonian* against the British *Statira* in battle but did not feel that the challenge should come from his, Decatur's, side.

Such an engagement would give the British an opportunity to recapture the *Macedonian,* something Decatur guessed Hardy badly wanted. He told the admiral that an encounter with HMS *Endymion* would be a more honorable one since her gun power approximated that of the *Macedonian.* "The only difficulty that appears in the way," Decatur added, "is from whom the formal invitation is to come." At any rate, "It is evident that [British captains] Hope and Stackpole have the laudible desire of engaging their ships with the *United States* and the *Macedonian.* You will be pleased to consider this an invitation." Decatur concluded with a superb display of chivalry. "We beg that you will assure Captains Hope and Stackpole that no personal feelings toward them induces us to issue this communication. They are solicitous to add to the renown of their country—we honour their motives."

Captain Biddle delivered Decatur's letter under flag of truce. The *Endymion* was lighter than the *United States,* carried twenty-six guns on her main deck compared with thirty on the American, which was also armed with heavier carronades on quarterdeck and forecastle. Against Hope's wishes, "I must consider it my duty to decline the

invitation on his part." Hardy then proceeded to surpass Decatur in the art of chivalrous rhetoric. "The captains of frigates under my orders, as well as myself, cannot too highly appreciate the gallant spirit that has led to the communication from you, Sir, and are equally convinced that no personal feelings towards each other can ever influence a laudible ambition to add to the naval renown of our two countries."

Into these exchanges, Captain Stackpole of the *Statira* had injected a political note about who was to blame for the war. Decatur brushed this aside. He told Hardy "whether the war we are engaged in be just or unprovoked on the part of Great Britain is considered by us as a question exclusively with the civilians, and I am perfectly ready to admit both my incompetence and unwillingness to confront Stackpole in its discussion." Besides, there was no future in separate individual duels. "This squadron is now under sailing orders from the government and I feel myself bound to put to sea the first favourable opportunity that may arise."

During the long period of inaction, Decatur had not had the comfort of Susan's presence. This was in part a sacrifice to avoid the possibility of gossip suggesting that her nearness, had she been in New London, accounted for his apparent failure to dare the English blockaders. But at any rate, tensions created by an enemy squadron off the New York coast had lessened, the British focusing their attention more on Baltimore and Washington. And in April, following the return of John Rodgers on the *President* from his fourth and again luckless cruise, Decatur was offered the choice of that frigate or the *Guerrière* (named after the British ship destroyed by Hull's *Constitution*.) He chose the former, saying that "the well-known rapidity of the *President*'s sailing places her in my estimation above all others." Also, he understood that the *President* was more ready for sea than the other ship. He could scarcely tolerate further delay. "Having been so long blockaded, I dread being placed in such an unpleasant situation."

The prospect of taking to the high seas again probably offset what dismay he felt upon hearing that an explosion had destroyed the gunpowder mills his brother John and John Bullus owned at Belleville, New Jersey. In May he moved to New York and took command of the *President* with most of his officers and men. From the press he learned that Washington was under attack and Baltimore besieged. Opportunity to get to sea appeared to have arrived. He was yet again frustrated, by orders to take command of New York harbor defenses. His duties included training seamen, supervising gunboats, manning forts, and even drilling militia. But by July his thirst for action had revived, as evident from a letter he wrote John Rodgers concerning the quantities of tablecloths, towels, and other linenware that should have been left on the *President* and had instead been taken to Philadelphia for Rodgers's latest command, the *Guerrière.* "Answer me by return mail," he wrote. "I am now nearly ready for a push."

But complying with a request from New York City officials, on July 12 he began sitting for Thomas Sully. The painter would take six weeks to complete Decatur's portrait. A letter from Secretary Jones on August 8 seemed to confine him still more firmly to his New York station. "You will take command of the whole of the United States Navy force in harbour, whether in force or in ordinary. You will freely concert with the United States military commander, state governor, and corporate authorities." Decatur could scarcely have drawn consolation even from a New York newspaper's glowing report of the "great pleasure [with which] we learn that Stephen Decatur has been directed to take command in this harbor and to remain here for its defense. . . . Where is the American sailor in this city that would not hasten to place himself under this accomplished officer?"

Not until December did Decatur receive directives he had so impatiently awaited. Threats of a British attack on New York had subsided. Peace negotiations were under way, although most Americans were unaware of them. Hostilities continued. Late in the month President Madison ordered six squadrons prepared for sea, their bold purpose

raiding England's worldwide lines of commerce. An early victim of this sweeping program was William Jones, who thought it a waste of money. Struggling with financial problems of his own, he left office at the end of the year.

Decatur had already been thinking up ways to best harry the British. On November 17 he had outlined two plans. One, an easterly cruise enabling him to intercept British ships sailing from the Windward Islands, overtaking them if need be as far as European waters. His second proposal was daringly ambitious, a distant voyage to India's Bay of Bengal to ravage the valuable traders and even the Royal Navy's cruisers. This latter plan was approved at the Navy Department, and Decatur began vigorous preparations for departure.

14

"Shall
Satisfy the
World"

The breakout began in the year's final weeks. On December 14
Captain Charles Stewart, commanding the *Constitution,* slipped
out of Boston. Ten days later on Christmas Eve a treaty signed at a
palace in the Belgian city of Ghent ended the War of 1812, but weeks
would pass before sailors of either side knew of it. On January 14,
1815, the *President* stood at Staten Island. By nightfall the frigate was
plowing through snowstorms south for Sandy Hook, New Jersey.
Three boats with lanterns lit had come out from the Hook and an-
chored in line to mark safe passage across the bar. The *President*
passed the first. And then, probably because of a guide-boat error,
she grounded.

For ninety minutes she took a pounding on the bar, lost much of
her copper, suffered internal strains to an extent Decatur could only
have guessed. But he knew his ship was hurt, and he considered re-
turning to Staten Island. He was denied this course by adverse winds
and a heavy swell. Yet he had to get over the bar before the tide began
to ebb. The elements helped him. A gale arose. All sails unfurled, his
ship was driven thumping across the bar, then the boats were taken
in, the anchors stowed, and by midnight the frigate was struggling
northeastward through rough seas.

Close to dawn on Sunday, January 15, his lookouts sighted three ships two miles off and dead ahead. A wintry daybreak brought a third, then a fourth, into view. Decatur would not yet know their names. But some fifty miles east of Sandy Hook his ship was surrounded on four sides by the fifty-six-gun *Majestic,* the twenty-four-gun frigate *Endymion,* and two light frigates *Pomone* and *Tenedos,* all of England's Royal Navy.

Decatur had only just dispatched a letter by pilot boat to Luke Wheeler and Littleton Tazewell. "I have a good crew, and although few can write, John Bull will find (if he gets alongside of them) that they can make their marks." But he had not bargained on this new predicament. Also, he more than suspected that the grounding had left him with a severely damaged vessel. Escape was his only option. Crowding all sail, he secured the weather gauge and held it. But identified now as British, the ships closed in and began a pursuit. The *President* must be lightened. Controlling his anger, Decatur ordered anchors, boats, and spare spars over the side, and kept his sails wet to catch every breath of wind. By noon the *Majestic* had fallen behind. But the *Endymion* drew closer, pulled slightly ahead, and gained a safe position on the *President*'s quarter to discharge her main-deck twenty-five-pounders.

The *Endymion*'s captain was Henry Hope, no relation to the dissident lieutenant on the *Macedonian* when she had flown English colors, but probably as eager as Admiral Hardy to avenge the loss of that ship to the Americans. In fact, at the Royal Navy's court of inquiry into Captain John Carden's conduct leading to the surrender, Hope had made clear his belief that defeat could have been avoided or at least crowned with honor.

That hearing had been held in May 1813 aboard HMS *Domingo,* moored at Bermuda. Carden attempted a detailed defense of his action. For one thing, the American ship had thrown a far greater weight of shot at one discharge than the *Macedonian* had. And although "some may have thought I was dealing with inexperienced

Americans. . . . The majority of the enemy's crew had been trained and disciplined in the British navy, said to be discharged American seamen." After this dubious assertion, Carden had concluded in a more defiant tone, "My country has lost a ship, but I conscientiously feel that is all she has lost. We could not obtain a superiority of force and I declare to the bravery and steady conduct of my officers and crew."

But under questioning, his first lieutenant, whom he would call "my impeacher," took a different tack. "Captain Carden said he wished to keep the weather gauge, and hauled to windward of the enemy." The Americans had given the *Macedonian* a broadside. "All her shots fell short. The *Macedonian* then wore upon the enemy's quarter and bore down upon her. It is my opinion if we had then, instead of hauling the wind, stood on, we must have passed under her stern or the enemy must have wore and brought us to close action. I attribute the loss of the *Macedonian* to our having kept at too great a distance from the enemy. . . . Our guns were disabled before we got alongside."

The court had guardedly agreed. "Because of over-anxiety to keep the weather gauge, an opportunity was lost of closing with the enemy." But this mistake had not sprung from any reluctance to engage the *United States,* and all hands served honorably. David Hope might not have agreed. But now, twenty months later, his namesake Henry was in command of a British warship and intent upon a more aggressive display than Captain John Carden's.

From the *Endymion*'s quarterdeck he eyed the American's desperate efforts to flee. His logbook told the story. "January 15, 1815. At 1 P.M. all hands at quarters, gaining fast on the chase. Observed the chase throw overboard boats, spars, casks., etc. At 2.30 the chase commenced firing her stern guns. At three returned the enemy's fire with our bow guns." Decatur had altered course southward, but so had the *Endymion.* And the *Pomone* was steadily coming up. Decatur knew his position was precarious. The *Endymion*'s opening barrage

had badly riddled the *President*'s top hamper. And his ship's surgeon, assisted by the purser, was already busy swabbing wounds and stemming blood.

Escape now was impossible. With more audacity than acumen, Decatur decided upon hauling close enough to the *Endymion* for boarding. The *President*'s complement numbered four hundred officers and seamen and fifty marines. Some cheered at their captain's announcement. The *Endymion* had ranged up to within pistol shot. But the cannonade continued at close range. The *President*'s armament consisted of thirty long 25-pounders on the main deck, two long 24s, and twenty 42-pound carronades on the quarterdeck and forecastle. But only a portion of the batteries could be brought to bear at once. And the *Endymion*'s fire was relentless.

Still Decatur thought of boarding. Once in possession of the *Endymion* he would scuttle the battered *President,* and to this end he ordered the frigate's single howitzer pointed down the main hatch. Trying to strike the English frigate with his own guns had proved exasperating, as Captain Hope yawed his faster ship to maintain a dominant position on the *President*'s quarter. Dusk approached. Decatur had sent men clambering into the freezing tops with buckets to wet the fully spread canvas. But now he decided to forfeit escape attempts and reckless boarding notions for a more reasoned chance to hit back. He put up his helm, the ship swung to starboard, her broadside guns blazed, and musket fire rattled from marines in the tops.

For four hours the two ships, rolling heavily, fought a running battle in blackness split by gun flashes. The *Endymion*'s thirty-two-pound carronades and the *President*'s forty-two-pounders thundered in dreadful unison, both ships enveloped by gunsmoke. The *President*'s main deck and quarterdeck ran with blood. A twenty-four-pound shot practically tore Archibald Hamilton in two. He was the lieutenant who had borne the *Macedonian*'s colors in triumph to Washington. Grapeshot and carronade fire ripped through Lieutenant Fitz Henry Babbit's abdomen and right leg, and he died within

hours. Yet another lieutenant toppled, a twenty-year-old named How-
ell. He was carried to the cockpit, and there died. Midshipman
Richard Dale, son of the Tripolitan War's first commander, would
lose a leg.

Large splinters opened Decatur's forehead and struck his chest.
After treatment below in the gorily busy cockpit he was back on the
quarterdeck upright, ignoring the pain of fractured ribs. Every fire
now from the *Endymion* cut away portions of the *President*'s sails or
rigging. The *Endymion*'s log had detailed the action. "At 5.30 the en-
emy brailed up his spanker and bore away, showing a disposition to
cross our bow and rake us. . . . Brought the enemy to close action, in a
parallel line of fire. At 6 the enemy commenced firing musketry from
his tops–returned it with our marine party. At 6.40 the enemy hauled
apparently to avoid our fire, [we] succeeded in giving him two raking
broadsides. At 7.15 the enemy shot away our boats from the larboard
quarter and lower main studding sails. At 7.32 the enemy hauled sud-
denly to the wind; we trimmed sails and again obtained the advantage
of giving him a raking fire. . . . The enemy much shattered."

With great reluctance Decatur acknowledged the hopelessness of
his position. His sails were in tatters; none of his officers and men
had rested for thirty-six hours; more than fifty were dead or wounded.
Three of his five lieutenants had been killed. The only sounds now
were the cries and moans of those who still bled, and the splash of
surf against battered hull. The *Endymion*'s guns were still. With her
sails stripped from her yards, badly dismantled, eleven of her crew
dead, she receded into the dark. Her log painted the final scene. Two
other English ships, the *Pomone* and the *Tenedos,* had come up. A
light arose from the American. "At 9 observed one of our squadrons
run up on the larboard beam of the enemy and fired into her, which
was not returned, but the light hoisted higher in the rigging."

The ship that fired was the *Pomone.* And the *Tenedos* had come
within a cable's length, two hundred yards from the *President,* and was
seen by Decatur as preparing to rake. The lantern aloft in the rigging

was Decatur's signal of defeat. He realized that to prolong the agony of his men would be of no avail. "We have surrendered." Still in pain, Decatur handed the trumpet to Henry Bowie, ship's schoolmaster, to hail the *Pomone* with those words, as if unable to utter them himself.

The time was three A.M. Decatur ordered a boat lowered and was rowed to the *Majestic.* He would not formally yield to an inferior ship. He offered his sword to the *Majestic*'s Captain John Hayes, who at once solemnly returned it. Back on the *President* he managed to rest awhile, then awoke to commit his dead to the deep. Standing on the gun slide nearest the gangway, he read the burial service. British marines fired a salute.

The wounded Americans were placed on different English ships. As a prisoner of war Decatur was escorted to the *Endymion,* where, on January 18, he performed "the painful duty" of reporting his surrender to the new secretary of the navy, a Salem merchant named Benjamin Crowninshield. "Thus situated," he concluded his account of the battle, "all that was left for me to do was to receive the fire of the nearest ship and surrender."

The *Endymion* took him to Bermuda. It was a stormy passage; the ship's main and foremast went by the board in an easterly gale. Otherwise Decatur enjoyed comparative comfort, and at St. George he was allowed an apartment of his own and sometimes dined with British officers and even the governor. There were sour notes. A controversy buzzed over whether the *President* had surrendered to a superior force, the British squadron, including the *Majestic,* or to a single and inferior ship. The Bermuda government's newspaper, the *Royal Gazette,* charged that Decatur, "an officer of first-rate abilities (the American Nelson as he is usually called)," had concealed sixty-eight men on the *President* who, if the frigate was taken as a legitimate prize, would spring from their hiding place in the sail room and recapture the ship. Decatur ignored the accusation but not so Midshipmen Robert Randolph and Christopher Emmet, who waylaid the *Royal Gazette*'s editor on a St. George street and soundly caned him.

By that time Decatur was on his way home, a parolee on board the British frigate *Narcissus.* In midocean he composed an intelligence report for his government describing British military troop movements to and from Bermuda. But the war had ended, as he learned upon landing at New London, where he was welcomed as a hero and driven in a carriage through streets lined with cheering crowds. He was honored at a ball that night in Brown's Hotel, toasted by American sailors and British guests alike.

Susan may have attended. Earlier, before the *Narcissus* anchored off New London, he had written to assure her of his safety and that his chest wound was healing, and the English captain John Hayes, under flag of truce, had seen to the letter's safe delivery in New York. Until then, Susan had heard nothing of Stephen except the capture of his ship. John Bullus was now able to personally hand him a worried letter the naval agent had received from her. "Have you heard anything of the *Endymion* since she sailed for Bermuda? I am extremely anxious about my husband." Now they were together again, but it was unlikely that Susan, or anyone else for that matter, could have fathomed the impact Decatur's surrender had had upon his innermost feelings, the determination already rooted to make sure, given any opportunity, that his supremacy as "the American Nelson" remained intact.

Benjamin Crowninshield applauded his "professional character as an officer whose brilliant actions have raised the national honour and fame even in the moment of surrendering your ship." This was all very well, but Decatur had to do what was expected of him, request a court of inquiry into his conduct. While having little doubt of its outcome, he felt the need for public declaration that nothing had occurred to sully his renown. Should official formality fail in this regard, he would seize every chance to secure it himself, whatever the odds.

On February 22 he wrote to Richard Dale, reassuring that commodore and his wife as to their son's condition. "I left him in as com-

fortable state of quarters as could be wished." The young midship-
man was considered "quite out of danger, time will restore health. . . .
He has lost his leg below the knee. I regret it most sincerely . . . a
more noble spirit never served his country." (The boy would die.)
And with those words Decatur might have rested his pen. But he
could not resist an urge to reveal what most preyed on his mind. "I
have lost a noble ship, sir, but I hope it will be considered that there
has been no loss of honour." Even this was not enough. Before seal-
ing the letter Decatur drew a line through the words "hope it will be
considered" and wrote above them "shall satisfy the world."

The opportunity for him to satisfy not just the world but posterity
came soon enough. North African corsairs had resumed their harass-
ment of American maritime commerce. On February 23, 1815, less
than a week after the end of the conflict with England, President
Madison asked Congress to declare war on Algiers. The Mediter-
ranean was the theater where Decatur had dramatically gained fame.
Glory now beckoned again, and to win it would spur him to a ruth-
lessness that startled friends and envenomed another commodore,
one who may have regarded that sea as his own by divine right, the
single place on the planet where he could free himself of the role in
which fate seemed to have cast him, in his own words, as that of "a
child of adversity."

During the war with England, construction had begun on two
seventy-four-gun ships of the line. One was completed at Charlestown,
Boston, launched in June 1814, and christened *Independence.* Three
days before the declaration of a new war, William Bainbridge had
written Secretary Crowninshield asking that he be selected to take a
squadron to the Mediterranean, with the *Independence* his flagship,
"to protect the trade against the depredations of the Algerian cruis-
ers." Just earlier, on February 14, Crowninshield had offered De-
catur three choices. He could succeed Isaac Hull as commandant of
the Charlestown Navy Yard, take the forty-four-gun frigate *Guerrière*
(named after the British ship destroyed by Hull's *Constitution*) in a

squadron bound for the Mediterranean, or command the other new seventy-four, *Washington,* as his flagship leading a second fleet to that sea. “In short, my dear sir, your wishes are to be consulted. Any service or any station that is at the disposal of this Department, rely upon it, you may command.” This was extraordinary largesse, for a court of inquiry had yet to absolve Decatur from blame for the loss of the *President.* But Decatur wanted something even more than any of the choices Crowninshield had put before him. And he was determined to get it.

15

Two
Squadrons

Forty-eight hours after the declaration of the second Mediterranean war, Susan Decatur wrote to Secretary Crowninshield. She had heard that the government contemplated sending out a squadron, and she did not want her husband to be a part of it. His prolonged absences had been difficult to bear. Often she had paced the floor of her bedroom unable to sleep. And as she told a friend, "My husband, you know, never writes." She pleaded with the secretary. "Commodore Decatur . . . has already had a very arduous tour of duty in that quarter [and] I know he has no wish to go there again unless it be deemed indispensibly necessary. . . . I have been so perturbed during the last two or three years that I really long for a little rest." So anxious was she about her husband's safety that "I have not yet been able to enjoy the glad tidings of Peace [with England]."

Crownshield sent her a sympathetic reply, which Stephen saw when they were reunited. His reaction was predictable and not to Susan's liking. "This is the second time she has suffered her feelings to get the better of her judgment," he told the secretary. When it happened before, he was away and had he been absent on the present instance "I would have felt humiliated lest it might be supposed possible that I had known what she had done." Her solicitude for him

was most gratifying. "But I cannot permit her to interfere in any way with my official duties." Any further letter from her to the secretary must be regarded as without his knowledge. "Should I have any indulgence to ask I will apply myself."

These words formed the last paragraph of a letter that mostly stated Decatur's aims. If he could not be given command of the first ships sailing for the Mediterranean, he would prefer a shore assignment. What he sought was unequivocal supremacy. "I have commanded a squadron for eight years." To settle for a subordinate role might be construed as evidence that the government had lost confidence in him. He asked for command of the *Guerrière* as flagship of the first squadron bound for the Mediterranean. He would not wish to stay out there but would hand over command to Commodore Bainbridge "upon his arrival with the second squadron."

Recovering from his chest wound while in New York, Decatur had shown Washington Irving his correspondence with the secretary. The two shared quarters at Bradish's, opposite the New York Navy Yard, a stopping place popular with naval officers. The historian and novelist offered advice he knew Decatur would relish. Get ahead of Bainbridge, "whip the cream off the enterprise."

Secretary Crowninshield and Decatur were both aware that Bainbridge, four years the latter's senior in rank, had clearest title to take the first squadron to Algiers. And they may have guessed how much Bainbridge ached for a triumph in the waters of his old torment. Others knew. Isaac Hull wrote to Commodore John Rodgers, "I think our friend B——— expects to command the squadron to the Mediterranean." The assumption was echoed overseas. In London, *The Times* ran a dispatch from its Philadelphia correspondent: "Commodore Bainbridge will be appointed commander of a very powerful force now fitting out for Algiers."

Meek and easily influenced, Secretary Crowninshield had even heard from his wife on the matter. Writing from their Salem, Massachusetts, home, she told him of her hope that he would not give the

Mediterranean assignment to William Bainbridge, "as some here think Commodore Decatur is the most fit for it." On March 24 the secretary gave him command of the *Guerrière* in New York with orders to prepare for sea at once. Inside a week, Decatur reported his whole squadron all but ready. "The Constellation and Epervier brig have arrived." And he wanted that court of inquiry into his surrender of the *President* as soon as possible.

None had been convened when he heard that the newly repaired and outfitted *Macedonian* was earmarked for Bainbridge at Boston. His peremptory letter was soon on the secretary's desk. The *Macedonian* wanted only "a little calking in her upper works, which can be done here in two days at most. I would suggest that she be ordered to this place. She would arrive here and be prepared for sea in less time than she would reach Boston."

It had begun to dawn on Bainbridge just what was afoot. On April 8 he wrote to his friend David Porter. Before leaving office, William Jones had established a three-man Board of Navy Commissioners, whose function was to advise the secretary of the navy on miscellaneous technical and other matters. The board's president was John Rodgers, for whom such bureaucratic eminence might have compensated for a lackluster combat record. Porter was a member of the board, and it was to him that Bainbridge displayed his sense of outrage. "I will be candid as saying to you that I do not think the secretary has acted properly towards me in keeping me in utter ignorance. . . . The public prints are reporting that Commo. Decatur is appointed commander-in-chief of the fleet for the Mediterranean. Although I do not believe in the probability of such an event yet it cannot be otherwise than rather mortifying to my feelings." His friends in the Boston area were expecting him to command. "I hope as soon as the Secretary, or the Board, informs me of my command, that the *National Intelligencer* will officially announce it."

The next day the president and the secretary of state formally appointed Decatur, Bainbridge, and William Shaler, United States consul

at Tripoli, as a three-man commission to talk or force the Dey of Algiers into an agreement on American terms. Each man would carry a letter laden with threat. Algiers would be confronted with the largest squadron that had ever sailed from American shores. Whether the ships directly blockaded the port or laid off some distance would be at the discretion of their captains. A neutral friendly flag would be hoisted to invite peace negotiations "before proceeding to extremities." Sweden would be preferred because of its pro-American consul, Mr. Norderling. And the Algerians had better see reason. "The honourable end to war with England must convince the Dey that he had much to dread from the continued hostility of the United States." When he knew "how rapidly we have grown–a sure presage of the destiny that awaits us–he will find no hope for any change in his favour."

The *President* court of inquiry convened in the middle of the month, on the *Constellation,* one of Decatur's ships at New York. All but one witness testified to his skill and courage under fire. The dissonant note was struck by Sailing Master James Rogers. Decatur cross-examined him. Could the *President* have been saved by any course or measures than those pursued? Roger's reply: "As it was found the enemy was going in one point of sailing, we ought to have tried [the *President*] on another."

"What kind of sailing would you have tried?"

"After dusk, before engaging the *Endymion,* I would have had the steering sails set before we bore away to engage her. Then I would have given the *Endymion* a broadside and kept the *President* dead before the wind. I think there was a chance she might have been saved."

Any damage this might have done to Decatur was decisively repaired by the court, which consisted of Captains Alexander Murray, Isaac Hull, and Samuel Evans, blind in one eye. Rogers had been slightly wounded during the sea fight. The court seized on this. What was the nature of his wound?

"I lost one finger and was bruised across the shoulders."

After his wound had been dressed had he remained in the cockpit?

"No, I went to my cabin."

"Were you able to return to your duty on deck?"

"I was, though in great pain."

Rogers added more. When he had asked the commodore for men to trim the yards, Decatur had shouted, "Damn you, do it yourself!"

Thereafter, the questions came rapid-fire, often giving Rogers little chance for utterance beyond assent. Was the commodore's conduct cool, collected? Did the officers do their utmost to defend the ship? Was the commodore's report correct as far as Rogers knew? And the remaining witnesses were unanimous in praising Decatur. The sailing master's testimony derived from "ignorance or the dictates of a culpable ambition." So much for the *President*'s sailing master. The court concluded that Decatur had struck his colors only when "resistance would have been a useless sacrifice of brave men's lives. In this conflict the enemy gained a ship but the victory was ours."

Within hours of the exculpation he needed before sailing out with confidence, Decatur had gotten Crowninshield's permission to alter the *Macedonian*'s original destination. And he ordered Master Commandant Jacob Jones, who as captain of the *Wasp* had fought one of the War of 1812's bloodiest sea battles, to bring the former British frigate into New York instead of Boston. That same week Crowninshield officially named Decatur commander-in-chief of the Mediterranean squadron. "As it is considered that the squadron presently under your command is not strong enough to try offensive operations against the town and batteries of Algiers, you may await an augmentation of force which will follow." Fortunately for Bainbridge's already upset peace of mind, he was unaware of this lame reference to the squadron he was rapidly assembling at Boston.

Decatur's fleet at New York was made up of the flagship *Guerrière,* the *Macedonian,* and the *Constellation*, whose captain, Charles Gordon, stubbornly ignored an unhealed duel wound, also the brigs

Epervier, Firefly, Flambeau, and two 12-gun schooners, *Spark* and *Spitfire.* Decatur had no difficulty in appropriating for himself whatever he wished. This included thirty men originally ordered to Boston, and a lieutenant Bainbridge felt sure belonged to his *Independence.* When he sent an order to New York summoning this officer to Boston, Decatur intervened with a tart letter. "I am satisfied you could not have known [the lieutenant] was under my command when you issued this order. I have directed him to continue on board the ship to which he is attached. No orders but those of the Department can remove him."

Two days later, May 5, he informed Secretary Crowninshield that the squadron had left New York and dropped south. "We are now ready for sea. I hope the government will not need to keep us long in port." Then three weeks passed before Bainbridge learned officially that his would be the second Mediterranean squadron. On June 5 he again wrote to Porter. The letter opened with "My Dear Beloved Friend" and closed with "God bless you," but the words in between bespoke an almost uncontrollable anger. "Am I to assume that it is intended to have two separate squadrons in that sea? If so, *I will not command* either of them." He was so disgusted with "the neglectful manner [in which] I have been treated . . . that I am totally indifferent about going out." But orders were orders, and he still clung to a hope that his ship of the line would reach the Mediterranean before Decatur. To complete preparations he drove his people almost to the brink of mutiny.

He was aware of doubts about the seventy-four's seaworthiness, and after sending his flag captain, William Crane, a few leagues out into Boston Bay to try her under sail, he was taken out himself and saw how badly she settled, even without her boats and spars on board. An officer who accompanied him told a Philadelphia newspaper that "in rough water her lower deck would be entirely useless."

Bainbridge also lacked competent seamen. His recruiting enticement consisted of two months' salary and no bonus. Belatedly, he learned that other commanding officers, Decatur included, were

allowed to pay enlistees three months' wages with a $20 bounty. He agonized over gun power. The lightweight model of thirty-two-pound guns cast for the *Independence*'s lower deck had been diverted to Commodore Isaac Chauncey for operations on Lake Ontario. They were replaced by guns heavy enough to endanger the *Independence,* whose ports were already low in the water. And they proved the wrong fit for the carriages Bainbridge had specially made of the most expensive well-seasoned wood.

He wrote desperately to the Navy Department. Could not Chauncey's guns at Sackets Harbor be shipped, as first expected, to Boston? The secretary said no, such change in plans would cost too much. By this time Bainbridge must have felt that he was no mere "child of adversity" but victim of a deliberate conspiracy to deny him any chance of triumph in those waters that were the scene of his unforgettable humiliations. Crowninshield told him that a committee composed of himself, Bainbridge, and the captains Crane and Charles Stewart must check on the seventy-four's fitness to sail. Bainbridge had other ideas. He would lighten the ship on his own. He ordered his weary crew to take all the heavyweight guns off the lower decks and replace them with lighter cannon, of the same caliber, from the main deck. The *Constitution* lay nearby awaiting repairs. Bainbridge had his men dismantle her twenty-four-pounders and transfer them to the *Independence*'s main deck.

Dutifully he sent a report of these adjustments to the Navy Board in Washington. That was his mistake. His having submitted a report at all placed the condition of his flagship in doubt. She must be razeed—stripped and cut down to a two-decker. The board recommended that for this purpose she be confined to port. Crowninshield wrote the commodore appropriate orders. They were returned unopened. Bainbridge had determined to wait no longer, was at sea with the second squadron, eight vessels led by the seventy-four-gun ship of the line *Independence.* Mercifully for the fuming commodore he did not know that Decatur, sharing cabin space with the emissary

William Shaler on the *Guerrière,* had been at sea since the end of May and on June 12 passed through the Straits of Gibraltar.

No good-bye letter to Susan would survive. Given his distaste for personal correspondence, Decatur may not have sent one. He had, however, revised his will. He had composed it on the eve of war with England, when his named beneficiaries included Lieutenant Stephen Decatur McKnight, his nephew. McKnight's father had died in a duel. In late fall 1814 the young McKnight was on the sloop *Wasp,* bound for the Spanish Main. The ship was never seen again.

Once Decatur reached the Mediterranean, his dash and deliberation were on full display. "Bringing to and boarding everything on sight," wrote Peter M. Potter, a musician on the *Spitfire.* "Every five minutes from the masthead came 'Sail-ho.' " On June 17 Captain Gordon on the *Constellation,* the headmost ship, sighted a strange sail. Upon closer examination it was seen flying English colors. Gordon's people hoisted the American flag prematurely. The stranger reacted by defiantly replacing its false flag with the red Algerian ensign and beat for the Spanish coast. Gordon gave chase, determined to deny him neutral shelter.

The vessel he pursued was the 20-gun *Mashouda,* flagship of Rais Hammida, the Barbary powers' most notable admiral. Gordon gleefully anticipated the high-seas victory he had longed for since the shame of the *Chesapeake.* The *Mashouda* did not make it to Spain. But neither did Gordon win glory. His gun divisions raked the Algerian, leaving dozens dead and Hammida wounded. Bleeding, the admiral remained seated on his quarterdeck dais continuing to command. Yet heavier fire struck his ship, but this time not from the *Constellation*'s gun crews. As Gordon later complained, "The Commodore reached between [the *Mashouda*] and myself, compelled me to cease."

16

The
Mediterranean
Factor

Decatur had indeed driven his flagship directly into the engagement. It was followed by the *Epervier,* and both craft hurled more broadsides into the *Mashouda.* A forty-two-pound carronade shot from the *Guerrière* almost cut Rais Hammida in half. Five men killed by a gun burst on Decatur's main deck was as nothing compared to the butchery on board the *Mashouda.* And still a third American ship, the *Ontario,* poured heavy shot into the stricken Algerian. Musket fire from stubborn Barbary topmen died away, and down came their ship's colors.

The American capture led to some revealing correspondence. Gordon told a cousin of the action and claimed credit for opening the attack. He asked that his letter not be published because Decatur was sure to proclaim the victory his alone. This Decatur did, making no mention of Gordon in his official report. Joseph Causten, the *Constellation*'s purser, was unsure whether anyone deserved credit "for drubbing a poor defenseless Turk with two frigates, a corvette, three brigs and two schooners." And so eager was Decatur to snatch the prize from Gordon that strict seamanship had momentarily deserted him. According to Causten, Captain John Downes of the *Epervier* "never saw a ship so shamefully maneuvered in all his life. Gordon

even told the Commodore to his face that such fighting would never take an Englishman . . . but such is [Decatur's] popularity his official despatches, be what they may, will remain uncorrected."

Within forty-eight hours the squadron had sighted another Algerian warship, the twenty-two-gun brig *Estedio,* off Cape Palos, in southeastern Spain. Trying to escape, the brig ran aground and surrendered under heavy fire from the *Epervier.* Several of Decatur's party took to looting. The musician Potter was disgusted to see a shipmate rob Algerians of their cutlasses, to wear about his waist. Decatur had the brig floated off and sent into Cartagena along with the *Mashouda.*

During this engagement, William Shaler had expressed concern. He was a veteran sea trader and diplomat whose travels had taken him across the Pacific to the China Sea. Uncomfortable as a joint commissioner with Decatur, whose self-confident manner struck him as arrogance, he feared that chasing the *Estedio* into Spanish waters was a violation of international law. But Decatur had no thought for diplomatic technicalities. A week's further cruising brought the fleet into Algiers. The Dey was awed by its size but not surprised by its arrival, a dispatch boat from Gibraltar having brought him news that the Americans were coming. As official envoys of the United States, Decatur and Shaler prepared to deliver a letter to the Dey from President Madison and reinforce it with diplomatic gestures of their own. Promptly on June 29, Decatur hoisted a white flag of truce and Swedish colors on the mainmast.

A felucca brought out the Swedish consul, Johann Norderling, and the captain of the port. Shaler told them of the capture of the Algerian warships off Spain. Plainly disconcerted, the port captain enquired as to the American terms for peace. He added that the Dey would prefer negotiations held onshore in his palace. Furthermore, the Dey would expect the *Mashouda* and *Estedio* restored to his navy. Decatur retorted that since the countries were at war with each other, talks must get under way on American decks. From what

Shaler would later imply, Decatur did most of the talking. If peace was secured, Shaler would settle in Algiers as American consul. But now Decatur could legitimately claim the initiative. The formal diplomacy Shaler represented depended for success upon the Dey's capitulation under the threat posed by American warships along the horizon.

Decatur offered the Algerians verbal guarantees not contained in the letter from James Madison that, with a copy of the president's war declaration, he and Shaler had brought out. This troubled Shaler. Decatur's performance during the proceedings on the *Guerrière* was clearly designed to impress. He had decked himself out in full dress uniform, looked "the very ideal of a hero," according to an eyewitness, with his "laced coat and hat, tight cassimeer pantaloons, long boots bound at the top with gold lace and having tassels of gold in front." Norderling, who probably sensed a tension between the two Americans, thought the commodore self-glamorizing, privately mocked him as "Bashaw Decatur . . . that spoiled hero . . . swaggering about with his Order of the Cincinnati."

Yet at least for the short term it worked. Madison's demands principally included the abolition of tribute payments, the release of imprisoned Americans, and compensation for seizure of American property. Otherwise, war would begin in earnest. The Dey sent out commissioners to negotiate. Shaler thought "they seemed extremely anxious to conclude the peace at once." They demurred on points they considered too stern and humbling. But on their next visit to the *Guerrière* they brought good news. All the Dey wanted now, as a face saver, was the return of the *Mashouda* and *Estedio.* Shaler pondered this. No one would buy the vessels in their sorry condition. To fit them out for passage home as prizes would not be worth the cost. He consulted with Decatur and agreed to "make a compliment to His Highness in the state they were then in." Decatur had promised, rashly as things turned out, to provide the ships with an American naval escort from Cartagena. His signature preceded Shaler's on

their report to Secretary of State James Monroe. The commissioners "returned onshore, and though the distance was fully five miles they came back within three hours, with the treaty signed as we had concluded it."

Decatur's crews rejoiced. On July 4 there was, Potter wrote, "a regular blow-out." Decatur selected the *Epervier* to carry his report and the signed treaty home, and he gave the brig a new commander, his own flag captain, William Lewis, whom he described as "an officer of great merit." Decatur also transferred a lieutenant from the *Guerrière* to the *Epervier*. This was a good-natured act, designed to permit the two officers an early reunion with a pair of sisters they had recently married. The *Epervier* was sighted on the fourteenth west of Gibraltar. And then she disappeared with all on board.

Unaware of this tragedy, Decatur reassembled his fleet and left Algiers–prematurely, as Shaler soon learned. He had taken up residence in Algiers and found himself wrestling with problems left in the squadron's wake. Exultant and eager to show the flag off every Barbary port, Decatur had sailed for Tunis. He had sent the *Spark* and the *Torch* to escort the battered pair of Algerian ships at Cartagena across the Mediterranean to their home port. And he had written to Secretary Crowninshield strong and prescient words. Peace with Algiers had been "dictated at the mouths of our cannon. And I beg leave to you my opinion that the presence of a respectable naval force in this sea will be the only guarantee for its observance."

William Bainbridge had sailed from Boston on July 3. His squadron was larger than Decatur's and distinguished by the inclusion of the largest American warship afloat. The other vessels were the thirty-six-gun frigate *Congress,* the sloop of war *Erie,* the brigs *Chippewa, Saranac, Boxer,* and *Enterprise,* and the schooner *Lynx.* But the commodore's thoughts were grim. His feeling of having been betrayed by Crowninshield and cheated by Decatur may have colored the program for naval reform that he composed on the

ocean passage. He wrote alone in his cabin. Shipboard discipline, for instance. The maximum sentence for insulting superiors or showing a mutinous spirit was one hundred lashes. Bainbridge thought it should be hanging.

Approaching Gibraltar on the last day of July, the *Independence* spoke a British brig. Its master told the Americans that Decatur had humbled Algiers. Bainbridge kept to his cabin for the rest of the week. According to the surgeon's log he was down with measles. He also had headaches, was bled for two days. But no medicine could quell his chagrin, some of which perhaps he took out on his crew. Aboard the *Independence* on August 15 he mustered all hands to witness the flogging of ten seamen and marines for drunkenness and sleeping on watch.

Four days later he dropped anchor off Algiers, where the newly installed consul Shaler looked forward to his support. The *Estedio,* driven by Americans into neutral Spanish waters, was still detained there. Hurrying off to Tunis, Decatur had shown little or no interest in getting the brig released from Spanish custody. The Dey of Algiers blustered about American bad faith, Shaler bearing the brunt of his wrath. Bainbridge proved of no help. So determined was he to overtake Decatur, he scarcely spoke to Shaler, instead sailed on eastward. Shaler cursed his country's navy for abandoning him in "the most dreary residence on earth." When he later protested to Decatur, the reply he got was a cheeky letter to the effect that surely he, Shaler, had not expected his consular post to be a bed of roses.

Decatur had reached Tunis on July 26. What he demanded of the Bey was reparation for the seizure of two merchantmen from British warships. Those vessels, Decatur insisted, were rightfully American, by virtue of their capture during the War of 1812 by an American privateer. As he later reported to Secretary of State Monroe, "the information of our having humiliated Algiers and brought her to our terms so speedily had preceded us and filled [the Tunisians] with alarm." The moment was ripe for making demands. Granted, he had

no legal authority to negotiate. But he had no need to act as a diplomatic envoy. He was allowed to land, and did so again in full regalia. "The Bey received me very civilly." And promised an indemnity amounting to $60,000.

Decatur's next stop was Tripoli. Yusuf Karamanli was still in power. But unlike fifteen years earlier when he defied one American naval squadron after another, he yielded to the threat of Decatur's cannon, pledged a payment of $25,000 and the release of "ten Christian captives." Decatur then took his ships to the Kingdom of the Two Sicilies to give his people a well-earned shore leave. The King himself hosted Decatur at his palace on the gorgeously scenic shore of the Bay of Naples. The squadron next sailed for Malta, then on to Spain, where, off Málaga, its commander-in-chief learned that the second squadron, under William Bainbridge, had struggled far behind him as if engaged in a game of catch-up. Bainbridge had shown the flag briefly before Tripoli, almost ignored Tunis, and refusing to pay Algiers a second visit had evidently given up the game and crowded all sail back to Gibraltar.

What Decatur could only have guessed at was Bainbridge's simmering fury. He could show off his proud ship of the line at every Barbary port of call yet could not avoid the mortifying sense of anticlimax and irrelevance. Bitterly he would write from the Mediterranean, "Peace having taken place prior to my arrival, I have been deprived of the opportunity of either Fighting or Negotiating. . . . Could possibly I have foreseen it, most assuredly I would not be here."

What must have felt like salt rubbed into the wound was the navy secretary's letter, finally delivered to the addressee three months after its date, declaring the *Independence* unseaworthy. Bainbridge wrote back defiantly that not a man on the seventy-four would have preferred serving on another vessel. On October 7, when Decatur's squadron rounded a promontory to join Bainbridge's, the assembly of warships off Gibraltar totaled seventeen, the biggest American

Decatur's leap to glory on February 16, 1804: the burning of the
U.S. frigate *Philadelphia* in the harbor at Tripoli.

At grips with the Tripolitans, August 1804. Decatur *(center foreground)* is shown in hand-to-hand combat, in a painting by Dennis Malone Carter.

Courtesy of the Naval Historical Foundation

American gunboats waging war against the Bashaw of Tripoli, 1804.

U.S. Navy Historical Center

The miniature that mesmerized Susan Wheeler: a watercolor on ivory by Olivio Sozzi shows Decatur at twenty-six years old.

Courtesy of the U.S. Naval Academy Museum

Susan Wheeler, from a portrait by Gilbert Stuart, two years before she met and married Stephen Decatur.

Pennsylvania Academy of Fine Arts

William Henry Allen, the lieutenant who was praised by Decatur for his gunnery against the British frigate *Macedonian* during a battle in the Sargasso Sea, October 1812. Allen had testified against James Barron at the commodore's court-martial.

U.S. Navy Historical Center

The *Macedonian* dismasted by broadsides fired by Lieutenant Allen's gun crew. Capturing the British ship was Decatur's principal victory in the War of 1812.

Courtesy of the U.S. Naval Academy Museum

Alexander the Great. Wood figurehead of the *Macedonian* by an unknown artist.

Courtesy of the U.S. Naval Academy Museum

Decatur was forced to surrender when the British frigate *Endymion* severely damaged the *President* in a battle off the New Jersey shore, January 1815. The war had ended, but news of the peace had not yet crossed the Atlantic.

Courtesy of the U.S. Naval Academy Museum

Decatur as commodore. Painting by John Wesley Jarvis, circa 1814.

Courtesy of the U.S. Naval Academy Museum

Stephen Decatur, portrait by Rembrandt Peale, circa 1815–1820.

Courtesy of the New-York Historical Society

Last victim of the *Chesapeake,* Captain Charles Gordon. Reprimanded by the secretary of the navy, Gordon fought two duels as a consequence of the *Chesapeake-Leopard* affair and died later of wounds incurred during the second.

National Archives and Records Administration

Commodore William Bainbridge. Stern, brave, but always overshadowed in his rivalry with Decatur, he became the latter's second in the fatal duel with Barron.

Collection of the City of New York. Courtesy of the Art Commission of the City of New York

The handsome commodore. Having tasted victory and defeat in the War of 1812, Decatur was determined to show the world he was still his country's hero when he commanded a squadron in the second Algerian war.

Collection of the City of New York. Courtesy of the Art Commission of the City of New York

Benjamin W. Crowninshield, secretrary of the navy, 1815–1818. Bainbridge felt betrayed by Crowninshield in favor of Decatur.

U.S. Navy Historical Center

James Barron, competent seaman, banished from the U.S. Navy yet restored to shore-based service after killing Decatur. Miniature by a court painter in Denmark, circa 1814.

Courtesy of the James Barron Collection, Eugene Swem Library, College of William and Mary

Ashore or on distant stations, Jesse Duncan Elliott qualified as the U.S. Navy's most controversial commodore. He served as Barron's second in the duel with Decatur.

U.S. Navy Historical Center

The Indian Queen, Bladensburg, Maryland, now called the
George Washington House. Barron breakfasted here
before walking to his meeting with Decatur.

The glade where Barron met
Decatur and struggled to voice
a truce, which was interrupted
by the duelists' seconds. Here
Decatur fell, mortally wounded.

armada yet assembled. But Bainbridge was in no celebratory mood. Hundreds of American tars cheered as their ships came abreast of each other, but no patriotic exchange occurred between their two commodores. Instead the crews were witnesses to an astonishing attempt to snub. Alexander Mackenzie was an officer on the *Chippewa* and as a naval biographer in future years described the scene:

The *Guerrière* hove to as she approached the *Independence*'s stern. In full dress uniform Decatur descended in his gig, broad pennant at its bow. His oarsmen pulled hard toward the ship of the line, which, however, got under rapid way. Bainbridge was bent on avoiding a meeting. But Decatur would not grant him even this much. "Determined to be courteous," he urged his oarsmen to pull harder. They were soon alongside the *Independence*. Decatur climbed on board, if not with the alacrity with which he had landed on Bainbridge's *Philadelphia* in 1804, certainly with no less intent. Bainbridge's only means of escaping Decatur's handshake would have been to jump over the other side. He gave his perceived usurper a chilly greeting. As Susan Decatur would describe it, her husband had visited the *Independence* simply to pay his respects, but Bainbridge "received him as a total stranger . . . never offered him the slightest hospitality."

Bainbridge on his seventy-four set course for home. Decatur on the *Guerrière* waited a full day before following but reached America three days before him, on November 12. He was nationally applauded. Commodore David Porter wrote admiringly of "your comet-like expedition." A Philadelphia journal boasted that Decatur had given the North Africans "an electric shock as it was never discharged from a Christian battery." President Madison honored him with a seat on the naval board, replacing Isaac Hull, who had resumed command of Boston's Charlestown Navy Yard, to the heightened rage of Bainbridge, who had come home believing himself entitled to that post. Decatur was credited with having settled the Mediterranean problem single-handedly, within six weeks, handing posterity a vision of the

American naval officer as seagoing diplomat, setting a bold example to European powers who had yet to end their policy of paying the Barbary rulers protection money.

Reports that his top-speed Mediterranean cruise had in fact left problems behind were too few or arrived too late to diminish Decatur's fresh renown. The American consul at Gibraltar told John Rodgers, head of the naval board, that Decatur would sacrifice his best friend to aggrandize his fame. "Had Bainbridge not been close at his heels, be assured that reasons for continuing the war would not have been found wanting."

No one would have agreed with this assessment more warmly than Charles Gordon, captain of the *Constellation,* who had not forgiven Decatur for robbing him of the *Mashouda*'s surrender. His frigate had remained in the Mediterranean as part of a much reduced American force left in support of Consul Shaler's efforts to mollify the Dey of Algiers. Gordon wrote to his cousin, Joseph Nicholson of Maryland, that "it is us who have acted wrong by Commo. Decatur's violating a sacred pledge." In early 1816 Gordon was joined by Commodore Oliver Perry, who came out in a new frigate, the *Java,* bringing the United States ratification of the treaty with Algiers. The Dey promptly disavowed it. Perry wrote that "the Algerians are extremely restive under the treaty made with Decatur, considering it disgraceful to the Faithful to humble themselves before Christian dogs." A new war threatened. Gordon was not dismayed by the prospect, for with his steadily ebbing strength he wished all the more fiercely to score a clear-cut victory in battle. That long-ago *Chesapeake* duel was taking its toll. The wound still drained. And Gordon had heard that back home Decatur was belittling his Mediterranean performance. He wrote to John Rodgers that "Commodore Decatur can injure me with his high standing as I have never whip'd an Englishman. But no man will ever suspect my character as an officer while I have some strength left to vindicate myself." He had no particular claims on the government "as I have never done anything. But as it is murder-

ing me to pass even one winter in a cold climate, I shall be compelled to solicit a southern station in the event of my return." Gordon never returned. Two months after that letter he died, put to rest finally in a Sicilian grave.

Supported by just two frigates, William Shaler was unable to appease the Dey. In a confidential letter to Secretary Monroe he blamed both Decatur and Bainbridge for failing their duty as peace commissioners. But no war broke out involving Americans. Spain at last released the *Estedio*. And in the summer of 1816 the combined fleets of Britain and Holland bombarded Algiers, destroying the Dey's navy and fortifications, in consequence ending the centuries-long era of Barbary piracy in the waters east of Gibraltar.

17

Perry
and
Elliott

The year 1815 would mark the genesis of the tragedy that lay five years hence for Stephen Decatur. Perhaps it could be traced earlier, to Barron's indiscreet remark on a Norfolk street, or his hapless performance on the *Chesapeake,* or even the *Philadelphia* disaster that stained Bainbridge's already blemished reputation and, through the frigate's fiery destruction, opened the gate to Decatur's glory. The events that sealed his fate accelerated after his final return from the Mediterranean.

His immediate postwar life was first a series of honorary celebrations, then a settling into a routine of professional duties and, most welcome to Susan, a childless domestic serenity blended with elegant social occasions. On December 26, 1815, on his way from New York to Washington, he had stopped at Baltimore to be fêted by local citizens at a dinner in Barney's Inn. Eighteen toasts were raised. The gathering typified the popular esteem that Decatur continued to enjoy into the new year. In the capital he bought one of the "Seven Buildings," an architectural septet just west of the White House. He paid less than $4,000 for it and enlisted the secretary of the navy's aid to put it "in comfortable and decent order." The wallpapering, he told Crowninshield, he would see to himself.

On January 2, 1816, he submitted to the secretary of the navy an excellent report on the defense of Chesapeake Bay. And it was just three months later, in April, that he delivered the toast that would echo down generations, often misquoted, and from future perspectives its import open to question. The occasion was a dinner at the Exchange Coffee House in Norfolk attended by a hundred navy and army officers and leading citizens, including Littleton W. Tazewell and Robert B. Taylor, protagonists at the Barron court-martial. Each toast rang with patriotism, and even had the word *chauvinism* been invented, no cynic would have dared criticize the prevailing emotion as such.

"National Glory—a gem above all price and worthy of every hazard to sustain its splendor." Another called for glasses raised to "The Star-spangled Banner—Long may it wave." Tazewell toasted Decatur. "Our distinguished guest. Most admired where best known." Then Decatur stood. He spoke as one who had indeed served his country heroically if not always with prudence, and his words were an acknowledgment of its admiration. "Our Country—in her intercourse with foreign nations may she always be in the right, but always successful, right or wrong." The toast touched off such a wave of applause he repeated it at least once, in August of the same year, while passing through Petersburg, Virginia.

During this blissful period, Decatur had no inkling of the danger looming ahead, and certainly would not have connected it with Oliver Hazard Perry, victor at the Battle of Lake Erie. In March 1817 Perry returned from a Mediterranean tour of duty that had been by no means trouble-free. Five of his crew had died when the frigate *Java*'s topmast broke in a strong gale. His other problems were partly self-inflicted and in a sense environmental. The Mediterranean, no longer a battle zone, had become a spawning ground for unrest within the American navy. In the fall of 1816 the acquittal of Captain John Orde Creighton, court-martialed for alleged shipboard bullying, had led to a massed midshipmen's petition to Congress for

protection against quarterdeck tyrants. The Washington lawmakers took no action.

Perry's bane at that moment was the *Java*'s marine captain, John Heath. Their quarrel sprang from Perry's perception of Heath's marines as a slovenly, undisciplined lot. During a heated confrontation in his cabin he punched or slapped Heath. "Passion became predominant" was Perry's excuse. But Heath refused his apology, whereupon Perry, knowing he had overstepped the line, requested that he be tried by court-martial. At the same time, he brought charges against Heath. The court convened at Port Mahón. Its members were the same as those who had judged Creighton, except that he took the seat previously occupied by Perry. Heath was convicted of neglect of duty and disrespect, Perry guilty of striking a subordinate officer. The court's partly deaf president, Isaac Chauncey, sentenced each to a reprimand.

Contention shadowed Perry after his return home. He had some dispute with a young lieutenant named Benjamin Booth. Again it was a matter of alleged disrespect. The thirty-three-year-old Perry genuinely wanted a quiet life devoted to his wife, Elizabeth, with their four small sons and a daughter. But, as he wrote to a friend in the Navy Department, "I have by some means made out a host of enemies about me." He and Booth both applied to Decatur, as a member of the Board of Navy Commissioners, for help in settling the affair before it reached pistol point. Booth had been placed under arrest. Decatur's intervention satisfied both sides. "Both parties have complimented me as a brother officer," he wrote to the navy secretary, who endorsed his action and ordered Booth freed with "I accede to the restoration of his sword."

About this time Decatur and Perry became friends. Their amity could not have developed earlier, and how binding it was must be conjectured. Anyway, Perry needed his help yet again, for he found himself attacked on two flanks. Captain Heath had continued to dog him, apparently bent on a duel, and he had also to contend with an

inveterate trouble seeker, Master Commandant Jesse Duncan Elliott, who had commanded the twenty-gun brig *Niagara* on Lake Erie. Decatur could hardly have relished unraveling Perry's tangled affairs. He had his own work cut out for him on the navy board, where his temper sometimes got the better of him. According to the board's president, John Rodgers, Decatur had once to be prevented from beating up an inventor who had tried to bribe him into approving a patent for a new firearm. He frequently quarreled with Rodgers and argued with the other member, David Porter, at whom he once snapped, "Since you and Commodore Rodgers always vote against me, I am of little use here." He stalked out of the room but was soon back, harmony restored.

Such clashes were usually resolved. In its flag-draped and trophy-ornamented special quarters at the Navy Department, Decatur attended faithfully to the board's business. He took a keen interest in the navy's modernization and drew from his considerable knowledge of foreign harbors. He wrote a report detailing the advantages of Hampton Roads and Chesapeake Bay as safe anchorages. He would prove instrumental in the establishment of Norfolk as a major naval base. Some of his proposals suggested the influence of Robert Fulton, even visions of an age when steam would replace sail. What he could not know was how little time remained to him.

A s a member of the Board of Navy Commissioners, Decatur was also in touch with William Bainbridge, only occasionally and in an official capacity. But certainly the connection did nothing to retard what was something approaching paranoia in Bainbridge's mind. He was still captain of the *Independence.* But he had long felt that the Charlestown Navy Yard, like the Mediterranean, was his to command. Upon returning from his latest humiliation in that sea and finding Isaac Hull firmly lodged in his old quarters, he at once set about having him ousted. Hull had financial motives for clinging to command of the yard, among them nearby property investments.

Bainbridge's efforts and Hull's resistance even became a topic of cabinet discussion. The outcome went against Bainbridge, who was compelled to stay on his seventy-four.

This blow was followed by harsh words he received from the department and the board for allegedly making improper appointments among his officers. And yet again he fell afoul of his Washington bureaucratic superiors when he tested the strength of the *Independence*'s lower-deck guns by striking them with a maul. It was a method quite different from that approved by the board's three commissioners, and John Rodgers reproached him in a tone more apt for chiding an errant midshipman. The commission felt that the *Independence* seemed unable to carry her deck guns far enough above water in heavy seas, and it recommended that she be placed in ordinary. Bainbridge fumed against this "unnecessary order," but it was repeated and President Madison himself, about to leave office, advised the commodore to obey.

Madison was succeeded in the White House by James Monroe. Bainbridge had not given up his efforts to get Hull out of the Charlestown Navy Yard, and he now appealed in person to the new president. But Monroe would not reverse his predecessor's decision. And the only member of the board who Bainbridge felt was sympathetic to anything he had to say was David Porter, certainly not Decatur. By spring 1817 he had again to taste defeat. At last he had given up the Charlestown Navy Yard fight. For the next two years Bainbridge's command, virtually his living quarters, would be restricted to the *Independence,* within sight of the navy yard to which he had so earnestly laid claim.

Decatur's friendship with Oliver Perry, drawing him closer into that officer's personal scrapes, was a distraction he could ill afford. There was Susan to think of. She was cheerfully content with their fresh life together, and it promised to be all the more permanent when her husband decided they would move from the old and

rather drab Seven Buildings into a mansion more fitting to their fast-rising social esteem. Decatur used a portion of his sizeable balance of prize money to invest in lots alongside the President's Square (later Lafayette Park) conveniently near the White House, now Monroe's residence. And for architecture he applied to Benjamin Latrobe, whose many creations included the United States Capitol.

Glimpses would linger of the private Decatur. Even approaching forty, he was still aware of shortcomings in his nonprofessional world and strove to match Susan's level of culture and education. He was at his most confident when in the company of officers who were, like himself, semiretired from seafaring, and among whom he could more firmly voice opinions. Once, the conversation had turned to British naval tactics. Trafalgar? Decatur conceded Nelson's courage but attributed his triumph to the poor gunnery of the French and the Spanish. But if less opinionated, Decatur shone most when at parties with Susan. As noted by a Washington press lord's wife at one of Dolley Madison's soirées, the Decaturs were "a handsome pair . . . very brilliant."

Oliver Perry, settled in command of the Newport, Rhode Island, naval station, was not permitted to enjoy domestic tranquillity with his wife and children. Captain Heath, "an impudent and insolent blackguard" Perry called him, had continued to publish vindictive pamphlets impossible to ignore. And Elliott was wondering out loud why the commodore, having officially praised his conduct on Lake Erie, had taken to circulating "*base, false* and *malicious* reports" about him. According to one of many certificates Elliott had somehow gathered, Perry had declared that Elliott had better keep his mouth shut as to what took place on Lake Erie. Instead of doing so, Elliott quoted from one of his cohorts to the effect that "you should lay before your country and the world your own share of the glory of that day. . . . Perry is endeavoring to rob you of all." Construction of Stephen Decatur's mansion was well under way. A fire, fortunately confined to its stabling, was of more concern to him just then than Oliver Perry's two-front war. But he was about to be caught up in it.

On March 9, 1818, Perry wrote informing Decatur that he had heard Heath was on his way to call him out. Should a duel ensue, he would not consent to return Heath's fire. He felt some guilt, having violated service rules by striking another officer. His acceptance of Heath's challenge he seemed to have divined as in the nature of an atonement. At any rate, he wanted Decatur as his "friend" and would give him "timely notice of the proposed meeting." Decatur replied hoping that Perry's information was incorrect, but acknowledged that the marine captain might be urged on by malcontents.

Perry had written another friend describing "this business with Heath almost farcical from the publicity which he and his partisans have given it." Perry's derision could justifiably have been extended to dueling in general. At least eighty-two duels involving naval officers would be recorded between 1798 and 1848. Thirty-six officers died on the "field of honor," half the survivors wounded. Most shots were exchanged from no farther than ten or twelve yards. Sometimes the distance was almost ludicrously shorter. Two *Constellation* midshipmen were to fire within a thirty-foot range on the understanding, solemnly agreed to by their "friends," that should they miss, they would fire at each other again, practically face-to-face. This extremity was avoided, the first exchange of bullets crippling one protagonist. The other's pistol misfired. So rigid, even revered, was the code governing affairs of insult and honor that absurdity was never a factor, leaving the only objective reaction one of sadness, since more than half of those eighty-two meetings involved midshipmen scarcely out of their teens.

That veteran officers with anxious families should consider gunfire the only honorable culmination to perceived attacks upon their reputation was a phenomenon that would persist throughout most of the nineteenth century, limited in certain locales only by legal prohibition. It would take the fatal shooting of a congressman in 1838 to produce a law forbidding duels in Washington. And why dueling appeared more prevalent in the U.S. Navy than in the army is one of the puzzles of this somber tradition.

Plain inaction might have offered a clue. Prominent Philadelphians had begun a subscription for a plate dinner service to be presented to the Decaturs. One such gift had already been awarded to Stephen by citizens of Baltimore, silver candelabra inscribed in Latin: *Renowned for his valor; beloved for his virtues.* Philadelphia's silver service, consisting of wine coolers and a dozen goblets (Susan's choice), was received by the Decaturs in February 1818. And the commodore already had a gold medal from Congress for capturing the *Macedonian.* These glittering prizes were all very well. But some yearning for action colors a letter Decatur wrote to Daniel Smith, at whose Philadelphia countinghouse he had worked as a youth. "After all this, my dear friend, what shall I do? We have no war, no signs of a war, and I shall feel ashamed to die in my bed."

But neither did his instincts for daring or audacity find gratification any longer in duels or involvement therein. Both dignified and distinguished as a neighbor of President Monroe, he had outgrown the passion for glory, despite his stated aversion to dying in bed. Yet he was drawn deeper into the Perry-Heath-Elliott skein, in the process inching inexorably along a path of direct danger to himself. Perry wrote to him the day after his letter to Daniel Smith. "I have been assailed from all quarters since this [Heath] affair became known and am at a loss how to act . . . it is questionable whether I shall disgrace myself by having anything more to do with him. I rely on your friendship for advice. I know you will not shrink from any responsibility. My reliance on your judgement is unbounded."

Jesse Elliott's contribution to the dilemmas besetting Perry hinged on the question of whether or not, at the height of the Battle of Lake Erie, he had, in Perry's words, determined to "sacrifice me by keeping his vessel out of action." But Perry had said nothing of this at the time. He spoke well of Elliott in his official report. On that morning of September 10, 1813, Perry had commanded a fleet of nine sail, his flagship, the twenty-gun brig *Lawrence,* named for the *Chesapeake*'s last captain and flying a blue flag, with the unforgettable

if futile deathbed command not to give up the ship sewn upon it in white muslin. The British flotilla was out too, four brigs, a sloop and a schooner, commanded by one-armed Robert Heriot Barclay (he had lost the other at Trafalgar) on the newest brig, *Detroit.* Small ships on both sides but fated for a pivotal battle.

Master Commandant Elliott, in command of the *Niagara,* was a good sailor who had performed effectively in previous action on the Lakes and was just the type who would resent following in the line of battle instead of leading it. By noon the two flotillas were at grips, Perry's flagship stormed with grapeshot and canister from both the *Detroit* and another powerful brig, the *Caledonia.* Blood ran all over the *Lawrence*'s pine planks and dripped through seams into Perry's wardroom below. And where was Elliott? According to Perry's planning, the *Niagara* should have taken on HMS *Queen Charlotte* until heavy shot ran out and she was then to close up and assist the flagship with her carronades. Instead the *Niagara* hung back.

By early afternoon the *Lawrence* was a near wreck, her guns silent. Elliott on the *Niagara* would say he presumed his commander was dead. But at 2:30 P.M. he saw him put out from the *Lawrence*'s port side in a boat manned by four oarsmen. Hidden from British view by settling gunsmoke, Perry reached the *Niagara* safely in fifteen minutes. Taking the undamaged quarterdeck from Elliott, he determined to continue the action. After dispatching Elliott to bring up gunboats at the rear of the American column, he bent all effort to overtake the *Detroit* and *Queen Charlotte.* Perry quickly put an end to their crews' celebration of the *Lawrence*'s surrender. The British were themselves beyond peak fighting condition, the *Queen Charlotte*'s captain dead, and Barclay on the *Detroit* semiconscious belowdecks, his remaining arm bleeding and useless. Then the two British ships collided. Perry seized the advantage, the *Niagara* raking them with starboard broadsides. The *Detroit* struck her flag. And Perry's victory resulted in a British army retreat back to lower Canada.

Though bodily exhausted, Perry had been so delighted by his success on Lake Erie that "there was not a person in the world whose feelings I would hurt," and he resisted friends' advice that he expose Elliott's failure to support him. Elliott insisted that his part in the battle had been misunderstood and actually merited greater approbation than Perry had given him. Thus began a controversy that would dominate naval historiography long after the departure of its main characters.

Elliott might have let the matter drop. His reputation stood unblemished. But then news reached America that Commander Barclay, court-martialed in England for the loss of his ships, had decribed the *Niagara* as "making away" from the battle. (Barclay was honorably acquitted.) Elliott appealed to the navy secretary for a court of inquiry. One was held on the sloop *Ontario* off New York on April 16, 1815. Witnesses were few. Perry was not summoned, the court accepting his report of the battle as testimony. The *Niagara*'s purser, close to Elliott in those crucial combat hours, had committed suicide. Captain Alexander Murray, the court's president, had no intention of appearing to endorse a British implication of American cowardice and concluded that the only vessel to retreat from the Battle of Lake Erie was the Royal Navy's *Queen Charlotte,* which did so under the fire of the U.S. Navy's *Niagara.*

Now, four years later, Perry was regretting that he had spoken favorably of Jesse Elliott. On June 18 he told him in writing that "the reputation you have lost was tarnished by your behaviour on Lake Erie." That was enough for Elliott, who wrote back in early July, "I now invite you to the field." There was no point in further wasting ink and paper. "I must resort to some other weapon more potent than a pen, one which will place me at once above your *cunning. . . .* I cannot think you so base as to have forgotten how you met me on *Niagara.*"

Perry was already facing the likelihood of a duel with John Heath. He had only one sure way of settling Elliott's hash, at least for the

time being, and that was to file official charges against him. Only when Elliott exculpated himself before a court-martial could his challenge be considered as issuing from a man of honor. Perry sent off his charges to the secretary of the navy on August 10. They numbered five and were meticulously detailed. Elliott was a liar and worse. He had beaten a seaman for laughing when he, Elliott, dodged an enemy chain shot. He had penalized sailing masters who had refused to sign certificates attesting to his brave conduct. He had spread perverted statements vilifying Perry and glorifying himself. Most serious of all, he had failed to close action and engage the *Queen Charlotte* as ordered, was therefore guilty of negligence and cowardice, responsible for the *Lawrence*'s toll of eighty-three dead and wounded. Why had these charges not been submitted sooner? Perry's explanation was that at the time he could not bring himself to accuse a fellow American officer of such base behavior. As he told a friend, Purser Samuel Hambleton, "Better to screen a coward than to let the enemy know there is one in the fleet." Indeed, he still would have remained silent, but "this Elliott will not allow me to do." So he had felt constrained to file charges against him.

The charges missed Secretary Crowninshield, who, like most sensible and sufficiently well-off Washington residents, had left the summer-scorched capital for healthier northern climes. On October 3 Elliott wrote to Perry that two months had passed since his invitation to the field and if Perry had indeed sent charges to the Navy Department, why was he, Elliott, not placed under arrest? Jesse Elliott's appetite for mischief making was insatiable. He had journeyed to Fall River, Massachusetts, and, he told Perry in a scoffing letter, queried Secretary Crowninshield, who expressed ignorance of any charges against him. What Elliott did not know, and Perry did, was that in the secretary's absence his chief clerk, deeming them of great importance, had forwarded the papers to the White House.

The country was at peace. It was the beginning of James Monroe's "Era of Good Feelings." The president was unlikely to intensify the

Battle of Lake Erie argument by acting on the charges, especially since Perry's original battle report had so clearly favored Elliott. Embarrassment would result for the navy and the nation. Moreover, the president had privately talked with Decatur and made apparent his anxiety for an adjustment to the Perry-Heath affair. When Perry wondered why Elliott was not under arrest, Decatur theorized that "the President has great exception to having the business brought before the public, and it is possible the charges will sleep on the Secretary's desk." Monroe may indeed have returned them to the Navy Department. At any rate, no action followed. The papers Perry had mailed disappeared. But a copy would soon rest in Decatur's hands. And he could never have foreseen where this entrustment would lead as he accompanied Perry, one gloomy October morning, to a dueling field on the heights of the Hudson, north of Hoboken, New Jersey, for the long overdue meeting with John Heath.

18

Barron
Returns

The pistols were loaded, the principals placed back to back. A chill wind crossed from the river. Decatur had avoided acting as Perry's chief second, perhaps conscious of the incongruity of such a role with his firmly established status as national hero, member of the Board of Navy Commissioners, a pillar of Washington society who was on excellent terms with President Monroe. Perry's friend was an army major and old school chum named James Hamilton. Heath's lone friend was Lieutenant Desha of the marines. Decatur gave the word. The duelists advanced at his counting, each man five paces. They wheeled. Heath fired and missed. Perry stood with arms at his side, pistol lowered.

Decatur stepped between the two and declared that his friend had come to the field determined to receive Heath's fire without returning it. Heath was probably informed of Perry's intention in advance. At any rate, Lieutenant Desha and Heath acknowledged that honor was intact. The parties bowed to each other and separated.

Decatur was soon at his desk, studiously handling matters large and small. Some issues for the board's consideration were of national importance. It had not always approved of Benjamin Crowninshield's performance as secretary. Sometimes, Decatur thought, he had to be

pushed. His successor, Smith Thompson, was hardly better informed on naval matters, deferring most policy questions to the Commodores Rodgers, Porter, and Decatur. Among service personnel, serious problems had arisen, especially at overseas stations. But in ships, the navy grew notably stronger. In 1816 Congress had voted for an annual expenditure of $1 million over six years to build new vessels, including steam batteries for coastal defense, and nine 74-gun ships of the line.

Lacking children of his own, in this sense unique among senior naval officers, Decatur may have felt a special sympathy for parents who worried about their seagoing sons. In the same week as the Perry-Heath meeting, a letter reached him from a Thomas A. Smith, who wanted his son, a midshipman recovering from fever, granted a short furlough at home before returning to active duty. His family had not seen him for two years, and since his desire was to serve on the frigate *Congress,* bound for the Indian Ocean, they could not expect him home for another two. Might they have the boy with them for a brief spell before departure? Decatur saw to it that they did.

Enriched by prize money, and shrewd in such business dealings as the purchase of land along the Anacostia River, Decatur was generous toward the less fortunate. He supplied the needy with groceries and fuel for the winter and acted kindly toward his sister's two daughters. And he did not wish his new home, under construction, to be palatial, would be content, he told Latrobe, with one "suitable for foreign ministers [and] impressive entertainments." As the premises grew, he busied himself organizing paintings and portraits, trophies, medals, swords, and sturdy furniture. And on January 16, 1819, he was able to tell his Philadelphia friend Daniel Smith, "I have just moved into my new house." He and Susan were at last able to entertain on a grand scale.

The Washington City Council had paid for gravel paving between Pennsylvania Avenue and H Street, facilitating the passage of carriages to the Decatur House. Guests would alight at the three-storied

hand-laid brick building with its four great chimneys and step through a stylishly arched entrance framed by side lanterns and a delicate fanlight. The vestibule they entered boasted a geometrically patterned floor and a vaulted ceiling and faced a circular staircase that led to the second floor. On that level were a suite of entertainment rooms, whose long windows opened onto wrought-iron balconies overlooking President's Square, a drawing room, and a dining room with fourteen mahogany chairs. The drawing room and dining room were connected by a sliding door, which, observed a guest, gave the effect of "two rooms thrown into one." The presence of a pianoforte and a pedal harp attested to Susan's love of music. The third floor's six rooms were sleeping quarters modestly furnished with feather beds and Windsor chairs, for family and guests. Heath rugs and Wiltons, so named for the English town noted for its carpetry, covered much floor space. Servants, their quarters in the attic, tended a garden at the mansion's rear bounded by a carriage house and stables.

Decatur liked to show off the place, and friends noted how pleasantly tempered he had become. His serenity derived in part from Susan's early success as a society hostess, also from an absence of serious discord between them, and his continuing efforts at non-maritime self-education. There were other redeeming factors. The Perry-Heath affair had ended, and President Monroe had effectively pigeonholed Perry's charges against Elliott. The latter had, in fact, been promoted to captain.

Shortly after the Decaturs moved into their new home, there did occur an incident that might have touched off Stephen's once combative spirit. The fiery General Andrew Jackson's brutal campaign against the Seminole Indians in Florida, and his execution of three Englishmen for trading with them, had aroused enough politicians in Washington to consider punishing him. Jackson stormed into the capital accompanied by tough aides and threatening violence in the halls of Congress. One February morning Decatur was walking along

Pennsylvania Avenue with Pennsylvania senator Jonathan Roberts when they met Jackson and what Roberts called "his dragonets . . . ruffians." Introductions turned hostile, with Jackson's party apparently unable to proceed and demanding space in order to do so. Decatur stepped to one side, turned to Roberts, and said, "What a pity this man will not act in such a way as we can approve."

The next day Decatur took Susan and their nieces to the Capitol, and he again ran into a blustering Jackson. One of Jackson's foes was John Wayles Eppes, a Virginia senator, and the two stood face-to-face in the Senate Chamber, close to fisticuffs. Decatur hurried the ladies up to the visitors' gallery. He came down in time to hear Jackson swearing to cut off Eppes's ears. Decatur thrust himself between the two and told Jackson that if he tried to do so, it would be over his dead body. According to Roberts, the general quailed at this, telling his entourage, "One is always safe in following the advice of a brave man. Let us retire."

After this episode on Capitol Hill, nothing appeared to disturb Decatur's contentment. At the close of March he freed a slave, Philis Ash, granting her and her posterity "all rights of freedom." Philis had probably been bought during the Decaturs' residence in Norfolk. Stephen's father-in-law, Luke Wheeler, witnessed his signature to the emancipation. (Under District of Columbia law all slaves had to be registered. There is no record of Stephen Decatur as an owner.) And Stephen had no immediate cause for concern when he heard that James Barron, after six years abroad, had returned to the embrace of his family in Hampton.

On April 1 Decatur was one of a party that boarded the steamboat *Richmond* for Hampton Roads. It was headed by James Monroe, and its mission had to do with the government's consideration of Norfolk as the site of a "grand Naval Depot." Among the other navy officers in the group was Jesse Duncan Elliott. The next day in Norfolk, at the Exchange Coffee House, a public dinner was held to

honor the president. Someone, perhaps Littleton Tazewell, proposed a toast to Decatur. "His laurels cannot fade, they are preserved by the gratitude of his countrymen." Elliott was there, and presumably raised his glass to the name of the officer against whom he would shortly be intriguing. Elliott was married to a Norfolk girl, spent much of his time in the Hampton Roads area working with U.S. Army engineers in a survey of suitable harbor locations. In the three months since Barron's return, Elliott, his one friendly witness at the *Chesapeake-Leopard* court-martial more than ten years earlier, had been in touch with him.

Barron's prolonged absence from his family and country had been far from happy. The outbreak of war with England had found him stranded in Copenhagen. Such was Britain's control of the seas, Danish shipping had declined and Barron was unable to find passage home. The only friend he had in the Danish capital was John M. Forbes, the American consul. He labored to profit from inventions, rented a small garret, and created several useful gadgets, including a rope-making device and a cork-cutting machine, both of which he managed to have patented and sold. His principal dream was to produce a steam-driven ship's windlass, which he felt sure would benefit the maritime world.

The war had continued to hinder transatlantic mail service, and Barron grieved over the lack of replies to the letters he wrote, especially to his eldest daughter, Jane, whose teenaged shoulders bore the weight of most domestic responsibilities. The family, unbeknownst to Barron, lived in a run-down Hampton house, the British having reduced Little England to ashes. Barron's suspension officially ended on February 8, 1813. For reasons he would find difficult to explain without embarrassment, five months passed before he wrote to William Jones, then secretary of the navy. "The first wish of my heart [is] always to render services to my country. Your command will find me here or St. Petersburg." He made several copies, to be carried by any ship that he had heard was about to head for America.

Never particularly discreet, his prudence now further impaired by stress and worry, he had lengthened the letter by protesting that the sentence at his trial was unjust, "the truly guilty [were] set at liberty . . . I was, to say the least of it, cruelly sacrificed." Barron, of course, knew nothing of that damning letter Lieutenant Lewis had written to the Navy Department concerning his alleged remarks to the British consul at Pernambuco. Neither William Jones nor his successors as secretary of the navy may have seen it. The missive rested in the department's files. Anyway, Barron got no response from Washington.

His more sorrowful letters were to his "beloved Janey." His Copenhagen lodgings were "miserable at best." What meager socializing he could afford were meetings with Forbes. "Did you expect, my dear child, to see your once gay father sit a whole evening without speaking one word?" He tried to get passage home on the *John Adams,* which in 1814 had brought American peace envoys to Europe for the negotiations at Ghent. One of them regretfully informed him that since the *John Adams* was at sea only as a cartel under British permission, she could not carry any army or naval officer of the nation with which England was still at war.

Early in 1815 Barron had managed to leave Denmark and via Sweden reach London for a business meeting with Armistead and Kelly's English agents regarding the blockaded *Portia* and her cargo. Then he was in Hamburg, writing another pathetic letter to Jane. "It is scarcely possible for any loving father to have more confidence than I have in you. . . . Kiss the children tenderly for me." He asked her to send "a perfect description of each of them, how tall they are . . . the colour of their eyes and hair." Yet after confirmation of the Treaty of Ghent early in 1815, Barron remained abroad for three more years. Work on inventions and lack of money would be his stated reason, also an "unconquerable reluctance" to expose his penury before foes. He could have benefited financially when the Armisteads secured a British license for him. But on September 8, 1815, he wrote,

"On no consideration can I be induced to sail under a British license while I hold my claim to the character of an American citizen."

With his company's permission he sold the *Portia* and cargo for $7,000, of which he kept $500 for living expenses. And his family's situation had somewhat improved. His half-pay of $50 per month had been restored at the expiry of his suspension, and he had sent a power of attorney to Jane so she could cash the checks. And she had married a wealthy Virginian whose manor, Bethel, stood near Hampton. Most important, Barron had at last gotten a passport for the United States, endorsed by the American minister in London. And from Elsinore, late fall 1818, he had finally sailed for his homeland, not knowing that almost from the moment he again set foot on American soil, there would begin a fresh period of frustration and despair.

According to one account, when Barron visited Washington early in 1819 to apply in person for an appointment to active service, he was met at the Navy Department by its chief clerk, Benjamin Homans, who referred him to the Board of Navy Commissioners. Told the names of two members, Rodgers and Decatur, Barron felt no urge to take that approach, and he was doubly dismayed when Homans informed him of a document on file that had prejudiced Secretary of the Navy Smith Thompson and predecessors against him. Clearly, the Lewis letter had surfaced, and this was the first Barron had heard of it.

He received on request word from John Forbes, testifying to having seen the letter Barron sent from Copenhagen to Washington offering his services. Forbes also confirmed that Barron had sought passage home in 1814. This was in Barron's favor but he was soon aware of what he was up against. Not only must he satisfactorily explain why he had stayed in Europe years after his suspension was over, but the harder task would be to convincingly refute the allegation in the Lewis letter of having made treasonable statements to an English diplomat. This must be the price of his rehabilitation. In February Smith Thompson showed him the letter and told him he

could only clear his name through a court of inquiry. This would require witnesses. The writer of the letter was beyond reach, lost on the *Epervier*. But what he had penned was doubly hearsay, conveyed by the Baltimore merchant Goodwin. At Barron's earnest request, Smith Thompson wrote to him.

Goodwin replied on March 4. He could not recall the precise wording of his 1811 Pernambuco conversation with the British consul Mr. Lyon, but what it amounted to was that Barron had declared himself "shamefully mistreated," had told the consul that "Mr. Jefferson caused him to go out in a defenseless state for the special purpose of having his ship attacked and disgraced, and thus attain his favourite object of involving the United States in a war with Great Britain. This is all the information I remember. . . . Mr. Lyon has since died." Another potential witness gone. And not long after Goodwin wrote his letter, ending it with "For how far this may attach credit to my testimony, I take the liberty of referring to my friend Commodore Decatur," Goodwin too died.

So Barron's vehement denials of the charges in the Lewis letter were getting him nowhere, likewise his attempts to explain why he had not come back to America earlier. He wrote desperate letters to Copenhagen, hoping to salvage some item that might put damaging charges to rest. These even included an allegation that he had sailed under a British license. About now, in April, Decatur returned from his Norfolk tour. Shortly thereafter, Oliver Perry arrived at his home as a guest. It was to be a farewell occasion, since Perry was under orders to sail for Venezuela on the *John Adams,* his mission to obtain Simón Bolívar's cooperation in the suppression of Caribbean piracy. While under the Decaturs' roof, Perry made of his host a sober request. Susan Decatur would recall some of his words. The subject was Captain Jesse Duncan Elliott.

The man was so devoid of honor and regardless of the truth that "there was no knowing what he might say if there was no person to keep him in check." Perry had papers documenting his charges

against Elliott. Would Decatur take custody of them and should Perry fail to return from his South American mission, make them public? Decatur said yes. When Perry left the room, Susan told her husband she was afraid that by consenting to do what Perry asked, he might get himself into some difficulty. Decatur said she should not worry, "it was his duty to watch over the reputation of his brother officers." This was not the first time Decatur placed a concept of duty above wifely advice.

After staying with the Decaturs, Perry went to Annapolis, where the *John Adams* awaited his command. He examined her fitness for sailing and hoisted his broad pennant. On June 5 he wrote a letter to a close friend and relative, Benjamin Hazard, a lawyer and politician living in Newport. He asked Hazard to "direct Benjamin Mason [Perry's hometown clerk] to make out a copy of the papers relative to Elliott and forward them to Commodore Decatur . . . sincerely a friend of mine who told me that Elliott was very busy defaming me among congressmen." For some reason the clerk failed to immediately act, and the material would not reach Decatur until the close of the year. By that time he was immersed in the most tragic and extraordinary correspondence in American naval history.

Events had assumed an ominous symmetry. Decatur knew Perry was being defamed by Elliott. Another officer was being defamed, this one by Decatur, who citied duty as his motive. He knew of the charges against Barron. Lieutenant Lewis had doubtless talked of them while flag captain on the *Guerrière* in the Mediterranean. And Decatur, along with his fellow board members, was now informed of them by the secretary of the navy. Already infected with an animus against his former mentor and father figure, Decatur readily and openly believed the charges against him. As he would write to Barron himself, he thereupon had "very frequent and free conversations regarding you and your conduct . . . said that in my opinion you ought not to be received again into the navy . . . [am] endeavoring to prevent your readmission." By acting thus he was "performing a duty I

owe the service." He had talked of Barron with "officers of our grade, superiors and inferiors, and all concur in the opinion that you ought not be employed again while the imputations that lie against you remain."

Barron had been home scarcely half a year. His wife was frail, his own health by no means perfect. The family still depended to some extent on the help of his now married daughter, Jane. But he knew that forces were at work to block his reinstatement, and he could not allow them to go unchallenged. There may have been, as suggested, some artful instigation on Jesse Elliott's part. But even without it Barron must have felt that he had no option. On June 12 he wrote to Decatur. "I have been informed in Norfolk that you have said that you could insult me with impunity, or words to that effect. If you have said so, you will, no doubt, avow it, and I shall expect to hear from you."

19

The
Letters

At the close of the nineteenth century's second decade, the United States was at peace with the rest of the world and was about to be internationally perceived as a naval power. There was still a long way to go. At home, a political bloc was still opposed to a national navy. But American ships and seamen had performed so commendably, if not always sucessfully, against some of the British navy's best, that only budgetary considerations could threaten the future development of an American naval force. United States warships were on foreign stations as distant as the far South Atlantic and the China Sea.

A new generation of seagoing personnel was emerging. Yesterday's heroes lived in fine mansions built with prize money and were forming into bureaucracies whose judgments relating to ship design and construction, squadron deployment, procurement and recruiting goals, could outweigh the opinions of whoever happened to be secretary of the navy. The members of the Board of Navy Commissioners, applying lessons learned in the Barbary Wars and the conflict with England, were laying the foundations of a naval force whose potential, by the date of the board's dissolution in 1842, would stir interest, and some concern, among the administrators of Europe's fleets.

In its early years the navy board had much to deal with, and Stephen Decatur's energies were as taxed as those of his fellow members, David Porter and the president, John Rodgers. But off duty he enjoyed a cordial relationship with the nation's chief executive, James Monroe, and accompanied by Susan adorned a succession of social events in Washington during the period immediately following his triumphant return from the Mediterranean. Of the diplomatic difficulties his "comet-like" sweep of that sea had left, and of Commodore Bainbridge's progressive misanthropy while confined to the ship of the line *Independence* at Boston, he knew or cared little. All of which adds a touch of mystery to the question of why he so witheringly and openly opposed James Barron's readmission to active naval service. Aboard the *United States* and on other occasions, Barron had demonstrated his professional initiative and seamanship. Did the animosity stem from whatever Barron had said on a Norfolk street twelve years earlier concerning the local object of Decatur's affection? Had Barron's words amounted to an infringement so galling to the young man who had formerly regarded him as a father? Was Barrons's conduct on the *Chesapeake* so unforgivable? Or his apparent avoidance of a duel with Rodgers? The answer could have been all of these, compounded by his failure to come home when the term of his suspension expired and his alleged sailing in European waters under British license. But underlying everything would have been Decatur's rigid concept of his duty.

He replied to Barron's letter on June 17, in terse words that, at least, made sense. Barron was entitled to what he requested but only "if you had been frank enough to name your informant." And he denied the story Barron claimed to have heard in a way not likely to have pleased the older man. "Whatever I may have thought or said, in the very free and frequent conversations I have had regarding you and your conduct . . . I never could have been guilty of such egotism as to say that 'I could have insulted you (or any man) with impunity.' "

And when Barron, disregarding the scorn in the other's words,

accepted the denial "which relieves my mind," he also wrote that while the source of reports of Decatur's "impunity" boast could not be traced, several gentlemen in Norfolk, "not your enemies, nor actuated by any malicious motive," had told him they were in circulation. Barron's admission that he had taken notice of unverifiable tales was enough to touch off a second, more contemptuous, letter from Decatur. "I meant no more than to disclaim the specific and particular expression." As to the motives of the unidentified rumormongers and of Barron's basing his inquiry on their gossip, "it is a matter of perfect indifference to me."

However brief, this exchange was soon broadly known among senior naval officers. And there was no dearth of message carriers. One was Master Commandant William Carter of Norfolk, who talked with Decatur while visiting the navy board in Washington. He returned to Norfolk and wrote to Decatur that to date nothing had transpired there regarding the letters but a certain lady feared they might lead to a duel. Decatur's friends in Norfolk did not think Barron would press his case that far. All the same, Carter thought that Decatur should send copies to Littleton Tazewell, "who I have just left" and would attend to his wishes. Carter's letter would eventually be published, with the name of the apprehensive woman blacked out. A clue provided by at least one newspaper described her as "a young lady living in the family of the father of Mrs. Decatur." (Carter would be cashiered from the navy in 1827.)

In September the *John Adams* arrived in Hampton Roads from her South American voyage and brought sad news. When the frigate reached Trinidad, Commodore Perry had gone up the great Orinoco River aboard the schooner *Nonesuch,* his destination the Venezuelan capital. Perry had sailed from home with no great zeal for his mission, troubled by the absence from his wife, Elizabeth, and their five children, and possibly full of the foreboding he had evinced when he committed his charges against Jesse Elliott to Decatur's care with the request that they be processed should he not return. Yellow fever

struck the schooner's crew. Perry returned to the *John Adams,* and, as the ship weighed anchor for home, he too fell victim. He summoned officers to witness the signing of his will and died within a week of his thirty-fourth birthday.

Jesse Elliott was still surveying off the Virginia capes. He and Barron were among the first to hear of Perry's fate. And within a few short weeks pens were once more active. Writing from his Norfolk home, Littleton Tazewell would inform Decatur, "But one opinion exists with all the Naval Officers here . . . that Elliott is the sole instigator of the renewal of the correspondence . . . has done everything in his power to stimulate his reluctant friend . . . that Barron would gladly now let the thing rest *if he can,* but that Elliott will prevent any sort of adjustment."

Those Norfolk naval officers may not have had irrefutable grounds for their suspicions regarding Elliott. And it can only be surmised whether Elliott actually had any inkling of the arrangement Perry had made with Decatur for the airing of the charges against him. But certainly the correspondence resumed. For four months Barron had been quiet, still relishing the reunion with his family. No doubt Elliott, a witness for his defense at the *Chesapeake* court-martial eleven years earlier, had made contact with him. And it was with a tortured evocation of that trial that on October 23 Barron began a letter to Decatur. "I had supposed that the measure of your ambition was nearly completed, and that your good fortune had rendered your reputation for acts of magnanimity too dear to be risked wantonly. . . . I had also concluded that your rancor towards me was fully satisfied by the cruel and unmerited sentence passed upon me by the court of which you were a member."

At his Navy Department desk, Decatur was busy. As a navy commissioner he had just drafted a circular directing that a study be made at shipbuilding yards of the suitability of iron to be used in constructing two ships of the line and a frigate "under the Act for the

gradual increase of the Navy." Barron's missive was likely addressed to him at the department instead of the mansion overlooking President's Square. Decatur may well have hesitated before reading beyond its opening paragraph. The letter from Hampton was long. Decatur could have read it in installments. Or he might have taken it home to read in the small room on the second floor he used as a private study. (Here too he might have read of the death, in late September, of his sister, Ann Pine Hurst, who had remarried after losing her first husband, Marine Corps Captain McKnight, to a duel.)

Barron expected that after his seven-year exile he would be allowed solace and tranquillity with his friends and family. But no sooner had he set foot on American soil than "I learnt that the same malignant spirit which had before influenced you to ruin my reputation was still at work," as he wrote Decatur. He had been told that Decatur had sent their June letters to Norfolk by "a respectable officer of the Navy" (doubtless William Carter) for showing to "some of my particular friends with a view of alienating them from me." Moreover, Decatur had "tauntingly and boastfully observed, that you would cheerfully meet me in the field and hoped that I would yet act like a man . . . or words to that effect."

Decatur had certainly sent the letters to Norfolk after Master Commandant Carter told him of a Hampton woman who had talked about them. That her name was excised from later published accounts may be of no significance, although oddly, newspapers placed her in Luke Wheeler's household, while Decatur quoted (Carter?) as saying she was a female of Barron's acquaintance. Might she perhaps have been both?

At any rate, Barron, almost certainly prompted by Elliott, had restarted the duel of words. They sped almost blindly along a path to confrontation. He was utterly convinced that Decatur was a bête noire that imperiled his career. Whether or not Elliott was the "sole instigator" of the renewed correspondence, clearly Barron felt himself at bay before a remorseless persecutor and believed everything

he was told to Decatur's detriment. He charged his long-ago protégé with conduct "towards an individual, situated as I am . . . oppressed as I have been, and that chiefly by your means [as] unbecoming you as an officer and a gentleman. . . . It calls loudly for redress at your hands, I consider you as having given the invitation, which I accept." He would be prepared to meet Decatur at any time and place "which our respective friends, hereafter to be named, shall designate."

He claimed entitlement to the choice of weapons and distance. Still more than that, "I flatter myself, from your known personal courage, that you would disdain any unfair advantage which your superiority in the use of the pistol, and the natural defect in my vision, increased by age, would give you." On the Sunday following his receipt of this impassioned document, Decatur, the commodore who detested writing letters, even to his wife, set about composing a reply, either while closeted at home, without interruption from Susan and servants, or in privacy at the Navy Department. Running to at least twenty-five hundred words, it would be by far the longest personal letter he had ever written.

The *Chesapeake-Leopard* affair? Barron seemed to have forgotten that a court of inquiry had preceded the trial, Decatur wrote, and from the evidence presented at that initial hearing, "I drew an opinion altogether unfavorable to you." Thus prejudiced, he had sought to be excused from sitting on the court-martial, but the secretary of the navy had insisted that he serve. He had informed Barron's counsel of all this "in order to afford you an opportunity, should you deem it expedient, to protest against my being a member [of the court] on the ground of my not only having formed, but *expressed* an opinion unfavorable to you. You did not protest. . . . Duty constrained me, however unpleasant it was, to take my seat. . . . You, I find, are incapable of estimating the motives which guided my conduct . . . [for which] I do not consider myself as, in any way, accountable to *you.*"

With those words, Decatur might well have set aside his pen. Instead: "Between you and me there never has been a personal difference,

but I have entertained, and do still entertain, the opinion that your conduct as an officer, since the affair of the *Chesapeake,* has been such as ought to forever bar your readmission into the service." Why had he voiced these views so freely and frequently? Because of the gravity of the facts on which they were based. Here Decatur brought up Captain Lewis's letter, its assertion that Barron had made treasonable remarks to a British consul.

Decatur deemed the honor and veracity of both the late captain and his informant, Mr. Goodwin, as "beyond question." Then he indulged in a twist of logic strangely cruel from one who, however uncontrollable in youth and ready to shed scruples in a thirst for glory, had never displayed ashore or afloat the merest hint of venom. "If, sir, the affair of the *Chesapeake* excited the indignant feelings of the nation towards Great Britain; and was, as every one admits, one of the principal causes which produced the late war, did it not behoove you to take an active part in the war, for your own sake? Patriotism out of the question! But . . . instead of finding you in the foremost ranks, it is said, and is credited, that you were, after the commencement of the war, to be found in command of a vessel sailing under British license!"

Here was a case of Decatur believing an unverified report. As he would shortly admit, no grounds existed for the assertion that Barron, while his country fought against the British, sailed a merchant ship under British license. But no sober thought stayed Decatur's pen as he wrote on: "You know, sir, that by absenting yourself, as you did for years, from the country, without leave from the government, you subjected yourself to be stricken from the rolls" and by intercourse with the enemy "become subject to the severest punishment known to our laws."

On his return to the homeland Barron had striven to reestablish himself in the navy. Other officers besides Decatur had opposed this. A number who had "faithfully discharged their duty to the country in the hour of trial" were inactive because of a shortage of service

employment. "To employ you, to the exclusion of any one of them, would be doing an act of injustice." And Decatur's motive in all this? Duty to the service and conviction "that I was contributing to the preservation of its respectability."

He lectured Barron that having been led into error by untraceable sources, one might have expected him to treat subsequent rumors with caution, or at least to seek their origin before swallowing them. A duel? "I never invited you to the field; nor have I expressed a hope that you would call me out." According to someone Barron had evidently spoken to in Norfolk, he had come to Washington even before the June correspondence "with the intention of calling me out." Decatur had told the informant that if Barron made the call "I would meet you, but that, on all scores, I should be much better pleased, to have nothing to do with you."

Even that was not enough to make Decatur sign, seal, and send the letter. He expounded his views on dueling. He did not think that such meetings, "under any circumstances, can raise the reputation of any man . . . it is not even an unerring criterion of personal courage . . . but, in my opinion, the man who makes *arms his profession,* is not at liberty to decline an invitation from any person, who is not so far degraded as to be beneath his notice. Having incautiously said I would meet you, I will not now consider this to be your case, although many may think so." Weapons, place, and distance? He was not "fastidious on those points, but should rather be disposed to yield to you any little advantage of this kind." His skill in the use of the pistol "exists more in your imagination than in reality; for the last twenty years I have had but little practice." As to a disparity in ages: "Not more, I believe, than five or six years [actually eleven]. It would have been out of the common course of nature, if the vision of either of us had been improved by years."

Decatur ended by declaring that should he decide it expedient, he would let others see the renewed correspondence as he had done that of June. And in this final paragraph he wrote, "From your manner of

proceeding, it appears to me that you have come to the determination to fight someone, and that you have selected me for that purpose; and I must take leave to observe that your object would have been better attained, had you made this decision during our late war, when your fighting might have benefited your country as well as yourself."

The correspondence did not end there. A brief November exchange reads as an incongruous interlude. Decatur had been told by John Forbes, the ex-consul, that Barron had not been afloat until after the peace. Decatur duly corrected himself. "Consequently, the report which I notice of your having sailed under British license must be unfounded." No apology. And Barron, on the twentieth, blamed his failure to answer Decatur's last two letters on "unavoidable interruption." But five days later he took on what he called Decatur's "very lengthy, elaborate, and historical reply" with a missive twice as long, allowing that "a much more laconic answer would have served my purpose, which, for the present, is nothing more than to obtain at your hands honorable redress for the accumulated insults which you, sir, have attempted to heap upon me. . . . Your last voluminous letter is *alone* sufficient proof, if none other existed, of the rancorous disposition you entertain towards me." He would not have bothered to write further other than to declare himself "prepared to meet you in the field." But since Decatur had said he intended to go public with the correspondence, he felt compelled to do likewise, "a duty I owe myself and to the world."

Decatur's actions had alienated no friends against him. "I have more friends, both in and out of the navy, than you are aware of; and it is not in your power, great as you may imagine your official influence to be, to deprive me of their good opinion and affection." As to Decatur's sending the correspondence to Norfolk because "a female of my acquaintance had talked of it," she had not known of it from Barron. "Females, sir, have nothing, or ought to have nothing, to do in

controversies of this kind." As to the *Chesapeake* court-martial, Decatur, so prejudiced, must have had a pliable conscience to have served on it. No power on earth (presumably including that of the navy secretary) could have forced a man to sit on a case that he had prejudged.

The Lewis story about treasonable remarks to a British envoy was "a ridiculous, malicious, absurd, improbable, falsehood." The envoy, named Lyon, happened to like Americans, and any conversation with him was perfectly innocent. Goodwin? Barron knew nothing of him; his recollection was dismissable hearsay. Of Barron's desire to return to the United States during the war, Decatur could, if so disposed, find his application for service among Navy Department records. "And one letter, above all, *you* should not have passed over unnoticed [was] that which you received from my hand of May, 1803, addressed to the Secretary of the Navy [which secured] the first command that you were ever honoured with." Decatur may have forgotten this, also that "by my advice and arguments, I saved you from resigning the service of your country." This, Decatur had threatened do when, in 1803, he was removed from the first lieutenancy of the *New York* to the *Chesapeake,* in effect a slight demotion.

As to the *Chesapeake-Leopard* clash having been a primary cause of the War of 1812, Barron took a different view of history. That conflict "did not take place, sir, until five years after, when that affair had been amicably adjusted . . . between the two nations. I mention this to show that, although it *did* happen to be your fortunate lot to have an opportunity to be in the foremost rank on that occasion . . . you are ignorant even to the causes which led to it." And the charge of having sailed under British license was one Decatur should have affirmed as fact, "not on rumor, which you so much harp upon."

Barron felt himself under no obligation to describe his attempts to return home during the war. Not to Decatur. His letter, nevertheless, supplied elaboration. Upon news of war's outbreak reaching Copenhagen, it was not expected to last six months. Even so, had the

Navy Department sent him the slightest intimation that it could use his services, "I should have considered no sacrifice too great . . . to obtain so desirable an object . . . a gunboat, under my own orders, would not have been refused; but what hope had I, when my letter of application was not even honoured by an answer?" Regarding the efforts he had since made for reinstatement, why had Decatur been "so particularly busy" attempting to bar them? "Was it because your inflated pride led you to believe that the weight of your influence was greater than that of any other officer?" Those who concurred in Decatur's derogatory opinion of him: "I suppose you are most commonly attended by a train of dependants . . . revolving around you like satellites."

The longest letter in the series, it ended ambiguously on the point of a meeting with pistols. "I consider you as having thrown down the gauntlet and I have no hesitation in accepting it." But he claimed no advantage to weapons or distance. "Could I stoop so low as to solicit any, I know you too well to believe you would have any inclination to concede them." He agreed with Decatur on dueling, it was "a barbarous practice which ought to be excluded from civilized society." But there might be cases making "an appeal to arms absolutely necessary." This was one such, "the only alternative which now seems to present itself for the preservation of my honour. . . . I never wished to fight in this way and had you permitted me to remain at rest, I should not have disturbed *you*. But you have hunted me out, have persecuted me with all the power and influence of your office, have declared your determination to drive me from the navy."

Decatur's only motive for "persecuting" him was "to obtain my rank: if my life shall give it to you, you have an opportunity of obtaining it." He asked for Decatur's determination and the name of his friend. He in turn would name his. So would be arranged "a final close to this affair." Barron ended this latest round with an apology for having replied so late. "Out of tenderness for [my family's] feelings I have written under great restraint."

His wife and children may have gleaned something of his letter writing. Decatur kept Susan uninformed. However cavalierly he had displayed his contempt for Barron among brother officers, he nursed no deep desire for a duel. He could talk in such a fashion convinced that he would be unable to find a second. When he spoke to fellow navy board members Rodgers and Porter of the possibility that he might need a "friend" in a duel with James Barron, they scoffed at the idea. Decatur's courage was already beyond question; he had no need to affirm it in a shooting match with Barron or anybody else. Other officers might have intervened with a view to a peaceful settlement, refusing any request by Decatur to act as his second. Thomas Macdonough was at hand but unwell, would die within five years of tuberculosis. Commodore Charles Stewart, an old comrade, would certainly have come to his aid but was at sea, returning from the Mediterranean.

Commodore Charles Morris was in Washington, about to embark for Venezuela to take up the task Perry would have discharged had he lived. Decatur showed him a Barron letter, and Morris acknowledged his dilemma, sure that Decatur was actually in no mood for a duel. But how could he refuse if directly challenged? Morris thought that a sensible letter to Barron could honorably close the issue. He drafted one but Decatur refused to sign it. "He appeared," Morris recalled, "to be governed by an apprehension that his reputation might suffer if he took any means to avoid a meeting . . . our talk lasted until dark." But without a second, there could be no duel. This was one safe loophole through which Decatur could honorably escape from the predicament he had written himself into.

He still had his navy board affairs, and other personal correspondence, to attend to. He was surprised and pleased to receive in November a letter from Gould Francis Leckie, the English diplomat with whom he had struck up a friendship at Syracuse. Leckie wrote from Genoa. "It is now 12 years since I returned to this part of the world to enjoy that domestic freedom under a monarchic government I never

could find in the boasted British system." An admirer of the young nation in the New World, Leckie had written a memoir dealing with America's future on the international scene. "The United States must either abandon foreign commerce to more enterprising nations and become simply an agricultural state like the Chinese or tread in the steps of the British and Dutch." Leckie focused on America's need to have a permanent naval base in the Mediterranean. This would be the first step toward the day when "America possesses the means to succeed Great Britain in the Empire of the Seas." For a start, the United States government should consider Lampedusa as a base; the island had "two decent harbours" that could be "America's home in the Mediterranean." Leckie offered his influence in the area should action be taken on his idea, and he had contacted Commodore Stewart, then Perry's successor as commander of the American squadron in that sea. Stewart's response was what a future generation would label distinctly isolationist. "My opinion is that the American government would not enter into any arrangement of that nature . . . to hold any possession in this sea, so remote from the U.S.A. There are, and probably will be at all times, friendly ports open to their commerce and ships of war in this quarter."

Leckie had decided upon direct communication with Washington and found there was a navy board on which Decatur sat. Hence his letter. "I know your attachment to the cause of your country, you have served her with honour and she has testified her esteem for you." If Decatur felt he was unable to do as Leckie wished, "at least this letter gives me an opportunity of hearing from you." He hoped that the many years since they had last met "have not obliterated from your memory your old friend and sincere admirer." Decatur read the letter with keen interest and probably discussed its contents with his colleagues. And it must have stirred personal recollections of his glory years in the Mediterranean. But his mind was still burdened, and his time much occupied, by the missives that continued to arrive from Hampton.

20

The
Friends

On November 29, four days from Barron's latest letter to Decatur, Commodore William Bainbridge handed over the *Independence* to Captain John Shaw and left Boston for Washington to take command of the other completed ship of the line, *Columbus,* under orders for the Mediterranean. One evening the following month Decatur was crossing Pennsylvania Avenue on his way home when a carriage drew up nearby. Bainbridge jumped out, and Decatur was startled to receive a double handclasp. Susan wasn't on the scene but was told by her husband of their exchange:

Bainbridge: Decatur, I behaved like a fool, but I hope you will forgive me. You have always contrived to reap laurels from my misfortunes.

Decatur: I have done nothing but duty, and if you are convinced of that, come along with me, to take a glass of wine.

Bainbridge declined, he had an appointment on Capitol Hill, but he promised to return and move in with the Decaturs as houseguest.

Susan was astonished. "It seems to me," she told Stephen, "an act of great assurance to invite himself to be our guest after allowing five years to elapse without writing or speaking to you." She was afraid Bainbridge had "some other motive than that of true repentance."

Decatur said not to worry, and by Wednesday, December 29, when he again turned his attention to the embittered broadsides from Hampton, Bainbridge was under his roof, conceivably looking over his shoulder as he wrote.

Barron's latest letter contained no direct challenge to a meeting. Indeed, throughout the prolonged correspondence thus far, neither man had displayed much zeal for the notion of replacing pens with pistols. Barron had never shown a taste for duels, and Decatur had long outgrown his. They were not hotheaded young midshipmen pursuing affairs of honor to a gory tragicomic climax but middle-aged commissioned officers, and after reading Barron's letter, "it was my determination," wrote Decatur, "not to notice it." Would that he had stopped right there. But he wrote as if trapped in what he called an "unprofitable discussion," forced to deal with Barron's "false coloring and calumnies. . . . Instead of calling me out for injuries which you insist I have heaped upon you, *you* have thought fit to enter into this war of words." Decatur had not challenged him, nor did he intend to. "I do not consider it essential to my reputation that I should notice anything which may come from you. If we fight, it must be of your seeking and you must take all the risks."

But if Decatur wanted to halt this epistolary jousting before it led to a sanguine consummation, he chose an unpromising course, continued to "harp" on points already gone over. Barron's denial of the charge that he had conversed with the British consul at Pernambuco was unacceptable. "The man capable of making such a communication would not hesitate in denying it." To Barron's assertion that he had been unable to secure passage home, Decatur replied: "The custom house entries in New York and Baltimore alone, from the single port of Bordeaux, will show nearly a hundred arrivals." And Bordeaux was "only a few days' journey" from Copenhagen. Decatur's desire to obtain Barron's rank? Were he disposed to "kill out of my way, as you insinuate," there would be other senior officers than Barron to be first removed.

Decatur denied as unfounded Barron's claim that his advice had prevented him from quitting the service. "I have never, since my first admission into the navy, contemplated resigning." And he was not ordered from the first lieutenancy of the *New York* to the second of the *Chesapeake*. He was asked to remain in the Mediterranean as first lieutenant and would have done so "had not the government of Malta demanded the delivery of the persons concerned in the affair of honour which led to the death of a British officer." Decatur had forgotten, assuming he knew, that Midshipman Joseph Bainbridge's victim was no officer. Anyway, "it was deemed necessary to send all the persons implicated in that affair out of the way." So he went home on the *Chesapeake* as a passenger. "Your offering your life to me would be quite affecting and might (as you evidently intended) excite sympathy, if it were not ridiculous." Barron's jeopardizing his life depended on himself, "is done with a view to fighting your own character up. . . . I shall pay no further attention to any communication you may make to me, other than a direct call to the field." The contents of this and all preceding letters were now known to William Bainbridge.

Still in that same December, the charges Oliver Perry composed against Elliott had reached Decatur's desk. They were sent him by Benjamin Hazard as Perry had requested the previous June. Hazard was preparing a biography of Perry and intended to mention the Battle of Lake Erie controversy although uncertain how to handle it, given Perry's misplaced magnanimity, his "sheltering Elliott from public animadversion as he endeavored to do in his official dispatch and a letter of approbation he furnished Elliott personally." Had Decatur any ideas?

William Bainbridge had moved in with the Decaturs three days after Christmas and stayed off and on for three weeks. Occasionally he had to be at St. Mary's City on a southern tributary of the Potomac River, down to which the *Columbus* had been towed to avoid ice. But he was on the scene in Washington when Decatur received a letter

Barron wrote January 16 as if goaded. "When you will consent to meet me on fair and equal grounds such as two honourable men may consider, you are at liberty to view this as that call."

In Decatur's exasperated opinion this still fell short of the point. On the twenty-fourth he wrote Barron, "I am at a loss to know what your intention is. If a challenge, I accept it and refer you to my friend Comm. Bainbridge who is fully authorized by me to make any arrangements he pleases as regards weapons, mode or distance."

This brought a final letter from Barron, its content concluding the long and profuse correspondence as a pathetically absurd anticlimax. He had been confined to bed with "a violent bilious fever" since the beginning of the year. Forty-eight hours after his letter of the sixteenth, about to recover, "I relapsed . . . have had a violent attack which has reduced me very low, but as soon as I am in a situation to write, you shall hear from me on the point." Nothing more was written between Barron and Decatur. And William Bainbridge, by offering himself as "friend," had effectively closed Decatur's escape hatch. The woeful war of words, a thirteen-letter argument, had ended. Matters were now in more purposeful hands.

Decatur attended conscientiously to his duties on the navy board, responding to other letters crossing his desk. An occasional application for professional help was made in person. In the first week of January he was visited by one Joseph Fogro, born in Corsica, not yet a naturalized American but eager to join the United States Navy. He showed suitable credentials including a record of unblemished service in the French navy. Decatur promised to do what he could to secure him a midshipman's warrant. The following week Senator Walter Lowrie of Pennsylvania, a social acquaintance, sent Decatur a request on behalf of his brother-in-law, a Scot named John MacDonald, whom he had seen only once in twenty-five years but who wanted his influence in getting him a position as a rigger on one of the new

seventy-fours under construction. MacDonald had told the senator to contact "my old captain and friend Commo. Bainbridge," who could testify to his shipboard rigging skills.

It was about two days later that Barron's ambiguous note of the sixteenth arrived. Decatur did not respond to it immediately, dealing just then with such appeals as that of a senior carpenter at the Gosport Navy Yard near Norfolk who wanted the naval commissioners' assistance appointing him to a position on board Bainbridge's *Columbus,* which would "enable me to act with more confidence and command more respect" from less experienced ship's carpenters.

Also among Decatur's incoming mail was a letter from Zacharia H. Jones, a molder and finisher at the New York Navy Yard, complaining that he had been fired "for a supposed fault." Would the commissioners consider it "a crime to take a glass extra with an old friend?" And the worried mother of Seaman Thomas Soper, who was "of an age and disposition extremely dangerous" for him to be abandoned on shore, wrote that it would be a pity if all the good her boy "has hereto acquired in the navy should be destroyed." Could a place be found for him on the *Columbus?*

About then Decatur had received Barron's last letter, the dismal report of his "bilious fever." Barron had removed from Hampton into Norfolk, placing him in more direct contact with Jesse Elliott. Decatur had said that *if* Barron meant a challenge, he accepted it but was "at a loss" to know just what Barron intended. Those words had become immaterial. Preparations for a duel were under way with nothing in view to interrupt them. Suspicions stirred of something sinister afoot. Samuel Archer, a U.S. Army colonel passing through Norfolk, told Captain Arthur Sinclair to warn Barron against dark plotting. He must be on his guard, "for if ever a man was jockeyed out of his life it will be him." Elliott should be cool, keep his temper in check. This warning reached Barron, who passed it on to Elliott. That second brushed it aside with "What can they do?"

The meeting was now inevitable. On February 10 Decatur, writing from Washington to Bainbridge, aboard the *Columbus* moored in the St. Mary's River, stipulated that "the place we are to meet is entirely at our option. Their convenience will not be consulted." The location should be reasonably close to the home of one or other of the contestants, given "the inconvenience of a man's lying wounded at a distance from his own house." Both men could not be thus accommodated, and on this point Decatur "should not like to yield." As to weapons, distance, and time, he left the choice to Bainbridge. And he would like the event held at Bladensburg, eastward just over the line from Washington. Bainbridge acknowledged this letter on the twentieth, adding, "In serving a friend, and particularly one I so sincerely esteem as I do you, inconvenience to myself will not be considered by me. As yet, I have not heard from them. God bless you."

The social scene in Washington was dominated by talk of an impending White House wedding. The president's seventeen-year-old daughter, Maria Hester Monroe, would marry her maternal first cousin Samuel L. Gouverneur, scion of a New York banking family. Invitations to balls and parties were soon circulating, some from Commodore David Porter's fine home, built with his prize money on Meridian Hill, others from General Van Ness's mansion near the White House and from the Monroes' even closer neighbors, the Decaturs.

Just returned to Norfolk from the north, Jesse Elliott wrote Bainbridge on February 20 that Barron had "put in my hands for perusal a series of letters which had passed between him and Commo. Stephen Decatur and solicited my friendly aid in bringing this matter to a final conclusion." Elliott enclosed a copy of each of two letters, probably the last exchanged between Barron and Decatur, which "make it only necessary" that he and Bainbridge should get together for the purpose of "settling the grounds on which they are to close." Elliott added that Barron was "rapidly recovering from an attack of bilious

fever." He then scored out words, inserted others, so that the line read that Barron was still "much under the effects" of it but would be able "to move in a few days."

On February 27 Bainbridge, aboard the *Columbus,* sent a copy of Elliott's letter to Decatur, also one of his reply to Barron's chosen second, which was "I will be ready, at any time, to receive you on board."

In this same wintry week Decatur, still attending to business, studied a letter from William Verner, a twelve-year-old boy of Berwick, Pennsylvania. "I almost fear you have forgotten your little friend." The lad was six when he had met Decatur in New London and was instantly awed by the commodore, who promised to protect him should he wish to join the navy. His eldest brother had helped educate him but recently died. Young William described himself good at grammar, arithmetic, and some Latin. Could Decatur assist in getting him into the service? A letter from his mother reached Decatur at the same time asking if he could be warranted a midshipman. "His attachment to you is ardent and sincere." Warm letters these, bound to have affected Decatur, who had lost the midshipman nephew named for him and upon whom he had looked as his only son.

Less felicitous papers lay before him, the Elliott-Bainbridge exchange, with the latter's accompanying note hoping that "the arrangements may be settled before [the *Columbus*] leaves here, which I expect will be in ten days." This one signed without "God bless you."

Bainbridge was now constantly in the great cabin or on the quarterdeck of his 193-foot-long, 1,480-ton, 74-gun ship of the line. Her full strength would be 780 men, but nowhere near that number were yet on board. The vessel was conveniently situated for the pair's private rendezvous, her anchorage several miles upstream on the St. Mary's River. Here she was flanked by tobacco plantations and the quiet little trading port of St. Mary's City, in colonial years Maryland's state capital.

Jesse Elliott, up from Norfolk in a jolly boat, was closeted with Bainbridge on March 8. He may have visited Bainbridge earlier, but this was the date on which they drew up an agreement. In a letter to Decatur with a copy of that document, Bainbridge, who had never fought a duel, wrote that to settle "your unpleasant business with Commodore Barron . . . the place, weapons, distance and mode were prescribed by me." He had first meant to leave the mode unfixed until on the field. But Elliott had pressed for an immediate settlement and "I thought it best to fix it, to avoid unfavourable suspicion against you by not doing so. I therefore acted for you precisely as I would have for myself and doubt not of meeting your approval." Elliott had spoken of Barron's imperfect vision. "But that had no influence on my mind, for I had resolved, a month since, that the distance should be eight paces. I observed to Captain Elliott that I presumed Commodore Barron's sight had not failed him since giving the challenge."

The agreement signed by the "friends" determined that Decatur and Barron should meet at nine on the morning of March 22 at Bladensburg. The weapons would be pistols, the distance "eight paces or yards." Before firing, the parties would be directed to present, and not fire before the word *one* was given or after the word *three,* and "the words *one, two, three* shall be given by Commodore Bainbridge." That night, Elliott probably slept on the *Columbus,* sharing cabin space with his opposite second.

Some fifty miles to the north in Washington, the drawing room of the president's mansion rang with music and gaiety. It was the eve of Miss Monroe's wedding. Stephen and Susan Decatur received a special measure of congratulations, for it happened to be the fourteenth anniversary of their own.

As Decatur's "friend," Bainbridge was traditionally obliged to secure conditions favorable to his principal. Decatur had, indeed, told him that the other side's "convenience will not be consulted." Yet the close range of eight paces to which Bainbridge had agreed benefited

the other side, even allowing for Barron's myopia. On the other hand, Decatur was younger than his opponent and unquestionably the better marksman. Decatur showed Bainbridge's terms to his fellow commissioners, saying that upon accepting the challenge it had been his intention to shoot his pistol skyward or not fire at all. Now he decided he would shoot to wound for his own defense but "take special care that it should not be in a vital place." He would aim for the hip.

By the middle of March, at least two members of Monroe's cabinet knew what had developed. So, probably, did the president, who could hardly have relished the prospect of notable bloodshed shattering a social season whose main event was his daughter's wedding. But no peacemakers intervened. There were officers in the navy who had long resented what they took to be Decatur's hubris, and some among those who had heard of his present awkward situation doubtless attributed it to that fault. And Bainbridge certainly knew when he sent the terms of the meeting that his principal's sense of honor would prevent him from raising any objection.

How much, if anything, did the family of each protagonist know of what was happening? Barron's was the larger, but whether any relative was aware of what was coming, of the emotional letterwriting, of Jesse Elliott's involvement, are among the unknowables. With just nine days before the event, Barron wrote to his beloved daughter Jane. Would the family keep "our dear Samuel," probably a young nephew, "in constant readiness for the [sailing] order of Commo. Bainbridge which may be constantly expected." A large quantity of clothes should be provided the boy, and while he may feel lonely when at sea "there is a midshipman on board the Columbus only nine years old and is said to be one of the most manly little fellows." Barron ended this letter with his opinion of how "Kentucky has taken our land [from Virginia]," a current political issue. The only hint he gave of the coming duel was "I shall go to Washington in a few days. I could wish to have seen you before I go but have so much to attend to that it will not be in my power." He did not elaborate.

Nineteenth-century historians echo one another's assertion that Susan Decatur was kept in the dark. About a week before the crucial date, Decatur wrote Luke Wheeler that he had an affair on his hands that might have a fatal ending. He asked him to come to Washington to be with Susan. We can only surmise how he explained her father's presence as well as Robert G. Harper's sudden arrival at the Decaturs' with his wife, Kitty, Charles Carroll's daughter and Susan's intimate friend. Outsiders who knew included two naval surgeons, Bailey Washington and Samuel Russell Trevett; Master Commandant William C. Bolton, a Bainbridge protégé who had killed a marine lieutenant in a duel six months earlier; and Colonel George Bomford, the army's chief ordnance expert, a friend with whom Decatur shared ownership of Washington real estate. That Barron and Decatur would duel was known even to Attorney General William Wirt, who may have tried to prevent the meeting. Commodore Charles Morris knew, but he had sailed to take command of the Brazil station.

President Monroe's daughter was married at a private White House ceremony on March 9, probably the same day Decatur received the duel program from Bainbridge. On the eighteenth the Decaturs hosted a party for the newlyweds, just returned from a brief honeymoon in Virginia. In the spacious drawing room they had decorated with portraits, gold swords and medals, gifts from Congress and grateful citizens, Susan sang, seated at the harp. During a pause in the music, the socialite gossip and chronicler Benjamin Ogle Tayloe saw Decatur drift over to Commodore Porter, whose own invitations were out, and heard him say, "I may spoil your party." Tayloe thought Decatur seemed "out of spirits and I was struck by the solemn manner and devotion to Susan as she played the harp, the company a semicircle in front of her, her husband, uniformed in the center, eyes riveted on her."

Oliver Perry's charges against Elliott, supported with affidavits, were in Decatur's hands. He agreed with Benjamin Hazard, who had sent them to him, that they should be made public or handed to

the secretary of the navy. On the twentieth, a Monday, he wrote Hazard that Elliott was still exhibiting certificates that "strike directly at Perry's character." Although a Norfolk friend of Decatur's had warned Elliott that this activity might backfire, Elliott was sure to continue his slandering of the late commodore. "It is due to [Perry's] memory that a full and faithful disclosure of all the facts in the case should be made."

That same day Decatur was observed by the ubiquitous Benjamin Ogle Tayloe on Pennsylvania Avenue. Tayloe thought he looked "ill, abstracted." Then Decatur ran into Commodore Thomas Macdonough and they chatted but, Macdonough later said, without allusion to any duel or he would have tried to prevent it. On Tuesday evening the Decaturs were at the home of John Quincy Adams, then secretary of state, and his wife, Louisa. In company with other guests the couple danced cotillions. As always when in uniform, gold braid against navy blue worsted, the Order of Cincinnati upon his chest, Stephen cut a handsome figure. Any anxiety he felt about next morning's outcome was not apparent. Susan may be pictured, passing from partner to partner in traditional quadrille fashion, as the woman whose radiant beauty not even Gilbert Stuart could capture when she sat for the renowned artist two decades earlier. It was nearly midnight when the guests said good night, many climbing into waiting carriages. The Decaturs lived within walking distance.

Did Susan have no inkling of the duel only hours away? Nothing in her future writings would show that she did. At home that night, after the reveling at John Quincy Adams's mansion, what passed between Stephen and Susan? At dawn, when he arose to dress, might she not have stirred from slumber? They may have occupied separate beds, hardly bedrooms if Robert and Kitty Harper were quartered under their roof, also Susan's father, who had come up to Washington from Norfolk. Remotely above, in the attic, the servants slept. An undated note apparently in Decatur's hand and signed was reproduced as a frontispiece of a nineteenth-century biography. It reads, "May angels

watch over you and protect you." Genuinely written by Stephen and placed beside her pillow in case she never saw him again? The questions intrigue. In bleak dawn light Decatur, clad in a heavy surtout for warmth and disguise, stepped from the house alone. How he did so without anybody else in it knowing must be imagined.

21

*The
Duel*

He strode along the poplar-lined, partially paved avenue. Traffic was meager, few horses and carriages. Most citizens were still in their beds. Within half an hour he had passed the scaffolded unfinished Capitol on the hill and reached Beale's Congress Hotel, where he was greeted by Bainbridge and an aide, Samuel Hambleton, the *Columbus*'s purser. They had come up the previous day and spent the night there. Over breakfast Decatur appeared cheerful, his demeanor hardly that of a man who wanted to kill anybody. He said he had brought his will but could not sign without the required three witnesses. Bainbridge had ordered a coach. Warmly clad, carrying a full pistol case and flasks of brandy, the three set out on the five-mile drive eastward to Bladensburg. It was Wednesday, March 22, 1820.

Barron, his nephew Edward "Ned" Latimer, and Elliott were already on the ground. Two days earlier they had come up to Baltimore on the overnight steamer *Virginia.* (Susan Decatur's father had taken the same packet, debarking at Washington.) Barron's party, which included an elderly doctor named Hall, had come down to Bladensburg from Baltimore by private coach and spent the night at the Indian Queen, a fifty-year-old hostelry where George Washington had stayed twice on his way to the Continental Congress in Philadelphia.

Barron awoke after a restful sleep, and Latimer had a servant light a fire before which his uncle could shave and dress. After breakfast Barron made out his will, "laconic" he called it, a page and a half. He strolled briefly in the garden and had to comfort Latimer, who was worried, aware that what lay immediately ahead was his fifty-two-year-old uncle's first duel.

Set on the south side of the Eastern Branch, a Potomac tributary later called the Anacostia River, Bladensburg had begun as a busy little tobacco port. During the War of 1812 it was the scene of a battle in which six hundred Americans fought but failed to halt the rocket-armed British descent on the capital. Since then the only sound of gunfire to disturb Bladensburg's serenity echoed from a shallow ravine half a mile away, concealed from the highway by trees and shrubbery, which would if not as yet acquire the title Valley of Chance. In all more than fifty duels were fought there. The most recent had been fought in a snowstorm a year earlier by two cousins using muskets. Coincidentally, the fatal victim was General Armistead T. Mason, probably kin to Barron's Armistead in-laws.

Decatur's carriage halted within sight of the ravine, and its occupants alighted. Jesse Elliott had appeared on the brow of a rise, silhouetted against the bleak March sky. Bainbridge and Hambleton strode up to him. The captain and the commodore probably exchanged salutes, then began a quiet talk as they led their principals down into the narrow valley. Barron walked slowly, with what a friend would describe as "a very elegant stick with an amber head representing a cloud and an approaching storm."

He was following the others when he became aware of a motionless figure in black who stood on a low ridge eyeing him closely. When Barron moved away the stranger said, "Don't be alarmed, sir." Barron said he was not but quickened his steps and the man disappeared. Barron did not know at the time that he was Robert Goodloe Harper, who had left his wife, Kitty, with Susan Decatur and had come to attend the duel, in sorrow but unable to prevent it.

The coaches had been dismissed. The men were on the ground, Elliott and Bainbridge with their heads together, still conversing. Barron and his nephew paused some fifty yards away. Elsewhere in the dale, Dr. Hall and the two naval surgeons Bailey Washington and Samuel Trevett carefully checked their scalpels, lancets, and probes. The seconds' conference lasted at least three quarters of an hour, during which period, and unnoticed by them, Decatur walked toward Barron, whose startled nephew asked what this meant. Barron said they would soon find out.

He and Decatur had not seen each other since the *Chesapeake* court-martial. Decatur fixed his eyes on the man he had once called a father and whose character he had since decried. Barron thought his object was "to menace me with a sneer." He jabbed his stick in the ground as if in defiance and stared back. After four wordless minutes of what Barron thought the other's "very indecent grimaces," Decatur turned, made for a nearby tree stump against which he leaned, head bowed. Barron and his nephew paced to and fro. Latimer said, "Why, uncle, that was worse than all he has done before." Barron replied, "My dear Ned, I concur with you, but I thank him for it as it will steady my hand, and in the event of a fatal result, I shall feel less regret."

That this incident occurred is hardly to be doubted, although it was seen by nobody else. And it compels a sadness exceeding any stirred by that harrowing thirteen-letter correspondence. Barron's assumption of why Decatur had come up to him may have been hopelessly mistaken. His nephew was too bewildered or nervous for his impression to be considered. But Barron's should be taken into account. He had interpreted Decatur's unexpected approach as intentionally intimidating when it might instead have reflected an inner confusion caused by some last-minute need for bloodless adjustment or even a wave of remorse for which Decatur was unable to find the right words. But then it mattered little. Decatur remained slouched against the stunted tree. Barron called to Elliott, were they not ready?

Elliott nodded and beckoned. Bainbridge was marking the ground where the duelists must stand. The seconds were in control.

Yet not entirely of themselves. Bainbridge had the task of charging the pistols. They were long-barreled, silver-mounted, and engraved, smart products of the gunsmith's art. But taking up the flask to pour powder into their chambers, Bainbridge's hands appeared to tremble. With Elliott's consent he asked Decatur to take over. Decatur, with more experience in duels than anyone else on the field, obligingly took each weapon, blew down its barrel, half cocked the hammer, and opened the cut-off lever of the powder pouch. He filled the chamber and inserted a strip of leather as a seat for the ball, which he rolled into the barrel and sealed in place with a ramrod. The priming completed, he handed the weapons back to Bainbridge and Elliott. Throughout these moments, Barron and his nephew watched in silence.

The seconds pronounced themselves satisfied with the weapons and the field. Bainbridge called for the toss of a coin. He won, which allowed his principal the choice of stands. Decatur selected that to the north, lower ground, from which he was more likely to achieve his stated intention of hitting Barron in the hip instead of delivering a killing shot. The duelists disappeared into the bushes to vent their bladders, a common practice in duels, reducing the risk of poisonous urine spilling into the abdominal cavity should the ball strike that low. Bainbridge marked eight paces and placed a short length of tree branch where each man was to stand. Then he announced how he would direct the gunplay.

The conditions that Bainbridge had set up with Elliott made some degree of bloodletting inevitable. There was the close proximity of the principals, standing face-to-face, no nonsense of back-to-back, pacing, wheeling to fire, the procedure adopted for the Perry-Heath encounter. "I shall give the word quickly," Bainbridge declared. "Present, one, two, three. You are neither to fire before the word *one*, nor after the word *three*."

Barron had detected Bainbridge's jitteriness. He made a request. Would Bainbridge pronounce the words exactly as he intended to give them for the actual shooting? Bainbridge consented, probably after some hesitation. But Barron then felt an urge for further words, his own and of a conciliatory nature. Before he could utter any, a surprising call came from his opponent. Decatur insisted on being searched. "I do not wish to be shielded." Barron had shed his greatcoat. Decatur still wore his, but he groped within and from vest pockets extracted a handful of flints.

Such items might deflect a ball, though their effectiveness as a shield was arguable. At any rate, Elliott protested. "Commodore, I shall have nothing to do with such dirty business." Barron intervened, saying he was willing to be searched. He emptied his pockets of a few half-dollars, a penknife, comb case, other sundries. Bainbridge stepped to him and went through the motions of proving his pockets were empty. Elliott, about to do the same with Decatur, shrank back instead, saying he would not indulge in such an unheard-of process. Both parties had been on the field an hour. Bainbridge stood behind Decatur to his left, Hambleton on the right. Elliott and Latimer mirrored these moves in back of Barron.

Those brief postponements of the actual shooting, unusual in the dueling ritual, seem almost to suggest that the two officers, each now gripping a pistol, were reluctant to go through with it. Then occurred an even more extraordinary exchange, a breach of the code that forbade any communication between duelists once the challenge had been made and accepted. The situation became surreal, or as if instinctively designed to force the seconds into dictating a settlement. Barron spoke first. "Now, Decatur, if we meet in another world, let us hope that we shall be better friends."

To which Decatur replied, "Sir, I have never been your enemy."

The words had scarcely left Decatur's lips when Elliott interrupted with "Gentlemen, to your places." Bainbridge immediately followed with "Make ready!" The two armed commodores faced each

other. Decatur still wore his surtout. Buttoned to the throat, it concealed the true shape of his figure, denying Barron a precise spot to aim at. Decatur was not so handicapped. Barron's greatcoat was hanging on a rosebush where Ned Latimer had carefully placed it. His uncle's profile offered Decatur a detailed target. Bainbridge called, "Present."

Each principal raised his pistol, cocked the flintlock, took aim along the barrel. Very likely, and pathetically, misinterpreting each other's thoughts, they stood still as statues, guns pointed. Bainbridge called "One." The duelests fired before two. A ball struck each man in the groin. Decatur's hit the edge of Barron's ilium, ricocheted down his thigh. Barron's tore into his opponent's entrails, cutting pelvic arteries. Decatur dropped the pistol, clutched his side, and fell, groaning, "Oh, Lord, I am a dead man."

The shots had shattered the morning stillness, were heard by locals at the Indian Queen, where Commodores Rodgers and Porter, for no clear reason, had also waited. They took to their horses and rode to the ravine. Surgeons were busy, Washington and Trevett attending to Decatur. Dr. Hall crouched beside Barron, seeking the ball. Conscious though in pain, Barron told Hall, "I really don't suffer from the probe you handle so delicately." Hall said the stem of the probe was too limber, could not reach as far as he wanted. But he assured Barron the wound was not mortal. Robert G. Harper, of Decatur's party, came up sighing and shaking his head. Another visitation was unwelcome. John Rodgers had dismounted, hung his bridle on a tree limb, came to within ten feet of Barron and asked if he was much hurt. Barron managed a hostile retort. When last he had seen Rodgers, touching his hat to him, the salute was not returned. Until Rodgers apologized, Barron said, "you may never expect an answer from me to any question you may ask."

Before Rodgers could respond, Porter was there to tell him that this was neither the time nor place for further altercation. Decatur lay on the grass about fifteen feet from Barron. Rodgers stooped to

support him. Decatur bled but with effort could still speak, and what followed struck surgeon Bailey Washington as the closing scene of a tragedy, Hamlet and Laertes. "Barron," said Decatur, "if I ask you a question will you answer?"

Barron had been told by Dr. Trevett that Decatur's wound was probably mortal. Without hesitation he said, "Certainly."

Decatur: What could have induced you to do this act?

Barron: My own sense of duty and the advice of every friend I consulted.

Decatur: What have I said more than that you should have come home, and why didn't you?

Barron: I had not the means, and neither I nor anyone else calculated on a continuation of the war.

Echoing points from their correspondence, the dialogue was brief, belated, even desperate. And it faded incoherently. Barron thought Decatur bent on further talk. And when the coach arrived for Decatur, who was carried into it by Rodgers, Porter, and the two naval surgeons, he was heard to bid a hoarse farewell to the man who had shot him. Porter remained behind with Barron. Both seconds had vanished. Bainbridge was hurrying with Hambleton to the Washington Navy Yard from where a tender would take him down the Potomac to his ship of the line. Elliott was in the carriage reserved for Barron but heading in the opposite direction, away from Bladensburg.

Assuming Elliott would return with conveyance for his wounded principal, Commodore Porter waited. A local magistrate rode up to ask what was going on—he had heard talk of a duel. Nothing of the sort, Porter told him. The official doubtless guessed otherwise but wanted to rid Maryland soil of the shooting party. He left, and by then, after an hour's vigil, Porter realized that shameful as it seemed, Elliott was not coming back. Climbing through bushes to the highway, Porter halted a passing coach. Helped by Ned Latimer and Dr. Hall, he lifted Barron into it. The party drove off. Bladensburg was

left behind, and with fresh blood on its turf, the Valley of Chance was once more silent and deserted.

Porter rode his horse alongside the carriage bearing Barron. They caught up with Elliott just short of the Washington district line. He had the gall to ask how things had gone back on the ground. Porter snapped contemptuous words at him. Elliott was quickly in the carriage behind the officer he had abandoned. Still brazen, he tried to engage Porter in talk blaming Bainbridge for not arranging an accommodation when words passed between the duelists. Porter ignored him, left the carriage, and spurred his horse into Washington.

As forenoon had advanced at Decatur's home, could not Susan have felt some anxiety, had some inkling of imminent catastrophe? Did she simply presume her husband safe and sound at his office? She had not long breakfasted with her two nieces, whom Stephen had informally adopted, her father, and Kitty Harper. Was there a conspiracy of silence to keep her from knowing where her husband had gone that morning? If he had indeed left a note, would she not have at least wondered? Shortly before noon, Commodore Rodgers knocked on the door, his uniform spotted with blood. And then she knew.

Decatur was taken into a room to the left of the domed entrance hall. Though in extreme pain, he was conscious. Dr. Thomas Sim, from a Pennsylvania Avenue row three blocks away, arrived to assist the naval physicians. But Decatur refused to have the ball extracted from his wound. And he gave orders that Susan not be permitted to see him. She and her nieces were ushered to an upper floor where Luke Wheeler tried in vain to console them. Decatur wished to sign his will. "I give and devise to my beloved wife Susan Decatur and her heirs all my estate, real, personal and mixed, wheresoever situated, and I appoint my friend Littleton Waller Tazewell of Norfolk, Robert G. Harper of Baltimore, and George Bomford of the city of Washington together with Mrs. Decatur my wife to be executors of this my will."

Rodgers, Dr. Trevett, and Dr. Sim signed as witnesses. Decatur's signature betrayed no indication of any tremor or weakness in his hand.

John Quincy Adams, at whose home the Decaturs had danced the night before, was preparing to leave for his State Department office when someone came to tell him that Decatur had been brought in from Bladensburg mortally wounded. Adams at once hurried to Decatur's home, where the growing number of callers included two generals, Colonel Bomford, and an apparently uncertain Dr. Lowell, "the Surgeon General who, I suppose, thinks it humane to keep Mrs. Decatur and her father, who is with her, in suspense as long as possible."

Decatur's ordeal lasted well into the evening. Dr. Trevett wrote to John P. Decatur at the Philadelphia Navy Yard. He told him his brother was "mortally wounded, I fear. Mrs. Decatur is here and she is as composed as one in her situation can be." According to a nineteenth-century writer able to contact her as well as other intimate contempraries, Decatur knew he was dying, "did not much regret his death itself as he deplored the manner of it; had it found him on the quarterdeck it would have been welcome." Decatur died at about eleven P.M.

John Quincy Adams wrote an early eulogy. The nation had lost one of its heroes, "one who has illuminated its history and has given grace and dignity to its character in the eyes of the world. . . . He had fallen in a duel and his dying breath was a sigh of compunction that it was not in his country's cause." News of Decatur's death spread quickly throughout the city, producing "unusually great sensation." But, Adams went on, "the lamentations at the practice of dueling were and will be fruitless, as they always are."

Barron was confined to a cot at Beale's Hotel. Bailey Washington and Edward Cutbush, another naval surgeon, attended to his wound. The ball was still in his body, but he was able to sit up, may have heard ships' guns off Washington's navy yard firing a salute every thirty minutes. Perhaps he read the next morning's newspapers,

brought by his friend and defender John Forbes or his nephew Ned. "Mourn Columbia!" lamented the *National Intelligencer,* "for one of thy brightest stars is set." Other reports were less florid. The *Georgetown Messenger* viewed the conflict between the commodores as "one of those unfortunate entanglements into which amiable and sensible men sometimes get unnecessarily involved and which false pride renders the means of their destruction." The *Baltimore Federal Gazette* chided those who would "excite public feeling in favour of the deceased officer who so wantonly threw away a life valuable to his relatives and his country."

In Washington planned social events to continue celebration of the Monroe wedding were canceled. Military and naval officers were ordered to wear crepe for thirty days. In the House of Representatives, John Randolph of Roanoke, Virginia, moved that colleagues do likewise for the balance of the session. This was opposed by John W. Taylor of New York on the grounds that Decatur had died in violation of the laws of God and of his country. But both legislative houses adjourned so that their members could attend Decatur's funeral.

While preparations were under way to make this one of the most elaborate ceremonies in the capital's history, some thoughts privately expressed were decidedly negative. Massachusetts senator Harrison Gray Otis, writing to his daughter, called Decatur "a victim to the inexorable laws of honour, which the men of the sword feel themselves bound to obey." Captain Arthur Sinclair shared the opinion of many officers, fellow Virginians, that Decatur was "ignoble" and Barron "a most persecuted man." According to Mrs. Seaton, related to the publisher of the *National Intelligencer,* "So many friends were privy to this intended duel . . . the President, [Attorney General] William Wirt, General [Robert G. Harper], Colonel Bomford," as well as the commodores Rodgers, Porter, and Bainbridge, and even Susan Decatur's father, "all kept it secret." And Mrs. Seaton judged the hero's death using a word his widow would angrily repeat: *murder.*

22

The
Widow

In the city of Washington, Decatur's funeral was the largest assemblage yet seen. Marines led the solemn procession with appropriate music. Clergy followed the detachment, and then the casket, pallbearers including the Washingon Navy Yard's commandant Thomas Tingey, and Commodores Rodgers, Porter, Macdonough, and Chauncey. Behind them rolled carriages containing relatives, Susan invisible behind a black-draped window, President Monroe, his cabinet, members of Congress, Supreme Court Justice John Marshall. Then army and naval officers, city officials, foreign ministers with their suites. Some ten thousand citizens lined what there was of sidewalks.

The procession slowly moved along Connecticut Avenue and around a desolate space that would one day be called Dupont Circle. Beyond it, an incline led to Kalorama, the property of Colonel Bomford, who had bought it from the poet and diplomat Joel Barlow. The cortège halted before the palatial home Barlow had built and surrounded with trees and plants collected from distant lands. Kalorama overlooked Washington, Georgetown, and the more distant Potomac River. Decatur's body was deposited in a vault. A short prayer and a volley from Marine Corps muskets concluded the ceremony. An

inscription placed on the tomb read in part, "His public services are recorded in the annals of the country, his private virtues in the hearts of his friends, and above all in the heart of who was fourteen years the happy partner of his life."

On March 25, the day after the funeral, John Myers, a Norfolk businessman and friend of Barron, still at Beale's Hotel, wrote to tell him that Ned Latimer had just come off the steamboat with details of the transaction at Bladensburg. Crowds thronging the wharf were pleased to learn that Barron was out of danger. Myers would see to press coverage, limiting it to a bare account of the meeting. Rumors abounded of a last-minute conversation on the field that might have offered both seconds an opening for a bloodless accommodation. Myers would see that nothing was reported of this, which might be considered "an effort to bias the public mind. . . . You have suffered injustice too long . . . to permit any to continue it."

But Barron had written to David Porter asking him to confirm precisely what Rodgers had said to him while he lay wounded on the ground. What Porter called an "unpleasant misunderstanding" had arisen. Both Rodgers and Porter recalled that the former had said to Barron, "I hope you are not much hurt, sir." Porter had also written to Bainbridge, who replied that Porter must have distinctly heard what passed between Rodgers and Barron, "since you were at the time nearer to Barron than I was." The officers were evidently apprehensive that something damaging to their reputation might leak out. Bainbridge had also heard from Decatur's friend and agent, Littleton Tazewell, and wondered what he was up to. Bainbridge told Porter that Tazewell should pause before taking any action. He ended his letter apologizing for its brevity, "feeling so deeply the death of my lamented friend Decatur."

Both sides, Barron perhaps excepted because still bedridden at Beale's, seemed to be racing to get their case first before the public. Elliott told his Bladensburg principal that he was trying to get two hundred copies published of the by now notorious correspondence

and that "conversation" on the ground. Others were getting into the act. Isaac Chauncey had told Elliott that it was important for Bainbridge to discover its real nature. Barron himself may not have cared about what Rodgers had said to him or his response. Weary but with his wound healing, he left Beale's and took the packet sloop *Ocean* for Norfolk, where Elliott assured him that after Bladensburg the world could no longer consider him a coward. Barron was probably more concerned for the loss of his cloud-headed walking stick, which had been left behind at Bladensburg and was, he had heard, put up for sale.

The correspondence leading to the duel was quickly before the public. In Washington it was published by Gales and Seaton of the *National Intelligencer,* to place things, they said, in their "true light," Decatur's "friends having learned that misconceptions injurious to him prevail." Barron's friends read the letters in the *Norfolk and Portsmouth Herald.* National reaction was mixed, ranging from praise for Decatur's patriotic rectitude to sympathy for an officer cruelly stigmatized.

Once Susan Decatur had regained enough strength and composure, she embarked upon a campaign that would consume much of her remaining life, its purpose to secure pecuniary reward for Stephen's fighting career, and to punish his "assassins." At first she pressed for the release of the unpublished proceedings of the *Chesapeake-Leopard* court of inquiry and Barron's subsequent court-martial. Littleton Tazewell promised to obtain copies from the Navy Department, also of Lieutenant Allen's scathing letter, which "speaks volumes." Tazewell reminded Susan that he had served as judge advocate at both hearings, thought Barron should have been cashiered. Susan confessed to no particular enmity against the man who had shot her husband but opposed any move to reinstate him. "I am unwilling that his character should be built up at the expense of the most zealous and devoted friend the Navy ever had." Barron had been pushed by Elliott to "the dreadful transaction." And it was

against Elliott that Susan next moved. She used the documents Stephen had taken charge of for Commodore Perry, a favor "which I have no doubt cost him his life." She would publish the papers anonymously, without even first consulting Perry's family. Besides fulfilling Stephen's promise to Perry, she wanted to expose Elliott's "base . . . cold-blooded, assassin-like conduct," so mortifying him as to place it out of his power "to injure any other human being by his wickedness and treachery."

Susan penned those words January 15, 1821. She had left the mansion on President's Square shortly after the duel and, following brief residence at Kalorama, settled in Georgetown. The house she had shared with Stephen was rented to a succession of European diplomats. On April 4 she told President Monroe her reason for wanting the *Chesapeake* court of inquiry and Barron's trial published. The nation could then judge his merit for itself. Her urgency sprang from the imminence of a court of inquiry into Barron's conduct after his suspension from the navy. She sensed, correctly, that since publication of the duel correspondence, public opinion had begun to favor Barron as the injured party. For Barron to survive this latest court without stain and consequently secure an honorable assignment in the navy would, in Susan's embittered vision, be an insult to her Stephen's memory. The hearing "will afford a very proper occasion to publish the proceedings of the court-martial hitherto omitted."

She was unaware that President Monroe, like Barron a native Virginian, had asked his secretary of the navy, John Branch, if Barron would agree to an appointment as commandant of the Philadelphia Navy Yard. The court of inquiry was to investigate whether Barron had engaged in treasonable talk with an Englishman, as alleged in the late Lieutenant Lewis's letter, and why he had failed to return to the United States upon the expiry of his suspension from the service. With Captain Alexander Murray its president, the court sat at the Brooklyn Navy Yard. The Pernambuco charge collapsed from lack of testimony. Principal witnesses had died. But Barron's attorney, the

respected Delawarean Caesar Rodney, had a hard time convincing the members that lack of funds alone had kept Barron in Europe during the War of 1812. Still, Barron emerged from the inquiry relatively unscathed, and not until 1822 did the government publish the proceedings of his 1808 court-martial.

Susan Decatur's ordeal had eroded none of her personal glamour. A William Lee of Massachusetts wrote in his diary on June 14, 1822, that "Mrs. Decatur has come out quite charming, handsome (they say) and brilliant. Therefore, some ill-natured things are said by the gossips." Two weeks later the same diarist wrote that "Mr. [Stratford] Canning is agoing to marry Mrs. Decatur. It is all stuff, though he visits her. She is ten years older than he is." The gossipy Benjamin Ogle Tayloe affirmed that there was a courtship initiated by Susan, who was forty-six. Canning's full title was Viscount Stratford de Redcliffe, British minister to the United States. Through her close friendship with Kitty Harper, Susan spent visits at Doughoregan Manor, owned by the wealthy Carrolls, some of whose heirs may not have taken kindly to the affection that had lasted many years between Susan and the now-aged Charles Carroll of Carrollton.

Susan's financial resources dwindled. The rent she received from Decatur House's tenants was her sole regular income. Stephen had invested $100,000 in Washington and Norfolk real estate, much of which by 1824 proved unproductive, and she was trying to sell it off. That year her father, himself almost pauperized by a decline in property values and working as a cashier in a Norfolk bank, made out his will. It stipulated that upon his death he be buried in Potter's Field. What property he left, "worn-out furniture, broken prints, old volumes of books, etc.," should be sold. Luke Wheeler would live four more years. The will listed no beneficiaries and made no mention of Susan.

She pestered the government for prize money she felt Stephen and his *Intrepid* crew were entitled to for burning the *Philadelphia*. She knew that had they captured the frigate and returned it to the

navy, instead of reducing it to floating embers, the legitimacy of her claim would long ago have been acknowledged. She argued that Decatur could have brought the *Philadelphia* into port as he did the *Macedonian,* but Commodore Preble had thought it in the national interest that the ship be destroyed on the spot. He had no idea he was depriving his small band of heroes of the fruits of their valor. Doggedly persistent, Susan wrote to Secretary of State Henry Clay, John Quincy Adams, Senators Daniel Webster and Andrew Jackson, and former navy secretary Crowninshield, only to see the "Bill for the Relief of Susan Decatur" fail in one congressional session after another. This, after reinforcing her claim by insisting that the 1815 Mediterranean peace treaties her husband had secured resulted from his 1804 exploit and forever protected American merchant vessels from Barbary plunder. The Islamic pirates "are only afraid of us thanks to Commodore Decatur's attack under their own batteries; a mode of war to which they were not accustomed from their Christian enemies."

While preoccupied with claims upon the government, Susan cherished memories of her short-lived status as mistress of the mansion she had shared with Stephen, and early in 1826 she was angered by a vandalism authorized by her present tenant, the Russian diplomat Baron de Tuyll. She was informed that he had allowed his domestics to tear up and sell all the flowers and shrubbery in the garden. On March 30 she protested to Henry Clay in a superbly worded letter declaring herself too much a democrat to treat European diplomats as princes. When the Baron's rental term expired, she extended it for six months because he was unwell and not up to the task of moving. Moreover, his steward had fitted up a parlor for himself and expected Susan to pay for it. When a friend asked the steward "not to let the servants injure the property, he replied that a foreign master's servants were quite as good as any American gentleman."

She kept up her volley of letters to the Congress, the cabinet, and the Board of Navy Commissioners demanding the *Philadelphia* prize

money. If ever there was an account to be setlled, she protested, it was this one. Her husband had brought glory to a navy then "at its last gasp." Susan often ended her bold letters with winning invitations to take afternoon tea with her in Georgetown. But there were questions. She had asked that $100,000 be appropriated. Should Captain Charles Stewart be allotted a portion of the money, inasmuch as he had taken a pivotal role in the *Philadelphia*'s burning by being on station to cover the *Intrepid*'s retreat? No, thought Susan, prize money should go only to ships' crews that were within sight of the capture.

Stewart gave only limited support to Susan's endeavors, and Captain Charles Morris, never conspicuous among Decatur's admirers, gave little or none. Morris, actually the first to board the frigate, was reported ready to furnish the Navy Department with documents showing that Decatur did not deserve supreme credit for destroying the *Philadelphia*. Susan's comment on this was that Morris's "mercenary feelings have tempted him to traduce his commander in hopes of getting more of the money for himself." She spent the summer of 1827 with Charles Carroll at his manor. Once back in Georgetown she invited Henry Clay and his wife to dine and meet with "some of my diplomatic friends. Most of the European corps who have come here since I have been out of society have brought letters of introduction to me." Susan was leading a semireclusive life, and a visit by the Clays with foreign envoys at her table would make it known that society had not abandoned her. The reason she no longer mingled with the capital's elite was that she might find herself in the same company as Bainbridge and Elliott, "my husband's murderers. . . . So I never go into the street or any public place or travel in any public conveyance. . . . I would rather live an *outlaw* . . . than find myself in the presence of those it is my strongest inclination to avoid."

Largely due to her association with the Carroll family, and perhaps to the holy fathers of Georgetown College, Susan joined the Roman Catholic religion. She was received into the church at Baltimore, and according to a priest who claimed to have been her confessor, she

practiced her religious duties punctually. But this brought her no rescue from indigence; she often survived on bank loans. The situation finally compelled her to pawn or sell her husband's awards and trophies. "I don't dare to violate his notions of honour by retaining such evidence of his patriotism and valour and remain indebted to poor tradespeople for my daily subsistence." On New Year's Eve, 1831, she wrote Lewis Cass, secretary of war, that she had been obliged to raise money by selling the medal voted Decatur by act of Congress. And the following year she advertised Decatur House for sale, complete with "spacious back building and stabling for six horses."

The following year she had to part with "the only articles I have left of all my comforts"–$500' worth of silver and china plates. "I am literally without one dollar to send to market." She offered this treasure to Andrew Jackson, just reelected president. He bought the lot for $350.

Although nothing transpired regarding Susan's claim to prize money, her improverished state did not go unnoticed. In 1834 Congress made her an appropriation of $7,000. She gave all of it to Georgetown College in return for an annuity that enabled her to spend the rest of her life in relative comfort. She was fifty-eight at that time, and by the date of her death the total return from the college exceeded three times the amount of her gift to it.

Susan outlived her husband's "assassins" and in her advancing years came to consider the man who had pulled the trigger as their innocent tool. A less charitable view of James Barron was held by Thomas Jefferson, who apparently continued to believe the Pernambuco story. Asked by President Monroe for advice on just what should be done about Barron, Jefferson wrote from Monticello that Barron was "a most unprincipled man, unworthy of any military trust."

But Barron was allowed a lengthy and profitable rehabilitation. As successively commandant of navy yards, including Norfolk, he continued to experiment and pressed for greater use of steam to replace wind and canvas. (His old foe John Rodgers, president of an increasingly

obsolete navy board, made no secret of his opposition to steam navigation.) Barron's final assignment was head of the Navy Asylum, a Philadelphia rest home for aged seamen. He died in Norfolk in 1851, having been senior officer of the U.S. Navy for more than a decade.

Jesse Duncan Ellliott benefited his country even while continuing to indulge his penchant for mischief making. In 1829 he had commanded a Caribbean squadron that made Spain think twice about trying to regain control over Mexico. On his own initiative he sent seamen and marines to help suppress Nat Turner's 1831 slave revolt along the James River. Andrew Jackson liked Elliott, favored him with choice assignments, in return for which Elliott used his likeness as a figurehead on the *Constitution* in port at Boston. A Bostonian who detested Jackson climbed aboard Old Ironsides one night and sawed the figurehead off. The ship was fitted with another Jackson head, and as her commander Elliott patrolled the Mediterranean showing the American flag while piling the ship's decks with looted gifts for taking home. They included a sarcophagus for an ailing Andrew Jackson, who rejected it as too imperialistic. In May 1840 Elliott was court-martialed on charges leveled by his junior officers and ranging from immorality to misuse of public funds. He was convicted and given five years' suspension from the navy, a penalty remitted by Martin Van Buren, Jackson's successor in the White House.

Elliott was untroubled by controversy that so often swirled about him. He may even have relished it, and was not much disturbed when Matthew Perry republished Oliver Perry's charges against him. James Fenimore Cooper, novelist and naval historian, sailed into print with a strong defense of Elliott, and the Battle of Lake Erie was fought all over again, with pamphleteering broadsides still echoing after Elliott's death in 1845 at the age of sixty-three.

William Bainbridge took his ship of the line *Columbus* into the Mediterranean five weeks after his service to Decatur on the Bladensburg field. He had mourned his principal's death with stoicism. "The vicissitudes of my life," he told the secretary of the navy, "have fortified

my mind for trying events." For his fifth voyage into the Mediterranean he had no Bashaw to fear, no Dey to shame him, and no rival to rob him of the redeeming glory he had sought in that sea. He had not, however, escaped the attention of what he once called "that damned jade misfortune." His official mission was to show the flag off Constantinople, the capital of the Ottoman Empire. The Turks refused to allow him east of the Dardanelles.

An officer on his seventy-four found him "fearful and uneasy . . . excited and alarmed at the smallest incident." When he voyaged home to his wife and seven children, Bainbridge was appointed president of the Board of Navy Commissioners. Before taking the office he wrote to General Henry Dearborn, a former United States ambassador to Tunis, that "the more I see of the world, the more I am confirmed in this belief. Man, instead of being as his Maker intended him to be—the noblest work of God—is a *machine,* molded by, and yielding to, the baseness and grovelings of his *lowest* fellow. . . . I am becoming a misanthrope."

He had, in fact, taken to drugs, was particularly addicted to opium. He had lost an only son. One of his daughters, on her own determination or at her father's directions, burned what a note written by his grandson described as "his most valuable letters and information." Bainbridge died July 27, 1833. More than a century later one of the U.S. Navy's first nuclear-powered frigates was named for him.

Fulfilling an agreement made years before, Susan Decatur consented to the transfer of Stephen's remains from Kalorama in Washington to St. Peter's Episcopal Churchyard at Third and Pine Streets, Philadelphia. Susan's most bothersome vexation during her last years resulted from the efforts of her three nieces, daughters of her husband's sister, Ann, to obtain a share of the federal money she had so earnestly campaigned to get. On January 28, 1850, she was required to certify for the Senate Committee on Naval Affairs that during all the fourteen years she was Decatur's wife, he "never conveyed

a thought, word or desire that I would, on his death, make provision for the ladies who have been brought forward as 'his adopted children.' " Two were married and well off; the third, aged fifty, benefited from her mother's estate and a pension connected with the death of her marine captain father. Susan insisted that whatever Stephen's fortune might have been, "it was all mine, that he did not consider any thing his own but 'his sword and his ship.' "

Nothing came of this to trouble the rest of Susan Decatur's life. She spent her last years at what became known as the Decatur Cottage, a frame house on the Georgetown University campus. Its owner was a Lucretia Hobbs, who let Susan rent it and became her friend and companion. Susan died in 1860 at age eighty-four. For well into the twentieth century she lay buried in a university-owned cemetery. In May 1988 her body was removed, placed in a mahogany casket, and taken to Philadelphia, where she was laid to rest beside Stephen and his parents.

All too often attempted assessments of historically heroic figures produce little more than romantic juvenilia, cardboard cutouts of the real thing, falling short of the true human beings they really were. This has been the case with American seafarers noted for their dash and courage, remembered only through slogans: John Paul Jones's "I have not yet begun to fight"; James Lawrence's "Don't give up the ship;" Perry's "We have met the enemy"; David Farragut's "Damn the torpedoes, full speed ahead." And Decatur's toast. Yet these men were not mere sloganeers, and the biographer's duty is to make them live and breathe on the printed page or other media, always being careful not to step across the line into hagiography.

The record on Stephen Decatur is not as copious as we might like, especially since his life was cut short. But we now know something of his human attributes. He could be as ruthless in rivalry with fellow officers as he was brave and audacious in combat with his country's foes. He was a loving husband, and had Susan borne him children (we

do not know why she hadn't), he would have been a stern but gener-
ous father. Also a mentor, perhaps in the fashion of the older man
fated to kill him. His concept of duty was uncompromising. The glory
he sought was his legacy to the navy he served. It has rewarded him
with seven warships, the first launched in 1898, that proudly bore or
bear his name.

And his famous toast? Because of its implication that patriotism
need adhere to no moral standards, it has long lost significance, is be-
yond taking seriously. But that fault lies only in its last five words.
Elaborated, they appear on the tall tapering marble column, sur-
mounted by an American eagle with wings spread, that marks De-
catur's grave: "He Cherished in His Heart, and Sustained in His
Intrepid Action, the Inspiring Sentiments Our Country Right or
Wrong." The toast is 190 years old. Shorn of its chauvinistic tagline,
it is by no means out of date. Surely it is more relevant today than
ever. *"Our Country! In her intercourse with foreign nations may she
always be in the right."* With fervor and genuine dedication, every
glass in the land can be raised to that one.

ACKNOWLEDGMENTS

A number of persons merit special thanks for assisting my own research while sharing some of theirs. Were it not for Virginia Steele Wood, reference specialist, Naval and Maritime History, Library of Congress, we would continue to erroneously believe that the victim of the duel in Malta dominated by Lieutenant Decatur was the island governor's secretary. Nicholas Scheetz, curator of Georgetown University Library's Special Collections, contributed not only valuable guidance but his characteristic zeal. Stephen Decatur, Jr., of Marblehead, Mass., allowed me to examine material that undoubtedly strengthened the story. And for her ever-ready assistance in my James Barron research, special thanks are due Margaret Cook, curator emeritus, Earl Gregg Swem Library, College of William and Mary.

Equally helpful when called upon were the curator and staff at Decatur House, Washington; personnel at the Library of Congress, Manuscripts Division; National Archives and Records Administration; Naval Historical Center (Washington Navy Yard); William E. Clements Library, University of Michigan; Henry Huntington Library, San Marino, Calif.; Peabody Library, Salem, Mass.; Lilly Library, University of Indiana, Bloomington; Fairfax County Library, Virginia,

Reference Division; Nimitz Library, U.S. Naval Academy. And while at Annapolis, special thanks to James W. Cheevers, curator of the Academy's museum, without whose aid I should never have nailed the identity of the Philadelphia lass loved by Decatur until he met Susan Wheeler. Edward H. Hammond, Jr., Berlin, Maryland, was informative regarding Decatur's birthplace, as was the staff at Worcester County Library, Snow Hill, Maryland.

Thanks are due to Robert B. Hitchings, Kirn Library, Norfolk, Virginia, and, in nearby Hampton, Thomas W. Sale, M.D., active member of the Hampton Historical Society. Welcome assistance came from Jan Herman, editor and historian, Naval Medical Command, Washington, D.C., André B. Sobocinski, and Edward Jenkins. Finally, my sincere gratitude must go to Douglas F. Greer, M.D., Jack Towers, Jean Guttridge, and, as always, to my devoted family.

NOTES

Biography has hardly neglected Stephen Decatur. Two years after his death there appeared S. Putnam Waldo, *The Life and Character of Stephen Decatur* (Hartford, Conn.: R. B. Goodsell, 1821). Later came Alexander Slidell Mackenzie, *Life of Stephen Decatur: A Commodore in the Navy of the United States* (Boston: Charles Little and James Brown, 1846). There followed Irvin Anthony, *Decatur* (New York: Charles Scribner's Sons, 1931); Charles Lee Lewis, *The Romantic Decatur* (Philadelphia: University of Pennsylvania Press, 1937); Helen Nicolay, *Decatur of the Old Navy* (New York: D. Appleton-Century, 1942). And some sixty years later James Tertius de Kay, *A Rage for Glory: The Life of Commodore Stephen Decatur, USN* (New York: Free Press, 2004).

All these books add more or less to our knowledge of the hero and deserve consultation. If they share a problem, it lies in the very concept of heroism, a tendency to portray the commodore as a hero above all things, which inevitably leads to hagiography. This certainly applies to Mackenzie, *Decatur,* whose content, however, most enjoys the merit of reliability. Himself a former (and controversial) naval officer, Mackenzie was able to personally interview many of Decatur's contemporaries, his shipmates, brother officers, friends, and relatives, Susan Decatur included.

1. Blazing Frigate

My account of the burning of the *Philadelphia* is drawn from official reports to the secretary of the navy, Naval Records, Record Group 45, National Archives and Records Administration (NARA); David F. Long, *Ready to Hazard: A Biography of Commodore William Bainbridge 1774–1833* (Hanover, N.H.: University Press of New England, 1981); William Ray, *Horrors of Slavery: Or the American Tars in Tripoli* (Troy, N.Y.: Oliver Lyon, 1808); *Charles Morris: The Biography of Charles Morris, USN, Proceedings of the United States Naval Institute* 6 (1880); and Christopher McKee, *Edward Preble: A Naval Biography 1761–1807* (Annapolis, Md.: U.S. Naval Institute Press, 1972). Bainbridge's anguished letters from prison and Decatur's triumphant report are among the Edward Preble Papers, Manuscripts Division, Library of Congress.

2. The Midshipman

Background for study of Decatur's forebears is provided by William Decatur Parsons, *The Decatur Genealogy* (New York, 1921). The Decatur biographers cited above agree that recklessness and pugnacity characterized his youth. But the murder charge in a column of the *Wilmington Daily Commercial,* 22 December 1874, is left unexplored. Recent examination of existing Philadelphia court records yields nothing. Assuming any truth to "Occasional"'s words, with their names of Bedford and Sergeant whose "skillful management secured Decatur's acquittal," one might consider the possibility that the case was settled out of court or perhaps in nearby Delaware, where Gunning Bedford was a politician and jurist of considerable influence.

The naval exploits of Stephen Decatur's father can be traced through Dudley Knox, ed., *Naval Documents Related to the Quasi-War Between the United States and France* (Washington, D.C.: Government Printing Office, 1934). Decatur in love: The identity of the Philadelphia maiden to whom

Decatur swore his undying devotion and whom he forsook when enchanted by Susan Wheeler has baffled previous biographers. Copy of letter to Sally (Sarah) Mason is in the Naval Academy Museum Manuscript Collection, Annapolis. John Barry's affection for the *United States* is apparent in his correspondence with the Navy Department, and letter, 22 July 1798, to the frigate's constructor, Joshua Humphreys, reproduced in *Pennsylvania Magazine of History and Biography* 30, no. 20. For Bainbridge and the *Insurgente,* see Knox, *Naval Documents,* and David F. Long, *Ready to Hazard: A Biography of Commodore William Bainbridge 1774–1833* (Hanover, N.H.: University Press of New England, 1981), James Barron in action: Indispensible to any study of this ill-fated officer are James Barron Papers, Earl Gregg Swem Library, College of William and Mary, Williamsburg, Va. Barron treating Decatur "as a son" is stated in Captain Arthur Sinclair to Caesar Rodney, 17 April 1820, Caesar Rodney Collection, Delaware Historical Society, Wilmington, Manuscript Library.

3. The First Duels

For Barron "fit to command any ship," see Commodore Barry to Secretary Benjamin Stoddert, 16 March 1798, Barry-Hayes Papers, Independence Seaport Museum, Philadelphia. The *George Washington*'s service to an Algerian despot is described in David F. Long, *Ready to Hazard: A Biography of Commodore William Bainbridge 1774–1833* (Hanover, N.H.: University Press of New England, 1981), and Dudley Knox, ed., *Naval Documents Related to the United States Wars with the Barbary Powers from 1785 through 1807, 6 vols.* (Washington, D.C.: Government Printing Office, 1939-1944), a mine of detail, which, if too intimidating to the researcher, may be supplanted by Gardner Allen, ed., *Our Navy and the Barbary Corsairs* (Boston: Houghton Mifflin, 1905). Bainbridge was a humorless tyrant according to John Rea, *A Letter to William Bainbridge, Esq. Commander of the United States Ship George Washington* (Philadelphia: Printed for the Author, 1802).

4. To the Mediterranean

For Thomas Jefferson's naval policy, see Leonard F. Guttridge and Jay D. Smith, *The Commodores* (Annapolis: Naval Institute Press, 1984). Occurrences onboard the U.S. Navy vessels engaged in the war with Tripoli are superbly detailed in *Naval Documents Related to the United States Wars with the Barbary Powers: Naval Operations, Including Diplomatic Background from 1785 through 1807* (Washington, D.C.: U.S. Government Printing Office, 1939–44, six volumes). For Decatur's inspiring attitude toward men under his command, see Charles Lee Lewis, *The Romantic Decatur* (Philadelphia: University of Pennsylvania Press, 1937) and Alexander Slidell Mackenzie, *Life of Stephen Decatur, a Commodore in the Navy of the United States* (Boston: Charles Little and James Brown, 1846). Midshipman William Lewis's opinion of Captain Barron as "a man of warm passions" is in a letter to his cousin, Edward Herndon, Fredericksburg, Va., 16 September 1802, U.S. Naval Institute Proceedings, 67, no. 11, 1941.

5. Loss of the Philadelphia

An article in a 1932 issue of the *Sunday Times of Malta* gives more accurate detail than previous accounts of the duel outside Valletta. Conclusive research was undertaken by Virginia Steele Wood and William M. P. Dunne through correspondence, 1992, with the library of the University of Malta and Professor Donald Sultana, University of Edinburgh, erasing the myth that young Bainbridge's victim was the Maltese governor's secretary. That Barron talked Decatur out of his impulse to quit the navy is indicated by ex-consul Cathcart's "Without Barron's Counseling Decatur Might Have Abandoned the Service," James L. Cathcart's Journal, 19 February 1803: State Department Records, Record Group 84, Foreign Service Posts, NARA.

The loss of the *Philadelphia* is described in David F. Long, *Ready to Hazard: A Biography of Commodore William Bainbridge 1774–1833* (Hanover,

N.H.: University Press of New England, 1981), and William Ray, *Horrors of Slavery: Or the American Tars in Tripoli* (Troy, N.Y.: Oliver Lyon, 1808). Bainbridge proposing that the frigate be burned is in his letter to Preble, 16 February 1804, Edward Preble Papers, Manuscripts Division, Library of Congress.

6. Bloodshed Off the Barbary Coast

Did Daniel Frazier or Reuben James save Decatur from a Tripolitan pike? The jury is still out. Lieutenant Commander R. C. Bartman, USN, wrote Captain M. D. Cooke, Boston, 5 August 1937, "The service of each might be worthy of recognition without detracting from the other." Naval Historical Center, Early History Branch, Washington, D.C. For Commodore Rodgers's frustrations, see Charles O. Paullin, *Commodore Rodgers, 1773–1838* (Annapolis, Md.: Naval Institute Press, 1967). A useful glimpse of the Decatur-Coleridge link appears in Donald Sultana, "Samuel Taylor Coleridge and an American Naval Hero," *Sunday Times of Malta,* 10 November 1957.

7. Stephen and Susan

For Decatur's arrival home with a Tunisian royal party and attracting Susan Wheeler, see Mackenzie, *Stephen Decatur,* an account generally followed by other Decatur biographies. Issac Chauncey congratulated Decatur on his wedding and four days later sent the Miltonian missive, which may not have sat well with the recipient. Chauncey to Decatur, 20 and 24 March 1806. Bill Dunne attributed the discovery of these letters in the New-York Historical Society to Henry P. Silka, with well-deserved thanks. Gunboats ridiculed in Stephen Decatur to William Bainbridge, 27 June (July?) 1808, Historical Society of Pennsylvania. For Gordon on the *Chesapeake,* see Herbert Baird Simpson, "Charles Gordon: Jacobite and Loyalist," *South Atlantic Quarterly,* October 1928. For Barron on Allen's "prejudices," see James Barron Collection, Earl Gregg Swem Library, College of William and Mary,

Williamsburg, Va. Also Ira Dye, *The Fatal Cruise of the Argus* (Annapolis, Md.: Naval Institute Press, 1994).

8. Chesapeake *and* Leopard

The fullest account of this tense Anglo-American crisis over British deserters on American ships, including the diplomatic give-and-take, is John C. Emmerson, Jr., *The Chesapeake Affair of 1807* (Portsmouth, Va.: private printing, 1954). Also see Leonard F. Guttridge and Jay D. Smith, *The Commodores* (Annapolis, Md.: Naval Institute Press, 1984). For Lieutenant Allen's account and harsh judgment of Barron, see his journal, "Occurrences and Remarks Aboard the United States Frigate Chesapeake," Henry E. Huntington Library and Gallery, San Marino, Calif., and a small collection of Allen letters at the Library of Congress, especially the emotional outburst to his father, 17 July 1807. "So many darts": Barron to John Bullus, 3 July 1807, James Barron Collection, Earl Gregg Swem Library, College of William and Mary, Williamsburg, Va. The "gifted attorney" is biographed by Norma L. Peterson, *Littleton Waller Tazewell* (Charlottesville: University Press of Virginia, 1983).

9. *Barron's Trial*

Decatur reporting on the duels that resulted from the *Chesapeake* affair is in Letters Received by the Secretary of the Navy from captains, microfilm 125, reel 9, November 1807, Record Group 45 NARA. Also see *Norfolk and Portsmouth Herald,* 26 September 1807. This chapter is largely based on *Trial of Commodore James Barron, Captain Charles Gordon, Mr. William Hook and Captain John Hall of the United States Ship Chesapeake,* January 1808, published by Order of the Navy Department, Washington, D.C., 1822, at the urgent request of Susan Decatur. Also see Leonard F. Guttridge and Jay D. Smith, *The Commodores* (Annapolis, Md.: Naval Institute

Press, 1984). Barron's request for the secretary of state as a witness is relayed to Washington by Littleton Tazewell, 11 January 1808, Miscellaneous Letters to the Secretary of the Navy, microfilm 124, reel 10, NARA. Captain Bromley's correspondence with Decatur is traceable in Public Records Office, Kew, London, Records of the Foreign Office, Bromley to Decatur, 11, 16, 17, 18, 21, and 27 January 1808.

10. The Captain Reprimanded

For more on Gordon, see William L. Calderhead, "A Strange Career in the Young Navy, Captain Charles Gordon, 1778–1816," *Maryland Historical Magazine* 72 (Fall 1977). "That unfortunate, unhappy ship": Charles Gordon to John Bullus, 4 April 1810, Miscellaneous Bullus MSS, New-York Historical Society. For Gordon's duel, see *Norfolk and Portsmouth Herald,* 26 September 1807, and Calderhead, "Strange Career." In his letter to Bullus, Gordon refers to "the orifice in my side."

11. Love and Glory

The American fleet: See William S. Dudley, ed., *The Naval War of 1812: A Documentary History,* vols. 1 and 2 (Washington, D.C.: Naval Historical Center, 1985 and 1992). Decatur's 30 October 1812 report of the engagement with the *Macedonian* appeared in *Niles Weekly Register* 111 (1812), also *Norfolk and Portsmouth Herald,* 18 December 1812, which notes that the New York naval dinner of 30 October 1812 was "electrified by the sudden appearance of two superb transparent paintings." More on the *Macedonian* in James Tertius de Kay, *Chronicles of the Frigate Macedonian 1809–1922* (New York: W. W. Norton, 1995).

For Decatur ending his prize-money partnership with Rodgers, see John Rodgers Papers, Manuscripts Division, Library of Congress. Box 20 contains revealing Decatur-Rodgers correspondence June–September 1812. The

Lewis letter calling Barron "a coward . . . traitor," is to Charles W. Goldsborough, 7 September 1811, copy in James Barron Papers, Earl Gregg Swem Library, College of William and Mary, Williamsburg, Md. Decatur's prize agents: 20 June 1812, Tazewell Family Papers, Library of Virginia, Richmond. Gordon "must have some hand in the war." Charles Gordon to John Bullus, 19 September 1812, New York Public Library. For Decatur's efforts to obtain fair prize money, see Tazewell–Luke Wheeler correspondence, March 1813, Lilly Library, University of Indiana, Bloomington.

12. Blockaded

Decatur's approving interest in Fulton's experiments is reflected in a letter or affidavit within the LeBoeuf Collection, New-York Historical Society. See especially Robert Fulton to Stephen Decatur, 15 November 1814. Fulton's letter to Jefferson, with Decatur's view of the inventor's "experiments on firing cannon under water," 6 May 1813, is in Thomas Jefferson Papers, Manuscripts Division, Library of Congress. Decatur blockaded: Lieutenant Commander D. S. Jordon, USN, "Stephen Decatur at New London: A Study in Strategic Frustration," *Proceedings of the U.S. Naval Institute,* October 1967. Also Joseph A. Goldenburg, "Blue Lights and Infernal Machines: The British Blockade of New London," *The Mariner's Mirror,* 1975. "We hauled and pulled back," W. M. P. Dunne, "The Inglorious First of June" *Long Island Historical Journal,* Spring 1990.

13. Decatur and Fulton

Susan uneasy: Her letter to John Bullus, 5 June 1814, Bullus Papers, Maine Historical Society, Portland. Decatur's keenness about Fulton's latest steamboat design is expressed in 29 July 1813 and 15 November 1814 letters, LeBoeuf Collection, New-York Historical Society. "Ready for a push," writes Decatur to Rodgers, 22 July 1814, Historical Society of Pennsylvania,

Philadelphia. And to Bullus, "John Bull and us," 11 January 1814, Leonard F. Guttridge and Jay D. Smith, *The Commodores* (Annapolis, Md.: Naval Institute Press, 1984). Admiral Hardy's challenge: Decatur to Hardy, 17 January 1814, Hardy to Decatur, 18 January Lilly Library, University of Indiana, Bloomington.

14. *"Shall Satisfy the World"*

"I have a good crew," Decatur to Littleton Tazewell and Luke Wheeler, 14 January 1815, U.S. Naval Academy Museum, Annapolis, Md. A copy of Carden's court-martial proceedings is in the New York Public Library. Also see James Tertius de Kay, *Chronicles of the Frigate Macedonian 1809–1922* (New York: W. W. Norton, 1995). Extracts from *Endymion* logbook: Official Letters with Comments and Observations Relative to the Capture of the *President,* American Frigate: Selected from *Royal and Weekly Gazette,* various dates (Bermuda: Edmond Ward, prob. 1815). See also *Proceedings of the Court of Inquiry to Investigate the Causes of the Loss of the Frigate President While under the Command of Commodore Stephen Decatur* (New York: Van Winkle & Wiley, 1815). Decatur's report of the battle was widely published. For instance, see *Niles Weekly Register,* 4 March 1815, and *Columbia* (Boston) *Sentinel,* 11 March 1815. "Satisfy the world," Decatur to Richard Dale, 28 March 1815, Dale Family Papers, Special Collections, Nimitz Library, U.S. Naval Academy, Annapolis, Md.

15. *Two Squadrons*

Susan's attempted intervention: See her letter to Secretary Crowninshield, 25 February 1815, Crowninshield Papers, Peabody Museum, Salem, Mass. Decatur's objection to her interference, and his request for command of the first Mediterranean squadron, 20 March 1815, in same collection. For Crowninshield's private letter to Decatur, 14 March 1815, offering him a choice of commands, see Alexander Slidell Mackenzie, *Life*

of Stephen Decatur: A Commodore in the Navy of the United States (Boston: Charles Little and James Brown, 1846). Also Decatur Manuscript Collection, U.S. Naval Academy Museum, Annapolis, Md. "Mortifying to my feelings," wrote William Bainbridge to David Porter, 8 April 1815, Naval History Collection, New-York Historical Society. "Wipe the cream off the enterprise": Irvin Anthony, *Decatur* (New York: Charles Scribner's Sons, 1931). For an official hearing replete with adulation and sympathy for the commodore who had surrendered his ship, see *Proceedings of the Court of Inquiry Held on Board of U.S. Frigate Constellation, New York April 1815, to investigate the Causes of the Loss of the Frigate President While under Command of Commodore Stephen Decatur* (New York: Van Winkle & Wiley, 1815).

16. The Mediterranean Factor

"Drubbing a defenseless Turk": Joseph Causten to James Causten, 14 August and 16 October 1815, Causten Papers, Special Collections, Georgetown University Library. For Decatur's "comet-like" Mediterranean sweep, see "Diplomacy in Barbary," *Pennsylvania Magazine of History and Biography,* January 1950. "Dictated at the mouths of our cannon." Decatur to Secretary Crowninshield, 5 July 1815, Crowninshield Papers Peabody Museum, Salem, Mass. "Bashaw Decatur": See Leonard F. Guttridge and Jay D. Smith, *The Commodores* (Annapolis, Md.: Naval Institute Press, 1984). "An electric shock," crowed *Poulson's American Daily Advertiser* (Philadelphia), 19 November 1815. For Gordon's frustrated desire for a victory, see Morris L. Radoff, "Charles Gordon of the *Constellation,*" *Maryland Historical Magazine* 67 (Winter 1972). Consul Shaler's discomfiture in the wake of Decatur's "peace" scoops is obvious from Shaler's words. See the extensive collection of William Shaler Papers, Historical Society of Pennsylvania, Philadelphia. Also, see Shaler to James Monroe, 4 July 1815; Shaler and Decatur to Monroe, 7 July and 31 August 1815; William Bainbridge to Monroe

5 September and 15 November 1815; Decatur to Shaler, 2 July and 7 October 1816, State Department Records, NARA.

17. Perry and Elliott

Decatur would see to the wallpapering: Decatur to Secretary Crowninshield, 14 June 1816, Crowninshield Papers, Peabody Museum, Salem Mass. The toast: The words were reported in two Norfolk newspapers, *American Beacon,* 4 April 1816, the day after the banquet, and next day *Norfolk Gazette & Public Ledger.* Eighteen toasts preceded that uttered extemporaneously by Decatur. Perry and Heath: See Leonard F. Guttridge and Jay D. Smith, *The Commodores* (Annapolis, Md.: Naval Institute Press, 1984). Perry and Elliott: See Richard J. Dillon, *We Have Met the Enemy* (San Francisco: McGraw-Hill, 1978). Also see David C. Skaggs, "Aiming at the Truth: James Fenimore Cooper and the Battle of Lake Erie," *Journal of Military History,* April 1995.

18. Barron Returns

For the near clash between Decatur and Andrew Jackson, see "Notes and Documents: Memoirs of Senator Jonathan Roberts 1771–1854, *Pennsylvania Magazine of History and Biography,* July 1938. Decatur frees a slave: Certificate bearing his signature, 30 March 1819, Annapolis, Md. U.S. Naval Academy Museum. For Decatur and Elliott in each other's company, conceivably not side by side, see *Norfolk Beacon,* 27 March, 1 and 2 April 1819. Barron finally at home: His business and family letters during and immediately after his return to the United States, his appeals to the Navy Department for readmission into active service, the letters to Elliott arranging terms for the approaching duel, and an account of the court of inquiry into his conduct while abroad, are in boxes 2, 3, and 4, James Barron Papers, Earl Gregg Swem Library, William and Mary College, Williamsburg, Va.

19. The Letters

"I shall expect to hear from you." The fatal Barron-Decatur correspondence that began 12 June 1819 and ran to a total of thirteen letters was eventually published in the *Norfolk Beacon* on 8 April 1820, later in other newspapers, and by Gales and Seaton, Washington, that same year, entitled *Correspondence Between the Late Commodore Stephen Decatur and Commodore James Barron Which Led to the Unfortunate Meeting of March 22, 1820.* Elliott the sole instigator: Littleton Tazewell to Stephen Decatur, 12 March 1819, Alexander Slidell Mackenzie, *Decatur* (New York: Charles Scribner's Sons, 1931), and a copy owned by Stephen Decatur, Jr., Marblehead, Mass. Other personal correspondence: While engaged in the emotional exchanges with Barron, Decatur attended to the following mail: From Gould Francis Leckie, 12 October 1819; H. Lee, 2 January 1820; Walter Lowrie, 13 January 1820; Zacharia H. Jones, 5 February 1820; Thomas S. Soper, 5 February 1820; William B. Verner, 21 February 1820; Ann Verner, 21 February 1820. All found in Decatur's desk after his death. Letters Received by the Board of Naval Commissioners from Commandants, Records Group 45, NARA.

20. The Friends

Charges against Elliott: see Benjamin Hazard to Stephen Decatur, December, n.d., Perry Papers, William E. Clements Library, University of Michigan, Ann Arbor. Hazard was a Rhode Island attorney and state legislator intending to write Perry's biography. Decatur wrote Hazard, 20 March 1820, two days before the duel, that he would "repel any insinuations" injurious to Perry's memory. "A full disclosure of all the facts should be made." The Decaturs at the Adams party: John Quincy Adams Diary, 21 and 22 March 1820, Massachusetts Historical Society, Boston.

21. The Duel

For more on the duel, see *Records of the Columbia Historical Society,* vols. 29 and 30; Charles O. Paullin, "Dueling in the Old Navy," *U.S. Naval Institute Proceedings,* December 1909; Samuel Hambleton, "Memorandum Respecting the Meeting Between Commodore Decatur and Commodore Barron," 22 March 1820, Hambleton Papers, New-York Historical Society; and Barron's "Account of the Meeting Between Commodores Barron & Decatur at Bladensburg on 22nd of March 1820," James Barron Collection, Earl Gregg Swem Library, College of William and Mary, Williamsburg, Va. Decatur's will is in the Office of Public Records, Washington, D.C. Barron's walking stick: Quartermaster's Office, Washington, D.C., to B. Jackson, Bladensburg, Md., 7 April 1820, Records Group 45, area file 7, NARA. "Inexorable laws of honour," wrote Harrison Gray Otis to his daughter, Harrison Gray Otis Papers, reel 7, Manuscripts Division, Library of Congress. *National Intelligencer,* 9 May 1820, reported that the cast taken of Decatur moments after his death would be exhibited in the Capitol, "Admission 25 cents." The sculptor Cardelli had exhibited busts in London the previous year. "My lamented friend Decatur": William Bainbridge to David Porter, 28 March 1820, John Rodgers Papers, Manuscripts Division, Library of Congress.

22. The Widow

Susan in widowhood: See her correspondence with philosopher and pharmacist Daniel Smith of Philadelphia, The Stephen and Susan Decatur Papers, Georgetown University Library. That she was forced by poverty to sell the gold medal awarded her husband is lamented in her letter to Lewis Cass, 31 December 1831, William L. Clements Library, University of Michigan. Her letters to Benjamin Crowninshield are in Crowninshield Papers, Peabody Museum, Salem, Mass, and those to Henry Clay in Henry

Clay Papers, Library of Congress, Manuscript Division. See in particular Susan's letter to Clay, 30 March 1826. Detail was kindly provided by the curator and staff of Decatur House on the items Susan sold Andrew Jackson.

Bainbridge letters: The New-York Historical Society holds a special edition of Cooper's *History of the United States Navy,* illustrated by John Barnes, the commodore's grandson. It contains a handwritten note stating that Bainbridge's daughter destroyed "his most valuable letters."

INDEX